THE FUTURE OF POLITICAL PARTIES

SAGE ELECTORAL STUDIES YEARBOOK

Series Editors

Louis Maisel
Paul M. Sacks
Colby College

Editorial Advisory Board

SAGE ELECTORAL STUDIES YEARBOOK

VOLUME I

The Future
of Political Parties

edited by
LOUIS MAISEL
and
PAUL M. SACKS

 SAGE Publications   Beverly Hills / London

For information address:

SAGE PUBLICATIONS, INC.
275 South Beverly Drive
Beverly Hills, California 90212

SAGE PUBLICATIONS LTD
St George's House / 44 Hatton Garden
London EC1N 8ER

Printed in the United States of America

ISBN No. 0-8039-0426-6 (cloth)
ISBN No. 0-8039-0570-X (paper)

Library of Congress Catalog Card No. 75-5016

Second Printing

JF
2011
. F87

CONTENTS

Introduction to the Series
    LOUIS MAISEL and PAUL M. SACKS   7

Introduction to This Volume
    LOUIS MAISEL and PAUL M. SACKS   9

1. Physical Change and Partisan Change:
    The Emergence of a New American Electorate, 1952-1972
    GERALD B. FINCH   13

2. Party Image and Partisan Change
    RICHARD J. TRILLING   63

3. Issues and Party Alignment
    JOHN E. JACKSON   101

4. Social Change and the Future of Political Parties:
    The Australian Case
    DAVID KEMP   124

5. Conservative Success in Liberal New York:
    Some Determinants of Conservative Party Support
    JOHN J. GARGAN   165

6. Party Reform and Political Participation:
   The Democrats in Maine
      LOUIS MAISEL   193

7. Clientele Markets, Organizational Dynamics, and
   Leadership Change: A Longitudinal Comparison of the
   Norwegian and British Labor Parties
      E. SPENCER WELLHOFER, VICTOR J. HANBY, and
      TIMOTHY M. HENNESSEY   221

8. American Politics in the 1970s: Beyond Party?
      WALTER DEAN BURNHAM   238

Contributors   278

INTRODUCTION TO THE SERIES

Whereas once men of learning viewed themselves as students of society, today's academic specialization has fragmented the search for knowledge about the way we live among a host of disciplines. And, while contemporary specialists may claim more exact understanding than their predecessors, this increased sophistication has not come without costs. Complaints about the problems attendant to specialization—the tendency toward trivial and narrow concerns, the concentration upon method while nearly ignoring substance, the lack of an overarching theory to bridge disciplinary gaps, the separate "languages" of each discipline which lead not only to mutual incomprehensibility but also to the near total exclusion of the lay audience—have become commonplace.

As professional political scientists (and therefore products of a specialized academe), we perceive this overspecialization as a real and ever-present problem. In the field of electoral studies, where we have both worked, the issue presents itself in a variety of ways. Political scientists, sociologists, statisticians, communications experts, historians, philosophers, and psychologists have all examined elections from their own points of view. While their studies deal with different aspects of the same social phenomenon, the goal of accumulating knowledge and relating one piece of research to another is often perverted by the very problems of specialization mentioned above.

Furthermore, much of the scholarly work on this subject appears to have little relevance to those involved in the practical aspects of elections: politicians; political consultants; speech writers; advertising specialists; radio, television, and print journalists; pollsters; and so forth. Their work is separated from that of scholars by gaps of purpose, assumptions, and language. The sociologist is often obscure to the speech writer; what is of immediate import to the candidate may be of only passing concern to the historian.

Of course, certain bridges span these divides. Politics creates the most unlikely bedfellows, and practical attractions overcome the most divisive obstacles. The lure of technique—in specialized skills such as polling, electioneering, and campaign fund-raising—has been felt by politicians at even the lowest level of government, and the purposes of specialists and politicians have thus been joined. However, while pragmatic considerations have both generated and overcome specialization at one level, such pragmatism provides little incentive for discussion of issues that transcend specialized concerns. Wherever the fundamentals of democracy are involved, as in elections, these issues are present. Yet, unfortunately, in the area of politics, where specialized skills have advanced so far, there are few compelling pressures (and accordingly few places) where these issues of broader import can be aired and where the voices of all concerned can be heard.

At the risk of some immodesty, we view this series as such a forum. Our plan is to devote each annual volume to some larger topic arising out of electoral politics, to select themes that involve not only the specialist but the wider public as well. Here issues such as the future of political parties (the theme of this inaugural volume), the implications of new electoral technologies for the democratic process (the theme chosen for our next volume), or the link between the electoral process and subsequent policy making will be discussed.

It is part of our purpose that the presentation of these themes transcend both territorial and disciplinary geography, that it move into the more meaningful territory of informed and general debate. Reduced to essentials, this involves urging academic specialists and practical politicians to bridge their divide, to test their ideas, and to speculate upon broader issues in this more open forum. Our goal is a series of yearbooks in which the general issues related to electoral politics, not just its particulars, will be examined and appreciated by a larger audience. We choose to cross national as well as disciplinary borders, to generalize about common findings and common experiences, to escape from our narrower shells.

We do not wish to sacrifice sophistication and rigor. We do not ask those who contribute to this series to desert their chosen fields. Rather it is our hope that this series will allow many who are concerned with this broad subject to share the understanding accumulated by a wide range of experts as it is drawn together and presented on a common ground.

ACKNOWLEDGMENTS

An introduction to this series would be incomplete without a word of thanks to those at Sage Publications who have been so helpful in launching this endeavor: Connie Greaser did much to encourage us in the early stages, and Betsy Schmidt served as a most understanding editor as this volume neared completion. We are also indebted to George Elison and Patricia Rachal, each of whom provided us with expert editorial assistance, and to Linda Martinek, who helped in typing the final manuscript. Finally, we have been most fortunate to extend the ties of friendship and draw on the recognized expertise of the men and women serving on our Editorial Advisory Board. Their willingness to join us in this experiment, to give their time to soliciting articles and their abilities to reviewing those that have been submitted, have made this series possible and have earned them our sincerest thanks.

L. M.
P.M.S.
Waterville, Maine
October 1974

INTRODUCTION TO THIS VOLUME

I

In most Western democracies, political parties have served as a stabilizing element over recent decades in which the electoral process has undergone rapid and far-reaching change. Political parties have acted as intermediaries between the voters and the decisions the voters must reach. In an age in which the government is playing an expanding role in citizens' everyday lives, in which scientific breakthroughs have led to vastly different methods of appealing to voters, parties have maintained their role as simplifiers. They limit alternatives to ones the voter can easily understand.

Most recently, however, evidence has been accumulating which leads one to question whether parties will continue to play the same role in the future as they have in the past. Walter Dean Burnham has talked about "the onward march of party decomposition." Observers of American parties have looked with alarm at the increasing percentage of voters not affiliating with either major party, at the extent of ticket-splitting, at the successes of third-party and independent candidates, and at the number of prominent political figures who have switched from one party to the other. Do these signs mean that the American parties, parties that have served as stable symbols to which a large majority of voters have attached themselves since the Civil War, are losing their meaning to the electorate?

Nor is this phenomenon a uniquely American experience. In Great Britain, generally considered the very model of a stable, two-party, parliamentary democracy, questions have been raised concerning the continued stability of the party system. Samuel Beer points to the decline in party organization at the local level, a weakening of attachment to party (as evidenced by the dramatic rise in "Don't Knows" in preelection polls), and a "striking increase in electoral volatility." In recent years the erosion of major party strength has been accelerated by the precipitous growth of local separatist parties in Scotland and Wales, an increase in separatist sentiments among Northern Ireland Unionists, and the revival of Liberal Party fortunes. The logical result from this fragmentation—minority government—was reached in the election of February 1974.

In Canada, for a somewhat different but parallel set of reasons, the Trudeau government was hobbled by the same affliction. Elsewhere in Europe, the warning symptoms of party weakness are in full evidence: the collapse of the Gaullist party in France following the death of Georges Pompidou, and the catastrophic regularity with which party governments collapse in Italy.

This questioning of the continued capacity of parties to aid in the electoral process led to our choice of the theme for the first volume of the Electoral Studies Yearbook. What will be the future of political parties? How will the electorate relate to parties? How will parties as institutions respond to challenges to their traditional roles? How will changes in the party function affect the governing process?

II

Each author in this volume approaches these issues from a slightly different point of view. Five articles deal with the party in the electorate, to use V. O. Key's familiar categorization of party activities; two deal primarily with party organization; and one deals with the party in government.

Several sorts of issues are relevant for those authors who are concerned with the future of party in the electorate. Probing the stability of party attachments in recent years, for which Survey Research Center data are available, two of the articles challenge the conventional assumption that party identification is some "predetermined, stable, exogenous variable which exists autonomously at the center of the electoral process." John Jackson argues that electors are governed less by traditional sentiments than by their evaluations of parties in terms of issues which are personally relevant. According to Jackson, the pattern which the process of realignment follows will depend on "which issues are important, the positions of the members of each group on these issues, and the policies associated with each party." In a related article, Richard Trilling asserts that "party image," a reflection of how voters perceive a party based on how it has performed in the past, leads to partisan choice. Both arguments have an important bearing upon any understanding of electoral change.

Evidence that the distinctive shape of parties in the electorate is changing, and their coherence dissolving, is discussed in several of the articles. Gerald Finch analyzes the breakdown of the New Deal Coalition by noting the aging of the electorate and the fact that specific segments of the American citizenry have moved from one geographic region to another in patterns that accentuate the breakdown, rather than the reinforcement, of old alliances. David Kemp, in a thoughtful discussion of Australian politics, examines the validity of several arguments about the effects of post-industrial society upon the parties in the electorate.

Both Kemp and John Gargan describe the growth of third parties. However, while each presents his findings as a response of a party system to post-industrial society, and thus each model might be used to judge the direction in which similar societies will go if decomposition is indeed upon us, it would be difficult to find parties more dissimilar in origin, composition, and issue concerns than the Conservative Party in New York State and the Australia Party Kemp discusses.

Parties, as organizations, have reacted variously to the challenges of modernity. Louis Maisel's article on party organization looks at the effects of recent reforms of the Democratic Party in leading to increased participation and to responsiveness by party officials in the state of Maine. Maisel feels that the desired impact of increased participation and party responsiveness can be achieved when local party officials make sincere efforts and address the controversial issues of the day. Spencer Wellhofer and his associates have traced several aspects of organizational change during the development of the labor parties in Great Britain and Norway. In a mood less optimistic than Maisel's, Wellhofer, Hanby, and Hennessey demonstrate that in some circumstances reforms succeed only until the reformers themselves reach a position of dominance and a new, conservative, not-too-participatory status quo asserts itself. They maintain that the types of inducements used to attract party members are a crucial variable. The stages of party development outlined in their article provide an important framework in which to view the nascent Australia Party Kemp discusses.

Finally, in an article that draws together many of the various issues implied by the title of this volume, Walter Dean Burnham takes a cold and sombre look at the future of American parties. Proceeding under the assumption that the period of "critical realignment" in which we now find ourselves is fundamentally different from any that have preceded it—in that it will lead to the decomposition of parties—Burnham raises important questions about the future performance of the party in government. If his assumptions about the future of the party in the electorate are correct, his discussion about the effectiveness or futility of a fragmented party as it attempts to govern has obvious relevance for many national party systems.

III

Just as these authors approach the subject from different points of view, so too do they employ different techniques to examine their data. To point to obvious differences, Wellhofer-Hanby-Hennessey have used a historical approach to the examination of party, while Kemp's analysis clearly reflects the views of a political sociologist, and Jackson has based his analysis upon econometric models. Many of the articles examine masses of data in aggregate form, while others look in more depth at individual cases. The diversity of methodological approaches represented in this volume, and indeed within some of the individual articles, reflects the spread of techniques and theories which have been applied to the study of the electoral process and with which scholars and students alike are becoming familiar. The authors, the majority of whom are political scientists, have attempted to present their findings and their judgments about the importance of these findings for the future of political parties in such a manner that the practicing politician and the layman can understand them as easily as the scholar who is more concerned with the techniques employed and the rigor of the proofs. This effort follows from their sharing of our belief that it is necessary to have one forum to which all concerned with the general area of electoral studies may turn.

IV

Is there then a common answer? What is the future of political parties? This much seems clear. That scholars the world over are examining this question, looking at different national systems, from different points of departure, with different methodologies, that they are arriving at different—often conflicting—opinions, attest to the fact that we are in the midst of a complex era in which parties are undergoing fundamental change. The electorate is more educated and, because government has an immediate effect on each person, watches politics more closely. To echo V. O. Key's dedication to *The Responsible Electorate,* "The voters are not fools." Society is undergoing vast changes as we move from the industrial to the post-industrial age. The interactions of voters and party officials, of party systems and governing systems, are currently in a state of flux. All aspects of these changes and all issues concerning the future of political parties are not discussed here. However, this much is evident: the continued stability of democratic systems may well depend on how political leaders respond to this evolving situation and on whether parties can continue to play the necessary intermediary role when a new equilibrium is reached.

Louis Maisel
Paul M. Sacks
Waterville, Maine
November 1974

Chapter 1

PHYSICAL CHANGE AND PARTISAN CHANGE:
THE EMERGENCE OF A NEW
AMERICAN ELECTORATE, 1952-1972

GERALD B. FINCH

The accelerated pace of social and political crises since the early
1960s has awakened a sense of history in American electoral analysis.
Every leading indicator of critical elections has appeared in the past
decade, and what remains of the New Deal party system seems
headed for realignment. In the past, realignments have been more
than random, isolated events that reshuffled party constituencies.
The critical election appears to be the chief instrument of American
political change, "America's surrogate for revolution," in Burnham's
words (1967: 289). Scattered evidence suggests, for example, that
critical elections are linked to changes in American political
institutions and the behavior of elites who occupy them (Westin,
1953; Shannon, 1968: 175-176; Burnham, 1970; Ladd, 1970;
Turner, 1970: 242-245; Forsythe, 1974). At the same time, critical
elections deflect challenges to regime legitimacy, and thus minimize
the likelihood of fundamental political change, by compressing
discontent into the confines of electoral politics.

AUTHOR'S NOTE: I am indebted to Keith Sours and Barry Warren for their assistance in
preparing this paper. Dall Forsythe, John Hammond, and Ezra Zask made helpful comments
on an earlier draft. I am also pleased to acknowledge the support of the Center for
Computing Activities and the Council for Research in the Social Sciences, both of Columbia
University. Survey data for this study were made available by the Inter-University
Consortium for Political Research, which of course bears no responsibility for my
interpretations.

[13]

Electoral behavior at the individual level has never been observed in a period of realignment. Survey data are necessary to achieve this sort of detail, of course, and surveys possessing the size and scope required for most academic studies of voting span only about half of the New Deal alignment. Still, an impressive amount of electoral change is apparent even in this abbreviated time series. Its broad outlines, which I will sketch in the following pages, suggest that physical changes in the national electorate—changes in its generational and racial composition and in its geographic distribution—have eroded the dimensions of cleavage that structured party loyalties in the New Deal party system.

The simplest and most extensive type of physical change, generational replacement, may help to explain the general pattern of American electoral change, particularly the measured intervals at which realignments occur. Generational turnover has weakened the New Deal alignment and increased the potential for realignment by adding large numbers of young independents to the electorate. In addition, geographic mobility since the New Deal has had significant partisan repercussions at both the regional and national levels. The southward migration of Northern whites, most of them Republicans and most with managerial or professional skills, contributed to the South's growing estrangement from the national Democratic Party. The northward migration and urban concentration of Southern blacks, most of them uprooted from a rural environment, increased their strategic importance as a source of votes and heightened overt racial conflict. Closely related to the latter population shift, the recent full-scale entry of blacks into electoral politics has expanded the size and diversity of the national electorate and disrupted party constituencies.

Based on age, less than half of the 1972 electorate was eligible to vote before the end of World War II. If the effective disenfranchisement of Southern blacks prior to the 1960s is taken into account, the discontinuity over time in electorates is even greater. Numbers such as these lead one to suspect that physical change in the electorate may be the principal source of partisan change at the aggregate level.

I. AGE, PARTY IDENTIFICATION, AND POLITICAL GENERATIONS

Realignments have occurred about once every generation. More precisely, those who were eligible to vote in one critical election have been a minority of the electorate when the next one occurred. Because evidence on the relationship between age and electoral behavior is quite plentiful, I will briefly review it and attempt to develop a rudimentary overview of generational succession and partisan change. I will then examine the impact of generational change on regional and class divisions in partisanship.

The inverse association between the length of time one has identified with a party and the likelihood that this support will change—a pattern commonly referred to as political immuniza- tion[1]—is among the best-documented findings of voting research (Campbell et al., 1960: 161-167; McPhee and Ferguson, 1962; Converse, 1969: esp. 142-145). Because the length of continuous party identification tends to increase with age, immunity to partisan change increases accordingly. Young voters entering the electorate in times of political normalcy tend to be disproportionately inde- pendent and weakly identified, and, under normal conditions, they become less independent and more strongly partisan with the passage of time. Figure 1 illustrates the relationship between age and party identification in periods of normal alignment (Inglehart and Hoch- stein, 1972: 348).

The process of political immunization implies that partisan change in general, and realignment in particular, occurs unevenly throughout the electorate. There is some empirical support for this suspicion. Survey studies since the New Deal realignment indicate that a "depression generation" was largely responsible for the sudden change in party strength that occurred in the 1930s. According to Campbell and his associates (1960: 155), "the Great Depression swung a heavy proportion of the young electors toward the Democratic Party and gave that party a hold on that generation, which it has never fully relinquished." A recent study by Abramson (1974) suggests that the social cleavages dividing an electorate during a critical election are most evident several decades later in the voting choices of those who were relatively young during the realigning period. He reports that class voting in presidential elections from 1948 to 1968 was highest among voters who were between 23 and 32 years old in 1936.

If it is true that the potential for realignment depends on the generational composition of the electorate, members of different generations must differ in their immunity to partisan change at comparable stages of the life cycle. The likelihood that a voter's party identification will change, in other words, must depend not

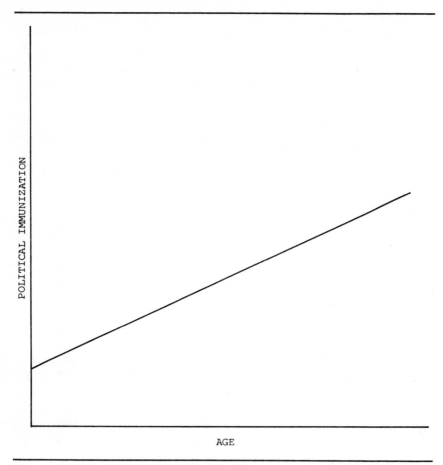

Figure 1: POLITICAL IMMUNIZATION AND AGE

only on his position in the life cycle, but on his membership in a particular generation. If not, the potential for realignment could not change appreciably over time, since the number of young voters in the electorate should be fairly constant (unless birth and mortality rates change radically from one generation to the next).

The existence of generational differences in political immunization would have to be the product of a learning process that reflects each generation's shared political experiences. One method by which such learning might occur is suggested by McPhee's model of electoral dynamics (McPhee and Smith, 1962; McPhee, 1963). As the voters "raised" by McPhee's simulation progress through a series of elections, their partisanship is weighted by the cumulative intensity of their past electoral involvement. In elections marked by an unusually high level of politicization, most voters manifest a surplus of partisan intensity that substantially modifies the strength, and in many instances the direction, of their party identification. Campaigns in which voters have little interest, on the other hand, leave no lasting impression on their party identification. McPhee leaves the basic relationship between age and partisan stability undisturbed by also providing for the effects of political immunization. The importance of his simulation for the present analysis, however, is that it postulates differences in partisan stability which exist independent of age and depend on the conditions of one's past electoral involvement.[2]

Based on this relationship, one possible account of generational change and electoral change can be outlined (also, see Sundquist, 1973: 33-34) as follows:

(1) Broadly speaking, the electorate will be composed of two different age cohorts fifteen to twenty years after a realignment: (a) the realignment cohort, which entered the electorate before or during the realignment, and which therefore was exposed to the intense conflict of the realigning period; (b) the postrealignment cohort, which reached voting age after electoral conflict had assumed more normal proportions.

(2) Given the diminished level of partisan conflict to which it is exposed, the postrealignment cohort is very likely to acquire party identification secondhand, as a result of intergenerational transmission.

(3) In the short run, intergenerational transmission will maintain the party balance and group cleavages established by a critical election, but it is unlikely to promote the long-term stability of an alignment; memories of the conflicts that realigned the party system are less likely to be transmitted across generations than the product of these conflicts, party identification.

(4) Members of the realignment cohort, who are more likely to have acquired partisanship firsthand, receive an added push toward political immunization which is lacking among members of the postrealignment cohort, who are more likely to have acquired partisanship secondhand; both types of voters proceed at the same rate toward political immunization, but those in the electorate during periods of realignment have a head start (Figure 2).

(5) The likelihood of partisan change is fairly high even among the oldest members of the postrealignment cohort, and fairly low even among the youngest members of the realignment cohort (Figure 2); consequently, realignment is more likely to occur after the postrealignment cohort is a sizable portion of the electorate.

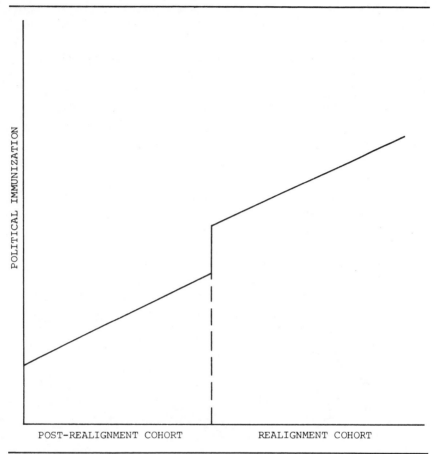

Figure 2: **POLITICAL IMMUNIZATION IN REALIGNMENT AND
POST-REALIGNMENT COHORTS**

(6) When realignment occurs, it will be centered almost entirely in the postrealignment cohort; the realignment cohort will remain frozen in the divisions established by the preceding critical election.

The group basis of an alignment can be maintained for some time by the intergenerational transmission of party loyalty along the lines of social cleavage that were politicized in the previous critical election. Barring dramatic rates of social, geographic, or ethnic assimilation, middle-class Republicans will raise middle-class Republicans, Southern Democrats will raise Southern Democrats, and Catholic Democrats will raise Catholic Democrats. As Converse (1966b) points out in his study of religion and politics, a stable socialization process can maintain a group's partisan distinctiveness long after the group's political self-consciousness has eroded. While the salient cleavages of a critical election will continue to run deep in the realignment cohort, few such cleavages are so obdurate in America as to become a conscious component of party identification in succeeding generations. The continued division of young voters along these lines is principally the result of political socialization, and is best regarded as a geologic feature of the alignment.[3] Such divisions should fade as new tensions emerge, however, and younger voters should gradually dealign until the conditions necessary to trigger a realignment are present.[4]

II. A NOTE ON COHORT DEFINITION

Cohort analyses abound in the literature of the social sciences (see especially Crittenden, 1962; Ryder, 1965; Glenn and Grimes, 1968; Converse, 1969; Crittenden, 1969-1970; Cutler, 1969-1970; Abramson, 1971; Klecka, 1971; Inglehart, 1971; Inglehart and Hochstein, 1972; Foner, 1972; Hyman, 1972: ch. 7; Abramson, 1974; more inclusively, see citations in Foner, 1974: 195-196), and it is rare to find much overlap between studies in cohort definition. In the analysis that follows, the realignment cohort includes those born before 1924 (who would have been eligible to vote for President by 1944), and the postrealignment cohort includes those born in 1924 or later (who would not have entered the presidential electorate until 1948 or later).[5] As Figure 3 indicates, the postrealignment cohort was a majority of the electorate by 1972, and some members of this cohort were in fact approaching middle age: the oldest members of the postwar cohort were 48 years old in 1972. Because there was a thirty-year range in age in 1972 among members of the postwar cohort,[6] this classification is extremely broad. All members of the young cohort came of age politically after the New Deal had ended, however, and its end marked a significant change in American electoral politics. Further subdivision of these cohorts is clearly possible, but this division seems adequate for exploratory purposes.[7]

The exact point at which cohorts are divided is not generally a matter of theoretical self-evidence. Roosevelt's long tenure in office suggests that the New Deal cast an unusually long shadow on American politics, one that did not finally disappear until after World War II. FDR's presence at the head of the national Democratic

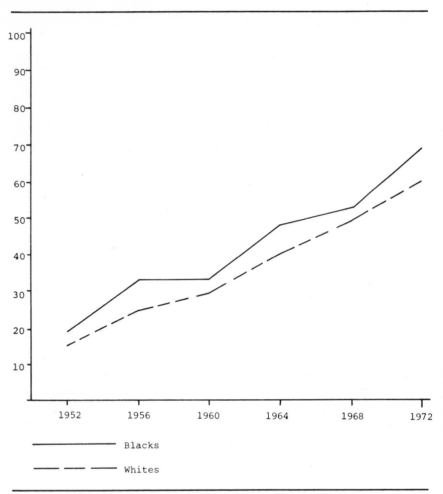

Figure 3: PERCENT OF THE ELECTORATE IN THE POSTWAR COHORT, 1952-1972, BY RACE

ticket in four consecutive elections kept alive memories of the New Deal, and exposed those entering the electorate before 1945 to its most visible symbol.

In addition, there is little question that American politics had entered a different era by 1948. Internal divisions within the New Deal Democratic coalition were symbolized by two splinter parties: a leftist third party and a segregationist states' rights party. The trend toward white prosperity had just begun in 1948, and foreign policy and anti-Communism had already entered election campaigns. Thus, despite the Democratic appeal to labor in 1948, those first eligible to vote in the Truman-Dewey election were confronted by political circumstances that differed clearly from those that prevailed during the Roosevelt presidency.[8]

The data analyzed here are taken from the presidential-year surveys administered by the Survey Research Center at the University of Michigan.[9] These surveys are cross-sectional, of course, which means that patterns of individual change cannot validly be inferred from changes in the marginal distribution of variables (Hyman, 1972: ch. 6). While net change can be examined, it cannot be disaggregated to reveal the gross change from which it is constituted. Because the basic thrust of this analysis involves relative changes in the alignment of groups, however, this is not a serious limitation.

A rather more serious problem is posed by changes over time in group composition (Hyman, 1972: chs. 6-7). The aggregate partisan change produced by cohort attrition, interregional migration, and social mobility can easily be confused with individual-level partisan change. While several methods for disentangling these processes are used in the following analysis, they are crude and necessarily presumptuous.

III. REGIONAL POLARIZATION IN THE WHITE ELECTORATE

Sectionalism has been the most abiding source of division in American electoral politics. North-South struggles over the expansion of state authority figured most directly in the party systems of 1860 and 1896, but the loyalties established in these years persisted well into the twentieth century.[10] Although sectional conflicts have shaped party systems in several Western regimes, the fiercest of these conflicts usually parallel ethnic, religious, or linguistic subcultures. The resilience of American sectionalism is all the more remarkable because it is not rooted directly in such easily identifiable traditions (cf. Burnham, 1968: 12-13).

The South's solidly Democratic composition after 1932 is generally regarded as a complete anomaly, "an astonishing tribute to the inertia of history and human institutions," in Converse's opinion (1972: 308). Appeals to social rank in 1932 were not sectionally oriented, at least not in any direct or deliberate way, and the rural, nativist South seemed totally out of place in a party whose non-Southern support was drawn principally from the urban working class and ethnic minorities. The South rejected the urban wing of the

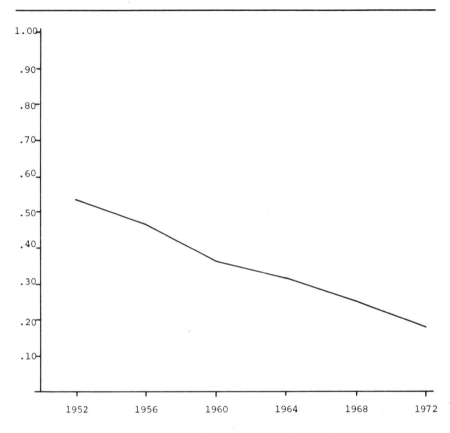

*South includes border states; polarization is measured by a gamma coefficient (a positive coefficient means that Democratic identification is more frequent among Southerners); all coefficients are based on at least 1,547 cases; weighted samples were used in 1960, 1964, and 1968.

Figure 4: REGIONAL POLARIZATION, 1952-1972 (whites only)*

Democrats in 1928, yet returned to its steadfast Democratic loyalty until after World War II.[11] The long-awaited realignment in Southern presidential voting finally occurred in the postwar years, and the South has recently been a regular source of electoral votes for Republican presidential candidates. I will discuss the erosion of Democratic loyalty in the South as a change in the New Deal alignment, not as a delayed adaptation to it (an "aftershock of the New Deal earthquake," in Sundquist's metaphor [1973: ch. 12]). Had a commitment to black civil rights not been made by the post-New Deal Democratic Party, it is likely that the South would still be strongly, if not solidly, Democratic.

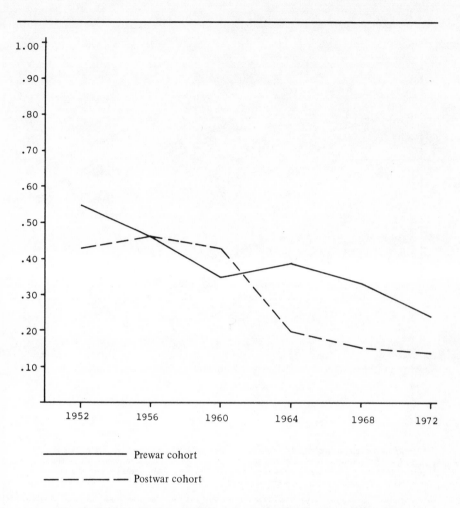

Prewar cohort

Postwar cohort

*South includes border states; polarization is measured by a gamma coefficient (a positive coefficient means that Democratic identification is more frequent among Southerners); all coefficients for prewar cohort are based on at least 950 cases; all coefficients for postwar cohort are based on at least 242 cases.

Figure 5: REGIONAL POLARIZATION, 1952-1972, BY COHORT (whites only)*

The sectional convergence of white partisanship has progressed steadily since 1952, as Figure 4 indicates. Although the growth of Southern Republicanism is one component of this trend, a more important component is the jump in independent identification in both regions. Independent identifiers nearly doubled in the South from 1952 to 1972, increasing from 16 to 31% of the electorate. The number of independent identifiers in the North showed a similar rise, climbing from 26% of the electorate in 1952 to 39% in 1972.

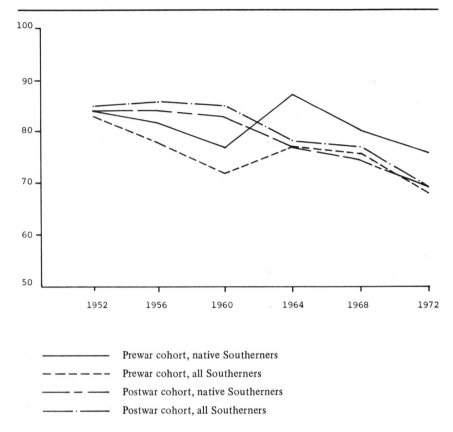

Prewar cohort, native Southerners

Prewar cohort, all Southerners

Postwar cohort, native Southerners

Postwar cohort, all Southerners

*Excludes independents; South includes border states; all percentages for prewar cohort native Southerners are based on at least 239 cases; all percentages for postwar cohort native Southerners are based on at least 50 cases; weighted samples were used in 1960, 1964, and 1968.

Figure 6: PERCENT DEMOCRATIC OF TWO-PARTY IDENTIFICATION, 1952-1972, BY COHORT, AMONG WHITE SOUTHERNERS*

There is not much difference between the two cohorts in the pattern of regional polarization. As Figure 5 shows, regional polarization dropped at a fairly similar rate in both cohorts over the twenty-year period. Although regional polarization is higher in most years in the prewar cohort, there is no evidence that party identification in this cohort was frozen along regional lines.

Because regions are not closed populations, some of the change in Figures 4 and 5 could reflect the assimilative effect of geographic mobility. There has been a substantial rate of population interchange between the North and South since World War II, and the southward movement of middle-class Northern Republicans has been shown by

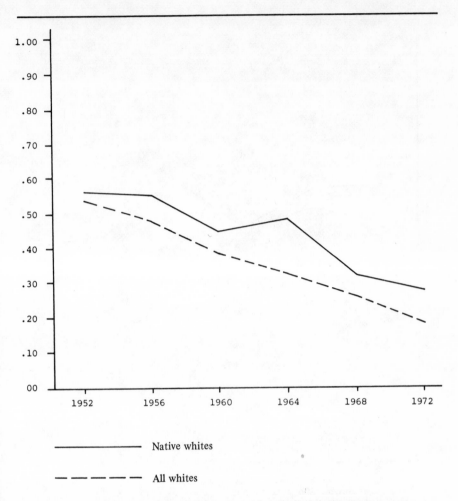

- Native whites

- - - - - - All whites

*South includes border states; polarization is measured by a gamma coefficient (a positive coefficient means that Democratic identification is more frequent among Southerners); all coefficients for native whates are based on at least 1,368 cases; weighted samples were used in 1960, 1964, and 1968.

Figure 7: REGIONAL POLARIZATION, 1952-1972, AMONG WHITES NATIVE TO THEIR REGION OF RESIDENCE AND AMONG ALL WHITES*

Converse (1966a) to be an important source of Southern Republicanism. The proportion of white Southern respondents raised in the North increased from 7% in 1952 to 18% in 1972; the fraction of the Northern electorate raised in the South was stable over the same period (12% in 1952, 11% in 1972).

The two streams of white migration were mirror images of one another in occupational and partisan terms. The South-to-North

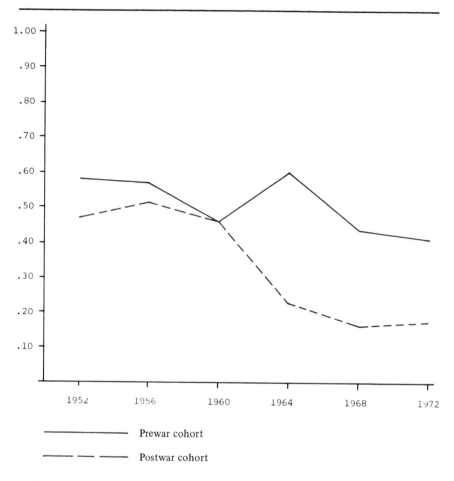

*South includes border states; polarization is measured by a gamma coefficient (a positive coefficient means that Democratic identification is more frequent among Southerners); all coefficients for prewar cohort are based on at least 807 cases; all coefficients for postwar cohort are based on at least 225 cases; weighted samples were used in 1960, 1964, and 1968.

Figure 8: REGIONAL POLARIZATION, 1952-1972, BY COHORT, AMONG WHITES NATIVE TO THEIR REGION OF RESIDENCE*

movement was largely blue-collar and Democratic, while the North-to-South movement was mainly white-collar and Republican. Perhaps more important for the present analysis, the migration in both directions affected the composition of the older cohort more than the younger cohort. As a result, much less movement toward Republicanism is evident in the South once geographic mobility is accounted for (Figure 6), but this is true only in the prewar Southern cohort: the younger cohort's drift toward Republicanism holds up even after controlling for the effect of in-migration.[12]

Regional polarization drops less sharply from 1952 to 1972 once the effect of in-migration is removed (Figure 7). Moreover, as Figure 8 shows, removing the immigrants from both cohorts reveals a pronounced intergenerational difference in the persistence of regional polarization: the regional convergence of party identification is much greater, and has occurred much more rapidly, in the postwar cohort. On the other hand, geographic mobility was primarily responsible for the downward trend of regional polarization in the prewar cohort; very little net partisan change is evident among members of the older cohort native to the region in which they reside.[13] Thus, two different sources of physical change have combined to lessen the sectionalism of the New Deal alignment.

Life-stage controls show that regional polarization was .31 less in 1972 than it was in 1952 among respondents between the ages of 29 and 48—an age grouping that in 1952 included the youngest members of the realignment cohort, and in 1972 included the oldest members of the postrealignment cohort.[14] Additionally, regional polarization fell more rapidly among members of the postwar cohort who were eligible to vote in 1952 than it did in the prewar cohort.

Given the probable importance of socialization for maintaining partisan alignments, the diminished level of regional polarization since 1960 in the younger electorate appears to signal a major disruption in the rate at which party identification was transmitted intergenerationally. Very sharp differences emerge, both in 1952 and in 1972, when recollections of paternal partisanship are compared regionally (Table 1). The fact that nearly 80% of the younger Southern cohort interviewed in 1952 reported having Democratic fathers, and that a scant 2% came from nonpartisan homes, gives a sense of how rigidly Democratic the South was. There is no doubt that the South would have remained heavily Democratic, and the post-1932 alignment sectionally divided, if Southern partisanship had continued to be transmitted intergenerationally with a high rate of success. The in-migration of Northern Republicans would have altered the configuration of Southern partisanship in any case, but the change would have been fairly marginal had the South's socialization process continued to function smoothly.

The extraordinary effectiveness of Southern socialization as late as 1952 can be seen from the data in Table 2. Over 70% of the prewar Southern cohort was raised Democratic, and nearly 90% of this

Table 1. REPORTED PARTY IDENTIFICATION OF FATHER, 1952 AND 1972, AMONG WHITES NATIVE TO THEIR REGION OF RESIDENCE*

	Prewar Cohort			
	North		South	
	1952	1972	1952	1972
Democrat %	46	50	77	77
n	340	231	213	167
Independent %	12	4	3	4
n	94	20	9	8
Republican %	42	46	20	19
n	316	209	56	21

	Postwar Cohort			
	North		South	
	1952	1972	1952	1972
Democrat %	60	53	78	73
n	97	401	39	214
Independent %	13	11	2	7
n	21	86	1	21
Republican %	27	36	20	20
n	45	275	10	60

*Excluding those whose fathers were floaters, apoliticals, or who cannot recall father's partisan behavior; South includes border states.

group had come to identify with the Democrats by 1952. By contrast, only about 60% of the older Northern cohort with Democratic fathers became Democratic identifiers. Almost 80% of the younger Southern cohort reported having Democratic fathers, and 78% of this group identified with the Democrats in 1952. A much smaller proportion of the postwar Northern cohort reported having a Democratic father, and only 62% of this group was Democratic in 1952.

For Democratic loyalty to have been transmitted so successfully from one Southern generation to the next obviously required a high degree of institutional and cultural reinforcement and an exceptional social structure. It was not simply that each generation was raised by an almost uniformly Democratic older generation, but that each generation was raised in an unusually well-insulated environment, of which parental partisanship is the element most accessible with survey data. The infusion of Yankee Republicans and the mobilization of blacks changed that environment radically, however, and, by 1972, the rate at which paternal partisanship was retained by members of the postwar cohort showed little regional variation

Table 2. INTERGENERATIONAL TRANSMISSION OF PARTISANSHIP, 1952, AMONG WHITES NATIVE TO THEIR REGION OF RESIDENCE[a]

| | Prewar Cohort | |
	North	South[b]
Father Democrat/		
Respondent Democrat, %	60	87
n	207	184
Father Republican/		
Respondent Republican, %	64	59
n	202	32
	Postwar Cohort	
	North	South[b]
Father Democrat/		
Respondent Democrat, %	62	78
n	59	29
Father Republican/		
Respondent Republican, %	60	c
n	27	3

a. Cell percentage is proportion of those adopting father's party identification.
b. South includes border states.
c. Too few cases for reliable estimates.

(Table 3).[15] The older cohort, on the other hand, was relatively stable over time. In 1952, 78% of the young Southerners with Democratic fathers were also Democrats; by 1972, this percentage had shrunk to 55. A change of this order is doubly significant in view of the highly skewed pro-Democratic distribution of paternal partisanship recalled by this cohort.

As Table 4 indicates, the breakdown of intergenerational transmission in the younger cohort of both regions has not been produced by the sort of party switching that would indicate a realignment. Indeed, the most important consequence of the younger cohort's increased rejection of paternal partisanship, both in the North and in the South, has been a shift toward dealignment. The Republican share of the postwar Southern cohort increased from 12% in 1952 to 18% in 1972; the independent portion grew from 18% to 40% over the same period. Both parties lost strength in the younger Northern cohort; and independent identifiers, who constituted 31% of the cohort in 1952, were more numerous (48%) than either Democrats (29%) or Republicans (22%) by 1972. Dealignment is also suggested by the fact that over 60% of the younger cohort raised by apolitical or independent fathers was not aligned with either party in 1972, a

Table 3. INTERGENERATIONAL TRANSMISSION OF PARTISANSHIP, 1972,
AMONG WHITES NATIVE TO THEIR REGION OF RESIDENCE[a]

	Prewar Cohort	
	North	South[b]
Father Democrat/		
Respondent Democrat, %	57	79
n	132	129
Father Republican/		
Respondent Republican, %	64	66
n	133	27
	Postwar Cohort	
	North	South[b]
Father Democrat/		
Respondent Democrat, %	50	55
n	200	116
Father Republican/		
Respondent Republican, %	44	58
n	119	34

a. Cell percentage is proportion of those adopting father's party identification.
b. South includes border states.

figure that should be somewhat lower in the wake of a realignment. The relationships in Tables 3 and 4 easily survive life-stage controls.

The trend toward sectional convergence produced by geographic mobility was spotted by Converse a decade ago, and his analysis needs no amplification. He was careful to distinguish convergence from realignment, because the latter would require a massive shift of party loyalty among native Southerners that did not appear to be forthcoming. The potential for realignment now appears to be much greater among native Southerners, but only because of generational replacement.[16] Over half of the native Southern electorate in 1972 was not eligible to vote before 1948, and all indications are that this electorate differs in important respects from the previous generation. It is clearly not a dependable source of Democratic presidential votes.

It is possible that regional polarization has subsided only temporarily and that the potential still exists for the creation of a new party system divided on sectional lines. The large bloc of white Southern independents in the postwar cohort raises the obvious prospect of their mobilization by a third party, particularly in view of Wallace's success among young independents in 1968 (Converse et al., 1969: 1103-1104). If no such party materializes, a cohesive and

Table 4. PARTISAN ALIGNMENT BY FATHER'S PARTISAN BEHAVIOR, 1952 AND 1972, AMONG WHITES NATIVE TO THEIR REGION OF RESIDENCE[a]

	Prewar Cohort			
	Father was Party Identifier		Father was Not Party Identifier	
	North	*South*[b]	*North*	*South*[b]
Percentage in 1952	80	89	61	59
n	532	238	125	19
Percentage in 1972	76	85	54	55
n	332	176	43	11

	Postwar Cohort			
	Father was Party Identifier		Father was Not Party Identifier	
	North	*South*[b]	*North*	*South*[b]
Percentage in 1952	71	78	46	c
n	101	38	16	2
Percentage in 1972	57	64	30	38
n	382	175	50	23

a. Cell percentage is proportion of respondents identifying with a party.
b. South includes border states; nonpartisan fathers include independents, apoliticals, floaters, and those whose partisan behavior could not be recalled by respondent.
c. Too few cases for reliable estimates.

lasting shift of young Southerners to either of the two major parties is unlikely. White Southerners in the postwar cohort are as favorably inclined as their Northern counterparts toward social welfare programs, as Table 5 indicates, but they are much less sympathetic than young Northerners to black demands for social change. Roughly the same contrast exists among older whites. If there is not much change in the platforms of the two major parties—if Democrats continue to be more liberal than the Republicans on both social welfare and race—then it is hard to believe that the South will, as a region, embrace either major party for an extended period of time.

IV. CLASS POLARIZATION IN THE WHITE ELECTORATE

The New Deal realignment perhaps best illustrates the tendency for potential threats to regime legitimacy to be diverted by the electoral process. The massive unrest that followed America's economic collapse "signaled political disaffection on a scale unparalleled in the American experience," in the phrase of Piven and Cloward (1971: 68):

Table 5. ATTITUDES TOWARD GOVERNMENT-GUARANTEED JOBS AND
SCHOOL INTEGRATION, AMONG WHITES NATIVE TO THEIR
REGION OF RESIDENCE*

| | Prewar Cohort | | | | | |
| | Percent Favoring Job Guarantee | | Percent | Percent Favoring School Integration | | Percent |
	North	South	Difference	North	South	Difference
1956	59	70	−11	46	25	+21
n	411	156		312	61	
1960	61	63	− 2	52	17	+35
n	390	181	−	309	52	
1964	29	35	− 6	50	14	+36
n	360	180		618	75	
1968	29	23	+ 6	40	19	+21
n	214	74		290	60	

| | Postwar Cohort | | | | | |
| | Percent Favoring Job Guarantee | | Percent | Percent Favoring School Integration | | Percent |
	North	South	Difference	North	South	Difference
1956	54	61	− 7	58	34	+24
n	122	54		129	31	
1960	59	59	0	63	41	+22
n	176	72		183	89	
1964	33	33	0	54	26	+28
n	321	78		540	69	
1968	33	27	+ 6	47	26	+21
n	252	72		346	70	

*South includes border states; question wording and coding was changed in 1964; 1972
data on school integration attitudes were restricted at the time this paper was written;
weighted samples were used in 1960, 1964, and 1968.

The people were turning against their leaders and against the regime
—against Hoover, against business, even against "the American way." What
direction that disaffection would take was to depend on the responsiveness
of political leaders and the adaptability of the regime.

The Democrats responded by enacting labor legislation and modest
social welfare programs, winning the loyalty of the working class and
reducing the probability of more radical economic change.

Because the American working class was not politically isolated in
the 1930s, it is not surprising that class voting responded in the
postwar years to the immediate circumstances of each campaign. The
short-term impact of class on electoral politics, gauged from voting

behavior rather than party identification, has varied widely since World War II, but has on the whole declined (Campbell et al., 1960: 356-361; Abramson, 1974). The level of class voting in 1948 was easily the highest in any of the postwar presidential elections: postwar prosperity had not yet been fully realized, and labor legislation (the Taft-Hartley Act) was a central issue of the campaign. As the success of Republican presidential candidates since 1952 would suggest, however, working-class support for the Democrats has been erratic. In Abramson's words (1973: 1):

> Unprecedented prosperity since World War II had eroded working-class support for the Democrats, and the mass mobilization of blacks further strained working-class loyalties. Today, a majority of working-class whites no longer support the Democratic Presidential coalition, and, without that support, the Democrats are unable to win.

The declining class basis of electoral politics since World War II is not confined to America. Several accounts have been offered for this trend, and each is based on the spread of Western affluence. As the pie grows larger, these arguments run, class deprivation becomes less acute; consumption supplants subsistence as the principal concern of working-class voters. The repeated Conservative successes in Britain during the 1950s and the consecutive landslide victories of Eisenhower suggested to some that increased affluence in the working class had led to its political *embourgeoisement,* its simultaneous acquisition of middle class patterns of consumption and partisanship (for a brief discussion and critical analysis of *embourgeoisement* in Britain, see Butler and Stokes, 1969: 101-104).

A generationally based account for the atrophy of class politics holds that the growth of "post-bourgeois" (i.e., nonmaterialist) values among Western European youth will slowly change the class basis of party alignments. According to this interpretation, the postwar cohort in Western Europe is more highly educated and less concerned with scarcity than previous generations were, and it is thus more responsive to expressive than to acquisitive issues. According to Inglehart (1971: 1013):

> the presence of post-bourgeois values is linked consistently with a relative tendency to remain loyal to the Left, among those who were brought up in that tradition, and with a tendency to shift to the Left among those who were raised in other political climates.

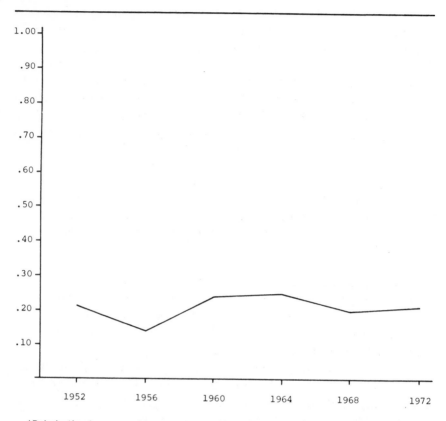

*Polarization is measured by a gamma coefficient (a positive coefficient means that Democratic identification is more frequent among blue-collar workers); all coefficients are based on at least 1,226 cases; weighted samples were used in 1960, 1964, and 1968.

Figure 9: CLASS POLARIZATION, 1952-1972 (whites only)*

Because middle-class youth are particularly likely to have post-bourgeois values, the diminished levels of class voting in Europe would mainly be produced by middle-class support of leftist parties.

Party identification is used here to identify patterns of class alignment in American since 1952. Despite the pronounced changes in class voting in postwar presidential contests, Figure 9 reveals very little change since 1952 in the occupational composition of the party coalitions. A comparison of class polarization[17] in 1952 and 1972 shows no change whatever. Although class polarization was the distinctive characteristic of the New Deal realignment, the electorate was more clearly polarized along sectional lines from 1952 to 1972.

It turns out, however, that changes in regional polarization have been closely related to changes in class polarization. The New Deal class alignment was strictly a Northern phenomenon, and it was not until the 1960s that the native Southern working class became more Democratic than the native Southern middle class. This lag is partly a result of the South's late industrialization. In 1960, according to Converse (1966a: 221-223), lower status respondents were more Democratic than upper status respondents in industrialized counties of the South, but the opposite relationship prevailed in intermediate and rural counties. One particularly important by-product of Southern industrialization, the settlement of Northern middle-class whites in urban areas of the South, greatly contributed to the spread of Republicanism in the Southern middle class. In 1964, for example, the prewar middle-class electorate raised in the South was 12% Republican, but the addition of ex-Northerners raised this figure to 23%.

As Figure 10 shows, class polarization in the native Southern electorate has followed an upward trend since 1952, punctuated by a sharp but partly temporary increase in 1964.[18] Most of the class-related partisan change in the South has occurred in the middle class, and this holds true even after the effect of Northern in-migration is removed. Indeed, the erosion of regional polarization since 1952 is mainly attributable to the sectional convergence of middle-class partisanship. The Democratic share of two-party identi-fication dropped in the Southern middle class from 1952 (92%) to 1972 (70%), while it inched upward in the Northern middle class over the same period (from 44% to 47%).

Generational change has figured prominently in the trend toward convergence, as Figure 11 indicates. Regional polarization in the postwar middle class fell precipitously from 1960 (.66) to 1964 (.20), and reached its lowest value of .15 in 1972. Although regional polarization has also declined in the prewar middle class, from .75 in 1952 to .55 in 1972, it actually increased slightly from 1960 (.66) to 1964 (.68). In 1972, the postwar middle-class electorate native to the South was more Republican (36% of two-party identification) than the prewar native Southern middle class (24%), and the postwar middle class raised in the North was more Democratic (53% of two-party identification) than the prewar Northern middle class (38%).

Class-related partisan change *within* each region also shows intercohort differences, but they run in opposite directions: class polarization has increased in the young Southern electorate, and has declined in the young Northern electorate. As a result, no consistent

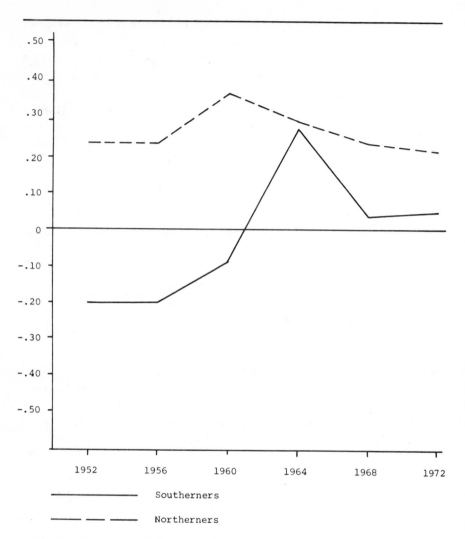

Southerners

Northerners

*South includes border states; polarization is measured by a gamma coefficient (a positive coefficient means that Democratic identification is more frequent among blue-collar workers); all coefficients for the South are based on at least 235 cases; all coefficients for the North are based on at least 848 cases; weighted samples were used in 1960, 1964, and 1968.

Figure 10: CLASS POLARIZATION, 1952-1972, AMONG WHITES NATIVE TO THEIR REGION OF RESIDENCE*

differences emerge on a national level (Figure 12). Class polarization increased fairly rapidly in the South, by .33 in the postwar cohort and by .17 in the prewar cohort. In the postwar cohort, the coefficient of polarization rose from −.20 in 1952 to .13 in 1972; it

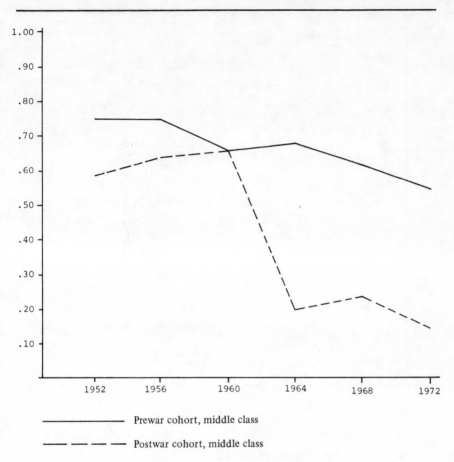

Prewar cohort, middle class

Postwar cohort, middle class

*South includes border states; polarization is measured by a gamma coefficient (a positive coefficient means that Democratic identification is more frequent among Southerners); all coefficients for prewar cohort are based on at least 377 cases; all coefficients for postwar cohort are based on at least 75 cases; weighted samples were used in 1960, 1964, and 1968.

Figure 11: REGIONAL POLARIZATION, 1952-1972, BY COHORT, AMONG MIDDLE-CLASS WHITES NATIVE TO THEIR REGION OF RESIDENCE*

rose in the prewar cohort from −.19 in 1952 to −.02 in 1972.[19] Predictably, class polarization registers a larger increase in the South when ex-Northerners are included in the computations.

Only the North was divided along class lines in the New Deal party system, and here generational replacement has weakened the relationship between class and partisanship (Figure 13). While class polarization was increasing in the young Southern electorate, it was decreasing in the young Northern electorate. Class polarization

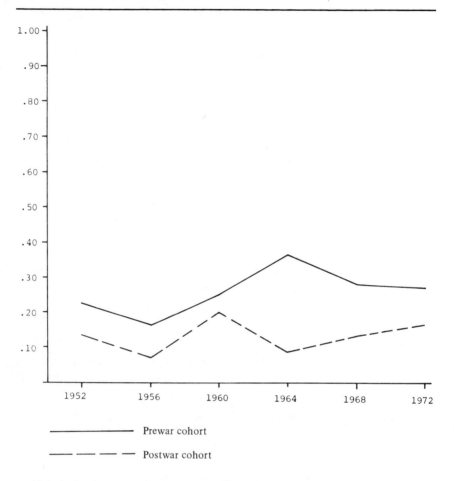

*Polarization is measured by a gamma coefficient (a positive coefficient means that
Democratic identification is more frequent among blue-collar workers); all coefficients
for prewar cohort are based on at least 885 cases; all coefficients for postwar cohort
are based on at least 204 cases; weighted samples were used in 1960, 1964, and 1968.

Figure 12: CLASS POLARIZATION, 1952-1972, BY COHORT (whites only)*

increased from 1952 (.24) to 1972 (.35) in the prewar Northern
cohort, but fell over the same period in the postwar cohort (from .23
to .13). Life-stage controls in the North reveal that class polarization
was .15 less in 1972 than it was in 1952 among 29 to 48 year olds;
the difference in the South is even greater (.56), and of course runs
in the opposite direction.

Unfortunately, examining class polarization within regions allows
the effects of mortality, out-migration, and occupational mobility to
intermingle with, and to produce the appearance of, partisan change

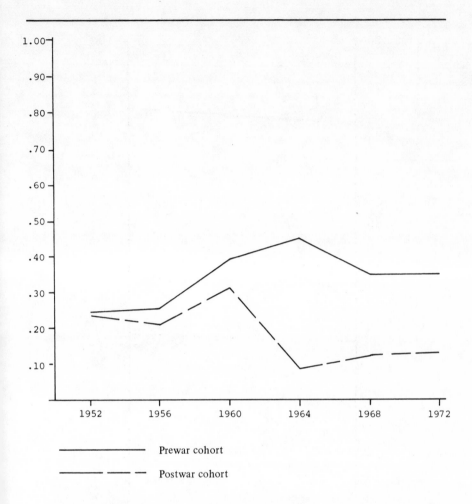

Prewar cohort

Postwar cohort

*North excludes border states; polarization is measured by a gamma coefficient (a positive coefficient means that Democratic identification is more frequent among blue-collar workers); all coefficients for prewar cohort are based on at least 524 cases; all coefficients for postwar cohort are based on at least 152 cases; weighted samples were used in 1960, 1964, and 1968.

Figure 13: CLASS POLARIZATION, 1952-1972, BY COHORT, AMONG NATIVE NORTHERNERS (whites only)*

at the individual level. It is therefore more risky than usual to venture a guess about the sorts of individual change that may have occurred within each region. Because the postwar cohort is more frequently employed in white-collar occupations than members of the prewar cohort were at the same stage of the life cycle,[20] the growth of Democratic strength in the postwar middle class may

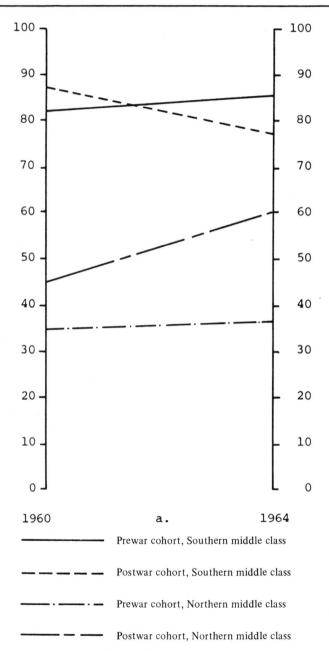

1960   a.   1964

———————— Prewar cohort, Southern middle class

— — — — — Postwar cohort, Southern middle class

——— · ——— · — Prewar cohort, Northern middle class

——— — ——— Postwar cohort, Northern middle class

*Excludes independent identifiers; South includes border states.

Figure 14: **CHANGES IN PERCENT DEMOCRATIC OF TWO-PARTY IDENTIFICATION, 1960-1964, BY COHORT, AMONG WHITES NATIVE TO THEIR REGION OF RESIDENCE***

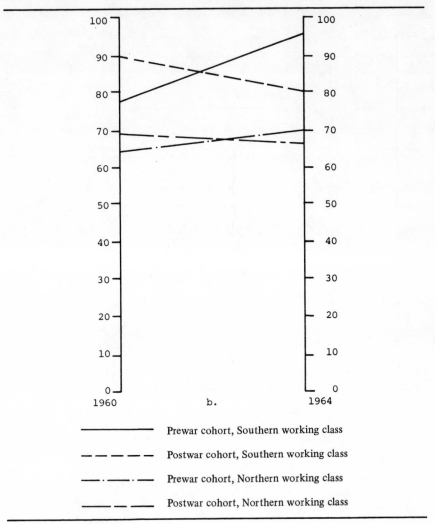

Legend:

————————— Prewar cohort, Southern working class

— — — — — Postwar cohort, Southern working class

—— · —— · —— Prewar cohort, Northern working class

—— — —— Postwar cohort, Northern working class

Figure 14: (Continued)

simply be attributable to upward mobility. This seems especially likely in the North, where many young middle-class respondents might have been raised by parents who were working-class Democrats. If these respondents retained their inherited Democratic identification after entering a white-collar occupation, intercohort differences in class polarization would largely be a result of intergenerational social mobility.

Controls for intergenerational social mobility actually sharpen the cohort differences in class polarization. In the North, for instance, the gap between cohorts widens—though the absolute level of class

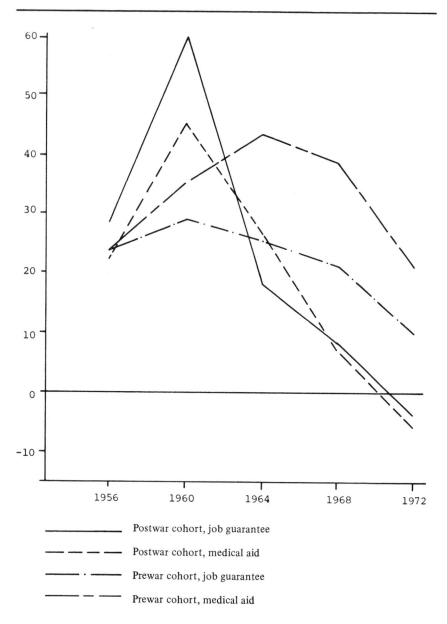

———————— Postwar cohort, job guarantee

— — — — Postwar cohort, medical aid

——— · ——— Prewar cohort, job guarantee

——— — ——— Prewar cohort, medical aid

*North excludes border states; polarization is measured with a gamma coefficient (a positive coefficient means that support for social welfare programs is higher among blue-collar workers); all coefficients for prewar cohort are based on at least 211 cases; all coefficients for postwar cohort are based on at least 205 cases; weighted samples were used in 1960, 1964, and 1968.

Figure 15: CLASS POLARIZATION IN SOCIAL WELFARE ATTITUDES, 1952-1972, BY COHORT, AMONG NORTHERN WHITES NATIVE TO THE NORTH*

polarization rises—when occupationally mobile respondents are removed from the analysis. The same holds true for the South, but small sample sizes in the postwar cohort are troublesome in the early surveys. Because the over-time trends are quite similar to those already discussed, there is no need to present them graphically.

The 1964 election stands out in each of these figures as a time of significant change in American partisanship. There was a sudden shift from 1960 to 1964 in the intricate patterns of regional and class alignment that had persisted in the white electorate since the 1930s (Figure 14). Pronounced cohort differences were first apparent in 1964, and the growth of the postwar cohort since 1964 has steadily narrowed the divisions established or reinforced by the New Deal realignment. Generational replacement in the North has blurred class distinctions in party identification, while in the South it has created a faintly New Dealish class alignment. Class polarization in the native postwar cohorts of both regions was .13 in 1972, compared to .35 in the native Northern prewar cohort, and −.02 in the native Southern prewar cohort.

Class differences in social welfare attitudes have subsided in the Northern postwar cohort (another change that can be traced to 1964), but they remain fairly strong in the prewar cohort (Figure 15). Although periodic changes in questionnaire wording and coding prohibit strict comparisons across election years, it is still possible to examine intercohort variation within each survey. As Figure 15 reveals, support for federal health insurance and a government-guaranteed job did not differ by class among young Northerners interviewed in 1972, but class differences were still apparent among older Northerners. Proportionally, the distribution of these attitudes by cohort has tended to be quite similar over time, but substantial differences between cohorts have developed within each class.

Fully accounting for the disappearance of class divisions in the young Northern electorate's partisan and social welfare attitudes requires a more detailed analysis than that undertaken here. The draft, the Vietnam War, and the cluster of life-style issues are obvious avenues of inquiry in the search for an explanation. So are political apathy and cynicism. Of the possible sources of discontent that come to mind, however, none seems to have the characteristics that realigning issues typically possess (see, e.g., Sundquist, 1973: 278-279), and none is likely to halt the partisan disengagement of this group.

Economic divisions in the Southern white electorate are embedded

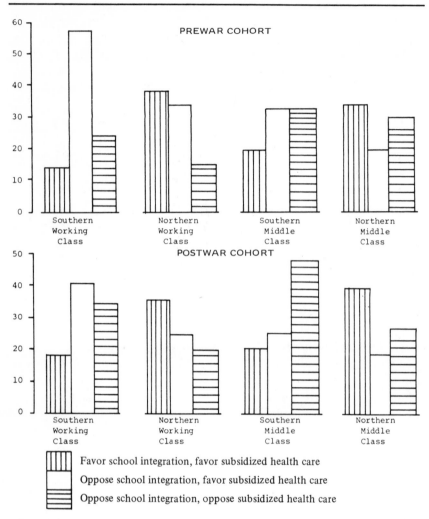

*Bars are the percentage of respondents with a given attitude combination of all those having an attitude on both policies; those favoring school integration and opposing subsidized medical care were included in the percentages but excluded from this graph.

Figure 16: JOINT ATTITUDE DISTRIBUTIONS ON SCHOOL INTEGRATION AND SUBSIDIZED HEALTH CARE, 1968, BY CLASS AND REGION (whites native to their region only)*

in a much broader conflict between the races, and there is no reason to suppose that the new Southern class alignment signals a delayed nationalization of the Northern New Deal party system. Despite the statistically similar levels of class polarization in the young electorates of both regions, significant regional differences in political orientation still exist. Most important, each class is split regionally on the question of black civil rights. In 1968, school integration was supported by 48% of the young Northern working class and by 23% of the young Southern working class (comparable data for 1972 have not yet been released), but there was only a 4% regional difference in support for federally subsidized medical aid (57% in the North, 53% in the South). Responses to both questions exhibited regional contrasts in the postwar middle class: there was a 19% difference in the proportion of white-collar respondents supporting school integration (27% in the South, 46% in the North), and a 12% difference in the proportions opposing federally supported medical aid (49% in the South, 37% in the North).

The opposition to subsidized health care and school integration among many Southern middle-class whites (Figure 16), including those in the postwar cohort, would seem to be ideally suited to the steady growth of conservative Republicanism in the South. A shift in that direction was evident in 1972, when the young Southern middle class was 15% less independent and 13% more Republican than it was in 1968. The tendency of the Southern working class to support subsidized health care and to oppose school integration appears to have little resonance with the social welfare and civil rights policies generally advocated by the two national parties. Wallace's considerable success among Southern working-class voters in 1968 (Burnham, 1972), the year from which the data in Figure 16 are taken, is a good measure of how isolated the Southern working class has become in the contemporary two-party system. Despite the absence of a Wallace party in 1972, there was no significant decrease in the number of young Southern working-class independents (about 40% in 1968 and 1972).

Generational replacement in the South has led to new class patterns of party support, but not to new attitudes on race relations. Race has always shaped class politics in the South, and the standing third-party constituency in the young Southern working class attests to the durability of that influence. Without an economic crisis of a high enough order to submerge racial conflict, this constituency is unlikely to be absorbed on a long-term basis by either major party.

V. RACIAL POLARIZATION

It would be impossible to discuss changes in the electorate since the New Deal without considering race. Although blacks have been among the most strongly Democratic groups since 1932 (Moon, 1948: ch. 1; Campbell et al., 1960: 160), the partisan significance of race as such was minimized during the New Deal by the restricted franchise of blacks and the predominance of economic appeals in party platforms and presidential campaigns. The national enfranchisement and mobilization of blacks in the 1960s[21] brought racial conflict to the surface, however, and race has been the dominant cleavage in American partisanship for the past decade.

Given the divergent implications of race and age for social conflict and the control of government power, it is clear that cohort succession and the expansion of black suffrage involve two very different types of physical change in the electorate. Events since the early 1960s, especially the wave of countermobilization in the white electorate (Hammond, 1974), suggest that the withholding of black suffrage should be added to the list of devices that have kept American politics within two-party bounds. While the strategic constraints imposed by the electoral college make a permanent third party improbable, there is also reason to doubt that black participation can be accommodated on a stable basis by a two-party system.

It is unlikely that a sizable black electoral constituency would have emerged at the national level in the 1960s had there been no postwar migration of Southern blacks to Northern urban centers. From 1940 to 1966, a net of 3.7 million blacks left the South, most of them settling in large Northern cities (Piven and Cloward, 1971: 215). The proportion of blacks residing in urban areas climbed from 27% in 1910 to 73% in 1960 (Taeuber and Taeuber, 1965: 14). More than 70% of the Northern black respondents in the 1952 survey reported that they were raised in the South, and it was not until 1968 that this percentage fell below 50%.

Blacks controlled enough votes in several large Northern states by 1960 to constitute an important political resource:

Uncertain that he could resurrect Southern allegiance, Kennedy made a vigorous appeal to the black vote in the industrial states by campaigning on strong pledges to deal with civil rights and poverty. . . . And, although black skepticism toward the Democratic party persisted, holding Kennedy down to 69 per cent of the national black vote, the ghettoes in a number of strategic Northern cities delivered overwhelmingly Democratic majorities, swinging several critical states to assure his election. [Piven and Cloward, 1971: 255]

The national Democrats continued to cultivate the support of Northern blacks, and they succeeded handsomely. In the view of Piven and Cloward (1971: 249, fn. 1):

> The Great Society programs were promulgated by federal leaders in order to deal with the political problems created by a new and unstable electoral constituency, namely blacks—and to deal with this new constituency not simply by responding to its expressed interests, but by shaping and directing its political future. The Great Society programs, in short, reflected a distinctively managerial kind of politics.

The legislative accomplishments of the Johnson administration in the fields of poverty and civil rights not only won the overwhelming support of Northern blacks, but also expanded the black constituency by extending the franchise to Southern blacks. Black voter-registration drives were conducted with Great Society funds (Piven and Cloward, 1971: 266), black turnout rose sharply, as Figure 17 indicates, and blacks became the most solidly one-party group in the nation.

A few cohort differences in racial polarization are apparent from 1952 to 1972, but they are entirely attributable to the cohort-related change in white partisanship which has already been described.[22] Black party identification varies so little by age that even the proportion of independent identifiers in the two black cohorts rarely differs by more than 5 or 6%. In only one year, 1960, does the corresponding difference between the two white cohorts fall below 5%, and it tends to hover in the 15 to 25% range.

It is not very surprising that age explains so little in black partisanship, since black electoral involvement was quite marginal nationally until the 1960s. Nearly 60% of the blacks interviewed in 1952 reported that they had never voted in a presidential election, and over 75% of the blacks living in the South, including the border states, had never voted for President. In effect, many members of the black prewar cohort came of age politically at about the same time as younger blacks, so the political learning that accounts for cohort-related differences among whites is unlikely to have occurred prior to 1960 among many older blacks. Blacks are essentially a newly enfranchised electorate, and this fact alone would lead one to expect their partisanship to exhibit distinctive characteristics.

It is generally believed that children who are familiar with the party identification of their parents are more likely as adults to

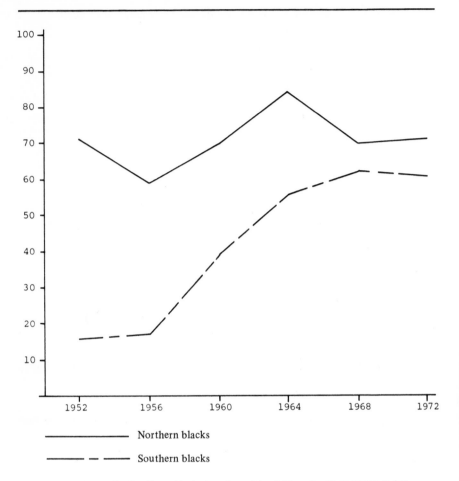

Figure 17: BLACK TURNOUT, 1952-1972*

maintain a stable party loyalty (Converse and Dupeux, 1962; Converse, 1969). Since there is little incentive for persons excluded from electoral activity to acquire a party attachment, partisanship will not often be transmitted intergenerationally in a disenfranchised population, especially in one as socially isolated as blacks.[23] This line of reasoning suggests that party identification will not crystallize in a newly enfranchised electorate until something like several decades after the extension of suffrage;[24] considerable potential will exist in the meantime for sudden changes in party identification.

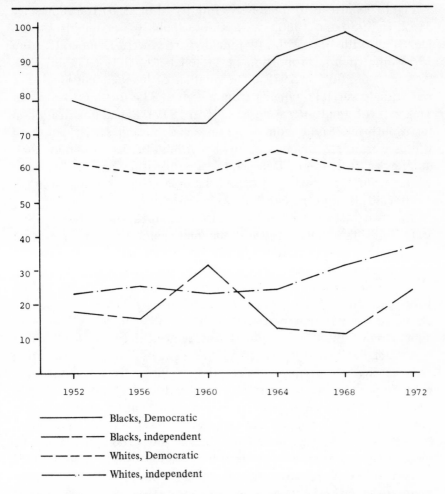

*Percent Democratic excludes independents; all percentages for blacks are based on at least 118 cases; all percentages for whites are based on at least 1,516 cases; weighted samples were used in 1960, 1964, and 1968.

Figure 18: PERCENT DEMOCRATIC OF TWO-PARTY IDENTIFICATION AND PERCENT INDEPENDENT IDENTIFICATION, 1952-1972, BY RACE*

A glance at the 1952 survey shows that partisan socialization was indeed weakly developed among Southern blacks. Only 49% reported that their fathers were party identifiers, compared with 77% of the national white sample (more generally, see the excellent description of party identification among Southern blacks during the 1950s in Converse, 1972: 301-311). Blacks native to the North were more likely to have been raised by a party-identified father (69%) than were blacks native to the South, but the percentage is based on only 16 cases.

Figure 18 attests to the relative fluidity of black partisanship since 1952. In 1956 and 1960, slightly more than 70% of the blacks who identified with one of the two major parties were Democrats; from 1964 onward, the proportion never fell below 90% (93% in 1964, 98% in 1968, 90% in 1972). The number of independent identifiers was equally variable, ranging from a high of 31% in 1960 to a low of 11% in 1968 (and increasing to 24% in 1972). Racial polarization in the South increased from −.10 in 1960—meaning that Southern whites were more Democratic than Southern blacks—to .46 in 1964, despite an increase in Democratic identification among Southern whites from 1960 to 1964.[25] Racial polarization was higher in the South (.80) than in the North (.72) by 1968.

The two races moved in very different directions between 1964 and 1968, the blacks toward alignment and the whites toward dealignment. Both movements are well summarized by Table 6. Large number of black party identifiers were recruited from those raised by nonpartisan (i.e., independent or apolitical) fathers, and by 1968 the rate of party identification among blacks was nearly unrelated to paternal partisanship. Over 80% of the blacks with nonpartisan fathers had acquired a party attachment by 1968, a rate so spectacular that it surpassed the frequency of party identification even among whites raised by partisan fathers. As has been noted previously, the dealignment of the white electorate originated primarily in the postwar cohort, and was particularly evident among young whites with nonpartisan fathers.

The near total alignment of blacks in 1968 proved to be momentary. The number of black independents more than doubled from 1968 to 1972, primarily, it appears, because those raised by nonpartisan fathers returned to more normal levels of independent identification. This move toward independence may also be temporary, and it is indicative of the continued potential for rapid shifts in black partisanship. To some degree this potential can be attributed to political socialization, but it also reflects the depth of racial cleavage in America and its uncertain expression in a two-party, majoritarian system. Both accounts will be discussed briefly.

Because panel data are unavailable for the 1964-1968-1972 sequence of presidential elections, partisan change is estimated here by comparing the marginal distributions of party identification from one cross-section to the next. This procedure yields very soft evidence, of course, since it is impossible to determine the amount of gross change in party identification that actually occurred. Never-

Table 6. PARTISAN ALIGNMENT BY FATHER'S PARTISAN BEHAVIOR, 1952, 1964, 1968, 1972[a]

| | Prewar Cohort | | | |
| | Father was Party Identifier | | Father was Not Party Identifier[b] | |
	% Blacks	% Whites	% Blacks	% Whites
1952	86	82	42	61
n	61	825	26	123
1964	90	85	79	61
n	112	1644	52	249
1968	90	79	86	59
n	60	912	37	148
1972	84	79	73	55
n	31	586	16	71

| | Postwar Cohort | | | |
| | Father was Party Identifier | | Father was Not Party Identifier[b] | |
	% Blacks	% Whites	% Blacks	% Whites
1952	c	74	c	46
n	13	152	7	20
1964	94	74	57	52
n	118	948	25	159
1968	87	65	81	37
n	93	662	21	92
1972	87	59	44	35
n	94	623	19	92

a. Cell percentage is proportion of respondents identifying with a party.
b. Nonpartisan fathers include floaters, independents, apoliticals, and those whose partisan behavior could not be recalled by respondent; weighted samples used in 1964 and 1968.
c. Too few cases for reliable estimates.

theless, the clarity of the patterns involved (which are presented in Table 7) seems sufficient to warrant further extrapolation.

As Table 7 shows, in each of the three surveys more blacks than whites reported that their fathers were not party identifiers. Table 7 also shows that the net change in party identification from 1964 to 1972 was greater among those reporting paternal nonpartisanship. But the net change that occurred from 1964 to 1972 among nonsocialized blacks easily surpasses the net change that occurred over the same interval among their white counterparts; it is clear, in other words, that partisan instability among blacks involves more than socialization. The movement of nonsocialized blacks from alignment to dealignment—from less than 10% independent in 1968

Table 7. PARTISAN CHANGE AND PARTISAN SOCIALIZATION, 1964-1972*
(among respondents 21 and older by 1964)

a. Percent with Party-Identified Fathers (by race)

	Blacks			Whites		
	1964	1968	1972	1964	1968	1972
	71	73	73	82	82	84
n	247	161	109	3,207	2,014	1,365

b. Party Affiliation of Blacks
(in percentages)

	Father was Party Identifier			Father was Not Party Identifier		
	1964	1968	1972	1964	1968	1972
Democrat	88	86	80	67	89	46
n	218	139	87	68	54	19
Independent	7	11	11	25	7	39
n	17	18	12	25	4	16
Republican	5	3	9	8	5	15
n	12	4	10	9	3	6

c. Party Affiliation of Whites
(in percentages)

	Father was Party Identifier			Father was Not Party Identifier		
	1964	1968	1972	1964	1968	1972
Democrat	52	45	42	40	28	27
n	1,656	906	574	279	120	67
Independent	19	25	28	42	48	51
n	615	508	375	294	206	128
Republican	29	30	30	18	24	23
n	936	600	416	129	104	58

d. Summed Absolute Values of Net Partisan Change
(in percentages)

	Blacks		Whites	
	1964-1968	1968-1972	1964-1968	1968-1972
Party-Identified Father	8	12	14	6
Non-Party-Identified Father	43	85	24	5

*Weighted samples were used in 1964 and 1968; nonpartisan fathers include floaters, independents, apoliticals, and those whose partisan behavior could not be recalled by respondent.

to almost 40% independent in 1972—strongly suggests that the different campaign contexts played a decisive role in this change. If this is so, pronounced short-term instability in party identification will be apparent in this group whenever the salience of race as a campaign issue changes as noticeably as it did from 1968 to 1972.

Because older blacks are especially likely to report being raised by nonpartisan fathers, black partisanship may stabilize somewhat as the prewar cohort passes from the electorate and the children of the postwar cohort begin to enter it. Yet is is doubtful that socialization is in itself sufficient to stabilize party identification in a group as socially and politically isolated as blacks. They are an electorally vulnerable caste that controls neither party, a situation that is likely to retard the growth of lasting party attachments in a system with two internally heterogeneous parties. Burnham's description of black gubernatorial voting in Baltimore (1968: 37) implies that blacks would leave the Democratic electorate as quickly as they entered it if the party's racist wing captured the presidential nomination; their interests are clear enough to ensure a high degree of electoral cohesion even in normally "low salience" elections. Such extreme insularity suggests that party identification among blacks will not evolve as it has in the white electorate, at least not in the absence of one party's explicit and irreversible commitment to the represen-tation of black interests.

It has in fact been suggested recently that the theory of electoral development and partisan stability is much less universally applicable than American analysts have generally assumed (Burnham, 1972; Shively, 1972). Shively's analysis of voting in Weimar Germany leads him to conclude that stable party identification, in the social-psychological sense that American scholars have developed that concept, is unlikely to develop in electorates that are deeply divided by social and economic cleavages and set in nonpresidential systems:

> Since in most other countries there are important and intense social cleavages, and rather more opportunity than in America for nonmajority parties to operate, we might reasonably expect that in these countries, learned and lasting party identification would be less common than in the United States. [Shively, 1972: 1223]

Recent trends in black partisanship would seem to broaden the applicability of Shively's findings.[26] To carry the argument a step further, it could be argued that the racial cleavage in America is comparable in intensity, and partly even in form, to class divisions in Western Europe shortly after the turn of the century. The analogy is far from perfect and does not account for national differences within Europe, but it is suggestive of the degree to which blacks are unlike other groups in the American electorate. They are, for example, the only American group with a social and political history that even roughly approximates the premodern feudal past and the late enfranchisement of Europe's working classes. If these conditions provided the sense of collective inequality necessary to sustain large working-class parties, a case some have argued for (see, e.g., Epstein, 1967: 135-145), then the comparison underscores the anomalous position of blacks in American electoral politics.

The physical closure of the black community is interesting for the same reason. The rapid urbanization, residential segregation, and communal insulation of the European proletariat, which promoted class consciousness and political solidarity, are conditions which also typify black urban life—apparently with comparable results. For example, Marx reports (1969: 117-118) that militant attitudes were most common in the 1960s among Northern blacks and those from urban areas, while Piven and Cloward note (1971: 239) that the cities in which ghetto riots were most severe during the 1960s were those where the black population had more than doubled from 1940 to 1960.

Perhaps more significant is the trend toward black ideological closure, of which black power is a leading example (Carmichael and Hamilton, 1967). The trend is of interest not only because it reinforces the physical isolation of blacks, but also because it has been widely accepted by black political elites. Peterson (undated manuscript) uses the latter point to develop a fascinating caste-class comparison, in which he observes that the tendency of black elites to abandon the civil rights ideology in favor of black organizational autonomy parallels changes that occurred after World War I in the ideology and organizational style of British trade unionists.

Despite these broad similarities, however, the strategic position of blacks in the American party system is obviously quite unique. As a small minority of the electorate in a two-party, majoritarian system, they lack the control of political parties that the European working classes were able to achieve. It is worth noting in this connection that 35% of the black respondents interviewed in 1972 said they would support a black third party, while 33% said they would not and 33% were unsure. This is an increase of 11% over the number of potential third-party constituents in 1970. It is difficult to know what positive responses mean when questions are posed in such hypothetical terms, but taken at face value they suggest a general absence of political immunization among members of the most strikingly one-party group in the nation.[27] This is certainly consistent with other evidence showing a very high potential among blacks for sudden electoral change.

While a third party for blacks would lead to a more durable alignment and suit the ideological emphasis on organizational autonomy, its encounter with the electoral college would probably increase black remoteness from government power. The system-level irony, of course, is that the same institutional forces working against an American three-party system cannot help but reduce the electoral stability of a two-party system which is forced to absorb latent third-party constituencies. Such constituencies clearly exist, and they are polar opposites where race is concerned.

VI. SUMMARY AND CONCLUSIONS

The data examined here indicate that the 1964 election dismantled the New Deal party system without replacing it. Many of the ingredients for a critical election were present in 1964, and the election outcome, in its broad outlines, fits the pattern of previous realignments (Burnham, 1968; Pomper, 1968: ch. 5; Pomper, 1972). But in retrospect it appears that the only lasting effect of 1964 was the Great Society antiparty system. A trend toward dealignment was started that has not yet been reversed, and there is growing reason to wonder, as Burnham does (1970: ch. 5), if we are witnessing "the onward march of party decomposition."

Two important sources of electoral change can be traced to 1964: the emergence of generational differences within the white electorate, and the creation and mobilization of a national black electorate. The first change is summarized in Table 8. Net changes in the two white cohorts from 1960 to 1964 are nearly perfect mirror images of one another, and there is no need here to recount them in any detail; it is sufficient to note that intercohort differences in party identification widened from 1960 to 1964 in every grouping of the white electorate examined in this analysis. The regional differentiation of partisanship in the postwar cohort was sharply reduced from 1960 to 1964 as class patterns of party support in the young electorate began to change in both regions.

Table 8. CHANGES IN WHITE PARTY IDENTIFICATION, 1960-1964 (in percentages)

	1960		1964		Net Change, 1960-1964	
	Democratic	Independent	Democratic	Independent	Democratic	Independent
*South**						
Prewar Cohort	65	16	77	12	+12	− 4
Middle class	66	21	70	18	+ 4	− 3
Working class	64	19	88	8	+24	+11
Postwar Cohort	66	23	56	28	−10	+ 5
Middle class	75	13	49	37	−26	+24
Working class	63	30	61	22	− 2	− 8
*North**						
Prewar Cohort	37	25	42	22	+ 5	− 3
Middle class	27	26	28	24	+ 1	− 2
Working class	47	27	53	23	+ 6	− 4
Postwar Cohort	41	28	44	31	+ 3	+ 3
Middle class	33	27	42	30	+ 9	+ 3
Working class	49	30	45	32	− 4	+ 2

*Only includes respondents native to their region of residence; South includes border states.

The attitudinal sources of dealignment in the young Northern electorate remain in doubt. Thus, it is not clear whether a bundle of specific issues or a general sense of political malaise, or both, prompted the spread of independent identification in this group. The origins of dealignment among young Northerners must be reckoned with before its long-term significance can be evaluated.

On the whole, there is considerable support for the hypothesis that generational turnover in the electorate is a principal source of partisan change, but it is important to stress the exploratory nature of this investigation, and especially to emphasize the need for finer discriminations among age groups. There is no evidence that the change which has occurred since 1952 can be accounted for by life-cycle controls, though the expansiveness of the cohorts does not lend itself to neat life-cycle distinctions. Further efforts are necessary to examine the suitability of other age groupings, since it seems likely that the broad division used here, while useful for identifying gross patterns of change, has blurred subtler effects of cohort succession.

The historical relationship between generational change and critical elections will remain unknown, so the historical applicability of this analysis can only be guessed at. Converse's theory of electoral development and partisan stability (1969) could be taken to imply that party identification was less common in nineteenth-century America than in the past several decades, and that the relationship between age and independent identification may in fact have been inverted until several decades after universal suffrage was extended to white males. It has recently been pointed out, however, that the equilibrium point in party identification predicted by Converse's theory does not fit recent survey data in America (Inglehart and Hochstein, 1972). Whether this reveals a theoretical fault or a temporary deviation is unclear, but if Converse is basically correct, it is probable that generational replacement has only recently become a source of partisan change.

Postwar change in American partisanship has been hastened substantially by physical change in the electorate, of which the inevitable generational turnover is but one component. Southern industrial growth stimulated a southward migration of Northern white-collar workers with managerial, professional, and technical skills, and Southern weather attracted affluent Northerners seeking a hospitable climate for retirement. The increase in Southern Republicanism during the 1950s and early 1960s is mainly attributable to the growing settlement of these middle-class ex-Northerners. Yet the solid South is dying in more than a figurative sense: the postwar cohort of native Southerners, now a clear majority of the native Southern electorate, was 40% independent and 41% Democratic in 1972, while the prewar cohort was 17% independent and 63% Democratic.

The most important postwar migration was northward. Agricultural modernization in the South pushed rural Southern blacks into Northern ghettos, and thereby radically transformed national politics. The Northern ghettoization of Southern blacks increased their strategic importance, and thus gave white political elites an incentive for encouraging black voting. It also fostered a sense of group consciousness for which no good American parallel exists. As Dunning (1972: 418) observes:

> Industrialization and urbanization have led, within the negro "caste," to what in some respects represents a closer approximation to the type of class formation process predicted by Marx than has occurred among the white working classes . . .

These physical changes in the electorate may have set in motion a self-sustaining process of partisan change: the more change that occurs, the more that is likely to occur. Generational replacement in the white electorate has swelled the number of independents to a point where independent identification is very likely to be transmitted intergenerationally to the post-1972 cohort. The numerical potential for realignment, gauged by the number of independents, may therefore continue to grow with each election. Black participation has created fissures within the Democratic leadership and electorate, thus increasing the likelihood that a leftist or Southern-populist third party will appear in each presidential election. Change in the composition of the Southern electorate, added to the apparent breakdown of white partisan socialization, has divided whites into Republican identifiers and independent/third-party/Southern Democratic identifiers (a division which heightens the importance of black votes in the South).

The likelihood that a two-party realignment would survive two presidential terms is fairly small. Intraparty factionalism has sharpened, particularly among Democrats, and changes in nominating rules increase the likelihood that parties will veer ideologically from one election to the next. Clearly, regular party constituencies are impossible to maintain when contestants for a party's presidential nomination represent large, mutually antagonistic segments of the electorate. A severe economic crisis, if it heightened awareness of class interests, might be sufficient to trigger a two-party realignment. Otherwise, the pattern of the last three presidential elections, which is to say no pattern at all, is likely to continue for some time to come.

NOTES

1. The term was first used, to my knowledge, by McPhee and Ferguson (1962).

2. One parameter that I have not discussed here is the "forgetting" function, which gradually reduces the weight of each previous election experience. Such forgetting undoubtedly occurs, even among the most traumatized and intensely partisan members of the New Deal generation, but I have ignored it for the sake of simplicity.

3. Political geology is a term I have borrowed from Elazar (1966).

4. Dealignment, as Inglehart and Hochstein (1972) use the term, refers to an increase in independent identification. They find that American and French survey data tend to support the hypothesis that dealignment is the result of "cross-cutting cleavages" in the party system.

5. Although 18-year-olds were eligible to vote in a few states prior to 1972, their small numbers did not merit special treatment in this classification.

6. I will use the term "postwar cohort" interchangeably with "postrealignment cohort," and I will use the term "prewar cohort" interchangeably with the term "realignment cohort."

7. Had a finer subdivision been used, sampling error would have prohibited setting aside regional and class groupings for special attention.

8. Abramson (1973) also uses the prewar/postwar cohort distinction to summarize changes in American voting behavior over the past few decades.

9. The 1948 survey was not used because it lacked a measure of party identification.

10. The North to which I refer throughout this paper is not a region in the same sense that the South is. It is simply the non-South, a residual and theoretically insignificant category except when used in comparison with the South.

11. Sundquist (1973: 259) observes, however, that Republican presidential voting in 1940 and 1944 increased in most Southern states at a rate higher than the national average.

12. In-migration had a much smaller effect on party strength in the North, largely because the distribution of party identification among native Northerners was much less skewed than it was among native Southerners. The small amount of partisan change that did occur as a result of Southern in-migration does not merit graphic presentation.

13. "Native" is used throughout the analysis in a loose sense: respondents who were raised in the region where they resided at the time of their interview are classified as natives.

14. Those who were between 21 and 28 years old in 1952 are members of the postrealignment cohort, so life-stage controls are not of interest for that age group.

15. Indirectly, the data presented in Tables 3 through 5 appear to illustrate the limitations of Converse's theory of partisan stability (1969) that Inglehart and Hochstein have pointed out (1972).

16. Converse did consider generational replacement (1966a: 226), but his analysis was confined to survey data gathered prior to 1964. The patterns described here indicate that

generational replacement had no effect on party identification in the South until 1964 (see Figure 14 for a good illustration of this).

17. I have used the customary distinction between blue-collar and white-collar workers as the measure of class. White-collar workers (a term I will use interchangeably with "middle class") include professional, technical, and kindred workers; managers, officials, and proprietors; sales, clerical, and kindred workers. Blue-collar workers (a term I will use interchangeably with "working class") include craftsmen, foremen, and kindred workers; operatives and kindred workers; private household and service workers; laborers (including farm laborers). Farmers, students, and members of the armed forces were excluded from all computations of occupational polarization. The head of the household's occupation was used for respondents who were not the head of the household.

18. There was an extraordinary increase in Democratic identification in 1964 among older members of the Southern working class. In 1960, 64% of the older Southern working-class whites were Democratic; in 1964, the figure increased to 88%; in 1968, it declined to 55%. It is possible that this increase in Democratic identification is at least partly attributable to sampling error, or that it is related to the unusually large overreporting of Johnson voting in the South in 1964 (Burnham, 1968: 33-35).

19. The increased Democratic identification of the prewar Southern working class in 1964 (note 18) raised class polarization in that cohort from −.08 in 1960 to .49 in 1964. In 1968, class polarization was again −.08.

20. Looking only at the North, nearly 60% of the whites who were between 29 and 48 years old in 1972 were employed in white-collar occupations. Less than 50% of those who were 29 to 48 years old in 1952 worked in white-collar occupations.

21. Converse (1972: 301-311) uses the term "re-enfranchisement" in his description of recent trends in black partisanship.

22. There are, however, strong correlations between age and nonelectoral attitudes. Regression equations using the SRC samples from 1968, 1970, and 1972 show that age is among the best predictors of "feeling thermometer" items on police, urban rioters, and black militants, and also of a racial consciousness measure constructed from the thermometer items on blacks and whites. On each of these measures, younger blacks tend to be more militant (i.e., "colder" on police, "warmer" on urban rioters and black militants, and higher in racial consciousness).

23. At least two qualifications are in order here. First, something loosely resembling party identification was probably quite common in the working class prior to its enfranchisement in Western Europe, especially where class organizations also served as political parties after the extension of suffrage. Second, the lack of social isolation among women in America may have increased the frequency of party identification beyond its "normal" level in a disenfranchised population. The same factor probably accounts for the relatively small impact of women's suffrage on American party politics.

24. This is suggested by Converse's theory of partisan stability (1969).

25. The figures cited here only include those respondents who are native to their region of residence.

26. Shively mentions blacks only in passing (1972: 1223): "The American governmental system, with its focus on the single, indivisible office of president, makes it impractical for any party to serve as a clearly 'appropriate representative' for nonmajority groups such as blacks, hardhats, or farmers, who might otherwise vote in the way suggested by the hypothesis [that group membership in itself can stabilize voting patterns in certain situations]." His emphasis on the centripetal effect of a majoritarian, presidential system with two parties has a corollary which he did not develop: such a system may destabilize party identification, and presumably voting behavior as well, in politically conscious groups which are outside the mainstream of social and political life and which are too small to control either party.

27. Contrary to what voting theory would suggest, the willingness of black respondents

to support a black third party was not affected by their strength of party identification in either 1970 or 1972.

REFERENCES

ABRAMSON, P. R. (1974) "Generational change in American electoral behavior." American Political Science Review (March): 93-105.

––– (1973) "Why the Democrats are no longer the majority party." Delivered at the 1973 Annual Meeting of the American Political Science Association.

––– (1971) "Social class and political change in Western Europe: a cross-national longitudinal analysis." Comparative Political Studies (July): 131-155.

BURNHAM, W. D. (1972) "Political immunization and political confessionalism: the United States and Weimar Germany." Journal of Interdisciplinary History (Summer): 1-30.

––– (1970) Critical Elections and the Mainsprings of American Politics. New York: Norton.

––– (1968) "American voting behavior and the 1964 election." Midwest Journal of Political Science (February): 1-40.

––– (1967) "Party systems and the political process," in W. N. Chambers and W. D. Burnham (eds.) The American Party Systems: Stages of Development. New York: Oxford.

BUTLER, D. and D. STOKES (1969) Political Change in Britain: Forces Shaping Electoral Choice. New York: St. Martin's.

CAMPBELL, A., P. E. CONVERSE, W. E. MILLER, and D. E. STOKES (1960) The American Voter. New York: Wiley.

CARMICHAEL, S. and C. V. HAMILTON (1967) Black Power: The Politics of Liberation in America. New York: Vintage.

CONVERSE, P. E. (1972) "Change in the American electorate," in A. Campbell and P. E. Converse (eds.) The Human Meaning of Social Change. New York: Russell Sage Foundation.

––– (1969) "Of time and partisan stability." Comparative Political Studies (July): 139-171.

––– (1966a) "On the possibility of major political realignment in the South," in A. Campbell, P. E. Converse, W. E. Miller, and D. E. Stokes (eds.) Elections and the Political Order. New York: Wiley.

––– (1966b) "Religion and politics: the 1960 election," in A. Campbell, P. E. Converse, W. E. Miller, and D. E. Stokes (eds.) Elections and the Political Order. New York: Wiley.

––– and G. DUPEUX (1962) "Politicization of the electorate in France and the United States." Public Opinion Quarterly (Spring): 1-23.

CONVERSE, P. E., W. E. MILLER, J. G. RUSK, and A. C. WOLFE (1969) "Continuity and change in American politics: parties and issues in the 1968 election." American Political Science Review (December): 1083-1105.

CRITTENDEN, J. (1969-1970) "Reply to Cutler." Public Opinion Quarterly (Winter): 589-591.

––– (1962) "Aging and party affiliation." Public Opinion Quarterly (Winter): 648-657.

CUTLER, N. E. (1969-1970) "Generation, maturation, and party affiliation: a cohort analysis." Public Opinion Quarterly (Winter): 583-588.

DUNNING, E. (1972) "Dynamics of racial stratification: some preliminary observations." Race (April): 415-434.

ELAZAR, D. J. (1966) American Federalism: A View From the States. New York: Crowell.

EPSTEIN, L. D. (1967) Political Parties in Western Democracies. New York: Praeger.

FONER, A. (1974) "Age stratification and age conflict in political life." American Sociological Review (April): 187-196.

––– (1972) "The polity," in M. W. Riley, M. Johnson, and A. Foner (eds.) Aging and Society. Volume III, A Sociology of Age Stratification. New York: Russell Sage Foundation.

FORSYTHE, D. W. (1974) "Taxation and regime change in America, 1781-1833: a taxonomy of political events." Ph.D. dissertation. Columbia University.

GLENN, N. D. and M. GRIMES (1968) "Aging, voting, and political interest." American Sociological Review (August): 563-575.

HAMMOND, J. L. (1974) "Race and electoral mobilization: white Southerners, 1952-1968." Unpublished manuscript.

HYMAN, H. H. (1972) Secondary Analysis of Sample Surveys: Principles, Procedures, and Potentialities. New York: Wiley.

INGLEHART, R. (1971) "The silent revolution in Europe: intergenerational change in post-industrial societies." American Political Science Review (December): 991-1017.

––– and A. HOCHSTEIN (1972) "Alignment and dealignment of the electorate in France and the United States." Comparative Political Studies (October): 343-372.

KLECKA, W. R. (1971) "Applying political generations to the study of political behavior: a cohort analysis." Public Opinion Quarterly (Fall): 358-373.

LADD, E. C., Jr. (1970) American Political Parties: Social Change and Political Response. New York: Norton.

McPHEE, W. N. (1963) "Note on a campaign simulator," in W. N. McPhee, Formal Theories of Mass Behavior. New York: Free Press.

––– and J. FERGUSON (1962) "Political immunization," in W. N. McPhee and W. A. Glaser (eds.) Public Opinion and Congressional Elections. New York: Free Press.

––– and R. B. SMITH (1962) "A model for analyzing voting systems," in W. N. McPhee and W. A. Glaser (eds.) Public Opinion and Congressional Elections. New York: Free Press.

MARX, G. T. (1969) Protest and Prejudice: A Study of Belief in the Black Community (rev. ed.). New York: Harper and Row.

MOON, H. L. (1948) Balance of Power: The Negro Vote. New York: Doubleday.

PETERSON, P. E. (undated) "The political functions of ideologies: Black Power and British Socialism." Unpublished manuscript.

PIVEN, F. F. and R. A. CLOWARD (1971) Regulating the Poor: The Functions of Public Welfare. New York: Random House.

POMPER, G. M. (1972) "From confusion to clarity: issues and American voters, 1956-1968." American Political Science Review (June): 415-428.

––– (1968) Elections in America. New York: Dodd, Mead.

RYDER, N. B. (1965) "The cohort as a concept in the study of social change." American Sociological Review (December): 843-861.

SHANNON, W. W. (1968) Party, Constituency and Congressional Voting. Baton Rouge: Louisiana State University.

SHIVELY, W. P. (1972) "Party identification, party choice, and voting stability: the Weimar case." American Political Science Review (December): 1203-1225.

SUNDQUIST, J. L. (1973) Dynamics of the Party System: Alignment and Realignment of Political Parties in the United States. Washington, D.C.: Brookings Institution.

TAEUBER, K. E. and A. F. TAEUBER (1965) Negroes in Cities: Residential Segregation and Neighborhood Change. New York: Atheneum.

TURNER, J. (1970) Party and Constituency: Pressures on Congress (rev. ed. by E. V. Schneier, Jr.). Baltimore: Johns Hopkins.

WESTIN, A. F. (1953) "The Supreme Court, the Populist movement and the campaign of 1896." Journal of Politics (February): 3-42.

Chapter 2

PARTY IMAGE AND PARTISAN CHANGE

RICHARD J. TRILLING

Why do some people change party identifications while others maintain them? This article will present evidence that an index of party image—a measure of the extent to which individuals like or dislike the two political parties—can help explain stability and change in the party identifications of Americans.

Various explanations of change in party identifications have been put forth in previous research. Crittenden (1962) and Cutler (1969; 1974) have debated the impact of lifespan changes. The effect of changes in social milieu has been studied by Campbell et al. (1960: 453-472) and by Lipset (1960: 267-273). The loosening bonds between political parties and voters have been discussed by Burnham (1965; 1970) and by Beck (1974). Key (1961: 442-455) and the authors of *The American Voter* (Campbell et al., 1960: 213-215) have examined the effect of political opinions on party identifications.[1] Social forces which produce eras of realignment—characterized by massive and durable changes in party identifications —have been analyzed by Burnham (1970) and by Sundquist (1973).

AUTHOR'S NOTE: I wish to thank Gerald M. Pomper for commenting on an earlier draft of this paper, which was presented at the Annual Meeting of the American Political Science Association, Palmer House Hotel, Chicago, Illinois, August 29 to September 2, 1974. See Trilling (1974c). I would also like to thank the Duke University Research Council for supporting the research which produced this paper. Needless to say, I assume responsibility for any errors which may remain.

Despite these studies, however, the examination of changes in party identifications has been inadequate for two reasons. First, there is relatively little change; indeed, the stability and enduring nature of party identifications among Americans is well documented (Dreyer, 1973; Converse, 1972; Stokes, 1966a; Campbell et al., 1960). Second, even when changes in identification are more frequent—for instance in times of electoral realignment (on realignment, see Key, 1955 and 1959; Burnham, 1964, 1968, and 1970; Pomper, 1970; Campbell, 1966b; Ladd and Hadley, 1973; Ladd et al., 1971; and Sundquist, 1973)—few individual-level data have been collected upon which to build theories of electoral change.

That scholars should be particularly concerned with changes in party identification is suggested by two trends. First, electoral patterns have been dramatically altered in the recent past, for instance in the South (Beck, 1974). Second, there is evidence that party identification is less important for American voters than it once was. Republican voting among Southern Democratic identifiers, increased split-ticket voting (see DeVries and Tarrance, 1972), a widening difference in opinions on issues between behaviorally defined and psychologically defined party members (Ladd and Hadley, 1973), and increased "issue voting" (RePass, 1971; Pomper, 1972; Boyd, 1972; Page and Brody, 1972; Brody and Page, 1972; Miller et al., 1973; and Kovenock et al., 1970) all constitute relevant evidence of this second point. It may be that both of these trends involve large-scale changes in party identifications.

If we imagine an individual voter who is about to change his party identification, say from Democratic to Republican, we can predict that the strength of his new Republican attachment will not be as great next year as it will be in ten years, assuming he does not switch identifications again in the meantime. Strength of partisan attachment is a function of the length of attachment.[2] Consequently, the behavior of this convert to Republicanism may not differ very much next year from that of the nonpartisan. That is, this new Republican identifier may split his ticket, may vote less frequently, and may be more like the Democratic identifiers he is leaving than long-time Republican identifiers are like those Democratic identifiers. These behavioral traits are the kinds of characteristics mentioned as evidence of the declining impact of party identification, but all that they actually manifest in this hypothetical individual is change in party identification.

It is therefore appropriate to ask whether the apparently declining impact of party identification really reflects patterns of change in party identification and whether there are any meaningful patterns in the changes which do occur. The pattern and meaning of change can best be appreciated in comparison with stable identifications. This paper accordingly investigates the role of party image in inducing stability or change in party identification. Using the panel study built into the national surveys of the Survey Research Center, Dreyer (1973) found that measurable change in party identification did occur, but the pattern of change was random. In the data below, however, we shall find evidence that party image seems to make the patterns of stability and change systematic and meaningful.

The sections which follow will discuss the concept of party image and its operationalization, stability and change in party identification among Americans, the role of party image in inducing this stability and change, and the ability of party image to affect both the amount of change and the resultant voting behavior of individuals who have experienced change. We shall also briefly review the movement of the electorate over the recent twenty-year period. Finally, we shall have the opportunity to speculate about the impact which party images are likely to have on future electoral behavior.

I. THE CONCEPT OF PARTY IMAGE

In periods of electoral realignment, Sellers (1965) speculates, individuals first adopt favorable images of the party with which they will come to identify before they actually alter their party identifications. This crucial role for party image in the process of electoral change has not yet been satisfactorily documented. Matthews and Prothro produced what is probably the best-known work involving the concept of party image. For them, party images are

> ... mental pictures of party—vague, often confused and contradictory.... Party image is not the same thing as party identification. Although the two concepts obviously are related, two people may identify with the same party but have different mental pictures of it and evaluate these pictures in different ways. Party identification is no doubt the more basic and less changeful of the two—the evidence is overwhelming that it is formed early in life and does not easily or often change. But, while party image is not so deeply rooted or so stable as party identification, it is

likely to be less ephemeral than voter attitudes toward the issues and candidates of specific campaigns. [Matthews and Prothro, 1966a: 378]

This description is compatible with the notion that party images constitute a "medium-term" force affecting electoral behavior, one somewhat different from the "long-term" forces which produce the "normal vote" or the "short-term" forces which cause defections from the "normal vote" (cf. Converse, 1966). Although there has been relatively little discussion of the concept of party image, and not many empirical treatments have appeared (see Matthews and Prothro, 1964, 1966a, 1966b; Abney, 1969; Stokes, 1966a; Key, 1961: 433-442; Meisel, 1973: 63-126; and Trilling, 1974c, 1975), my own work suggests a tentative theory of the "medium-term" force of party image (Trilling, 1974a). *The hypothesis is that individuals alter party images or develop party images favorable to a new party before and as part of the process of changing identification to that new party.*

Matthews and Prothro (1966a: 392-396) demonstrated that individuals who report a change of party identifications have party images which favor the party of their new identification. Abney (1969) stated that negative images of the Democratic Party contributed to many individuals' forsaking their Democratic identifications. Neither of these studies, however, possesses enough longitudinal scope or is comprehensive enough to provide us with a definitive statement of the theoretical role of party image in electoral behavior.

Matthews and Prothro went on to investigate the issue components of party image and found that Southern White perceptions of the Democratic Party's treatment of Blacks contributed to the greater pro-Republican party images found in 1964. My own more recent and longer longitudinal study (Trilling, 1974a) reveals, however, that the race issue component of party image was significant only in 1960 and 1964, and not significant for the concept of party image either before or after the time of the Matthews and Prothro study. It would appear that the generalized index of party image—how much people like and dislike the two parties—is more important for electoral behavior than the substantive components of party image—that is, what people like and dislike about the parties.[3]

II. OPERATIONALIZING PARTY IMAGE

Party image will be operationalized, as in Matthews and Prothro, by the use of four open-ended questions which ask the respondent what he likes and dislikes about the Democratic and Republican Parties. These questions are drawn from the national surveys conducted by the Survey Research Center (SRC) in each presidential election year from 1952 to 1972.[4] These items have been discussed by the authors of *The American Voter* (Campbell et al., 1960), by Donald Stokes (1966a) in an examination of the components of American electoral politics, and by V. O. Key, Jr. (1961) in his analysis of American public opinion. In a manner similar to procedures used by Matthews and Prothro, each response favorable to the Republican Party and unfavorable to the Democratic Party was assigned a value of +1 and each response unfavorable to the Republican Party and favorable to the Democratic Party was assigned a value of −1 for each respondent. "Don't knows" and other missing data categories were coded zero. Up to five responses to each question were recorded by the Survey Research Center, except in 1972, so that the "index of party image" ranges from +10 for most strongly pro-Republican to −10 for most strongly pro-Democratic.[5] Then this scale was collapsed into five categories, as was also done by Matthews and Prothro.

The Survey Research Center has also collected information on changes in party identification. Present Democratic and Republican identifiers have been asked whether they ever identified with another party and present Independents have been asked whether they ever identified with either the Democratic or Republican Parties.[6] Unfortunately, the questionnaire items do not permit one to determine whether present Democratic and Republican identifiers were formerly Independents. Furthermore, past identifications can only be measured imprecisely ("Democratic," "Republican," or "Independent") rather than with the more desirable SRC seven-point summary party identification scale.[7] Consequently, in cross-tabulating present identification against past identification, there is no point in using the seven-point scale for present identification, and it has been collapsed below into Democratic, Independent, and Republican.

Table 1. CROSS-TABULATIONS OF PRESENT PARTY IDENTIFICATION BY PAST PARTY IDENTIFICATION, BY YEAR
(in percentages; numbers in parentheses)

	Past Party Identification											
	1952				1956				1960			
Present Party Identification	D[a]	I[b]	R	Totals	D[a]	I[b]	R	Totals	D[a]	I[b]	R	Totals
Democratic	81.6		21.0	58.6	79.7		14.4	51.3	79.0		22.2	52.3
Independent	2.0	(63)	2.9	6.3	3.6	(97)	2.4	9.0	4.4	(113)	3.9	10.2
Republican	16.4		76.2	35.0	16.7		83.2	39.7	16.6		73.9	37.5
Totals	100.0		100.1[c]	99.9[c]	100.0		100.0	100.0	100.0		100.0	100.0
(N)	(964)	(63)	(491)	(1,518)	(926)	(97)	(577)	(1,600)	(955)	(113)	(689)	(1,797)

	1964				1968				1972			
	D	I	R	Totals	D	I	R	Totals	D	I	R	Totals
Democratic	86.3		28.7	62.0	78.1		23.0	55.6	81.0	24.6	14.2	52.7
Independent	1.5	(259)	2.8	7.9	4.8	(203)	1.7	10.6	7.2	56.5	5.3	15.7
Republican	12.2		68.5	30.1	17.0		75.3	33.8	11.9	18.8	80.5	31.6
Totals	100.0		100.0	100.0	99.9[c]		100.0	100.0	99.9[c]	99.9[c]	100.0	100.0
(N)	(2,628)	(259)	(1,429)	(4,316)	(1,779)	(203)	(882)	(2,664)	(573)	(191)	(282)	(1,046)

a. D = Democratic, including Strong, Weak and Independent Democrats; R = Republican, including Strong, Weak and Independent Republicans;
I = Independent.
b. For discussion of empty cells, see text.
c. Columns do not total 100.0% due to rounding error.

III. STABILITY AND CHANGE IN PARTY IDENTIFICATIONS

Although our interest is in changes in party identification, these changes can be best appreciated in proper perspective. It is clear that changes in identification are relatively few in number. Table 1 presents cross-tabulations of present party identifications by past identification for each year. The single most impressive fact about these data is the stability in partisan attachments which they display. Because the past attachment of present Independents is not fully probed in the questionnaires, producing the empty cells in Table 1, our emphasis throughout this analysis will be on present partisans.[8] Among present partisans, in any one of these six surveys, three quarters or better remember always identifying with the party they currently identify with. Except for 1956, a higher percentage of Democrats than Republicans manifests stable attachments.[9] Because Democrats have outnumbered Republicans throughout this electoral period, and since stable attachments should be more conducive to party voting, these data indicate one further obstacle the Republican Party has had to overcome in trying to muster an electoral majority.

In any given year, the percentage of Democrats recalling their past identifications as Democratic represents the percentage of stable Democratic attachments within the entire electorate. We would expect this figure to remain fairly stable from year to year unless large-scale social and political forces arise to cause realignment. At the same time (to the extent that these figures are reliable), no more than 20% or so of present Democrats remember a different previous identification, whatever year we are dealing with. Consequently, the increase in the proportion of stable Democrats in 1964 accompanied by the decrease in the proportion of stable Republicans—both to record levels for this period—lend credence to the argument that 1964 was a critical election. Pomper (1970) and Campbell (1966c) have both noted the increase in the proportion of Democratic identifiers in 1964, leading Pomper (1970: 99-125) to expand the traditional classification of American elections (Key, 1955; Campbell, 1966b) by adding the category of "converting" elections, in which a given majority party alters its electoral base but retains its majority status.

These data reveal a "normal" range of stability, against which patterns of change can usefully be compared. We can pursue this comparison by examining more carefully the patterns of change in

Table 2. STABILITY AND CHANGE IN PARTY IDENTIFICATIONS, BY YEAR
(in percentages)[a]

Party Identification		Year					
Past= *Republican*	*Present=* *Democratic*	*1952*	*1956*	*1960*	*1964*	*1968*	*1972*
1. Democratic	Democratic	81.6	79.7	79.0	86.3	78.1	81.0
(N)		(964)	(926)	(995)	(2,628)	(1,779)	(573)
2. Republican	Republican	76.2	83.2	73.9	68.5	75.3	80.5
(N)		(491)	(577)	(689)	(1,429)	(882)	(282)
3. Democratic	Republican	16.4	16.7	16.6	12.2	17.0	11.9
(N)		(964)	(926)	(995)	(2,628)	(1,779)	(573)
4. Republican	Democratic	21.0	14.4	22.2	28.7	23.0	14.2
(N)		(491)	(577)	(689)	(1,429)	(882)	(282)
	Difference	−4.6	+3.3	−5.6	−14.5	−6.0	−2.3
5. Democratic	Non-Democratic	18.4	20.3	21.0	13.7	21.8	19.1
(N)		(964)	(926)	(995)	(2,628)	(1,779)	(573)
6. Republican	Non-Republican	23.9	16.8	26.1	31.5	24.7	19.5
(N)		(491)	(577)	(689)	(1,429)	(882)	(282)
	Difference	−5.5	+3.5	−5.1	−17.8	−2.9	−0.4

a. Entries are the percentages of those with the given past identification who have the given present identification, based on the number of cases (in parentheses) with the given past identification.

Table 1, which have been removed to Table 2 for closer scrutiny. The conversion of former Democrats to present Republicans (row 3 in Table 2) is reported at a constant rate of approximately 16 percentage points, with the elections of 1964 and 1972 falling closer to 12 percentage points. For all years except 1956, there is a higher proportion of present Democrats who remember having been Republican (row 4) than that of present Republicans who remember having been Democratic (row 3). This is consistent with the data in *The American Voter* (Campbell et al., 1960: 155), which indicate that the last known electoral realignment up to 1960 occurred in the 1930s, converting Republicans and potential Republicans to the Democratic Party.

It is not apparent from these data that the Democrats have lost consistently more than the Republicans during this electoral period. If we compare Democratic to non-Democratic conversion (row 5) with Republican to non-Republican conversion (row 6), we see that the Republican loss has in fact generally exceeded the Democratic loss, with 1956 an exception again. Consequently, the data of Tables 1 and 2 would not support the contention that a present realignment is benefitting the Republicans.[10] In fact, the only evidence of realignment so far is the indication that in 1964 many more Republicans than usual were converted to the Democratic majority.

These cross-tabulations are also useful for discussing the topic of "party decomposition," the loosening bonds between electorate and party, which Burnham (1965; 1970: 91-134) discusses. The increasing number of Independents, which many scholars have observed, is often cited as evidence of party decomposition. If decomposition is taking place, then we might expect to encounter

Table 3. STABLE COMPONENTS OF THE AMERICAN ELECTORATE, 1952-1972

	1952	*1956*	*1960*	*1964*	*1968*	*1972*
1. Independents as % of electorate	5.9	9.2	10.1	7.9	10.8	12.4
(N)[a]	(1,729)	(1,690)	(1,864)	(4,561)	(3,049)	(1,342)
2. % of Independents recalling some previous party identification (Democratic or Republican)	34.4	32.6	38.6	23.6	33.2	34.1
(N)[b]	(96)	(144)	(184)	(339)	(304)	(164)
3. Stable Independents as % of electorate: (1) X [1 − (2)]	3.9	6.2	6.2	6.0	7.2	8.2
4. Democrats as % of electorate	58.7	51.9	52.9	61.4	55.7	52.2
(N)[a]	(1,729)	(1,690)	(1,864)	(4,561)	(3,049)	(1,342)
5. % of Democrats recalling past party identification as Democratic	88.4	89.9	83.7	84.7	87.3	84.2
(N)[c]	(890)	(821)	(939)	(2,677)	(1,593)	(551)
6. Stable Democrats as % of electorate: (4) X (5)	51.9	46.6	44.3	52.0	48.6	44.0
7. Republicans as % of electorate	35.4	38.9	37.0	30.7	33.5	35.5
(N)[a]	(1,729)	(1,690)	(1,864)	(4,561)	(3,049)	(1,342)
8. % of Republicans recalling past party identification as Republican	70.3	75.6	75.5	75.3	68.7	68.6
(N)[d]	(532)	(635)	(674)	(1,300)	(967)	(331)
9. Stable Republicans as % of electorate: (7) X (8)	24.9	29.4	27.9	23.1	23.0	24.1
10. Stable partisans as % of electorate: (6) + (9)	76.8	76.0	72.2	75.1	71.6	68.1

a. Based on all respondents assigned by the Survey Research Center to one of the seven categories on the summary party identification scale.
b. Based on Independents for whom past identification is available (see Table 1).
c. Based on Democrats for whom past identification is available (see Table 1).
d. Based on Republicans for whom past identification is available (see Table 1).

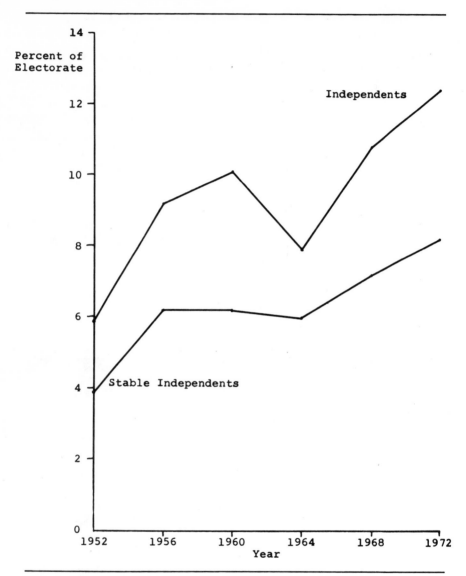

Figure 1: INDEPENDENTS AND STABLE INDEPENDENTS AS PERCENT
OF ELECTORATE

smaller proportions of stable partisans within the electorate. The
data of Table 3, Figure 1, and Figure 2 offer mixed evidence about
party decomposition.[11] The percentage of Independents has
increased throughout this period (serial regression coefficient =
1.003, p < .05) with only one figure (for 1964) less than the figure
for the preceding presidential election year. Within this growing

group of Independents, the group of stable Independents—present Independents recalling no former partisan identification—has grown fairly steadily and dramatically since 1952, so that the group of Independents recalling *some* partisan attachment has shrunk. Finally, the group of stable partisans—stable Democrats and stable Republicans combined—has decreased over this time period, as Figure 2 reveals. This decrease would seem to suggest the presence of party decomposition, as would the increase in the proportion of Independents, but the increase in the proportion of stable Independents would not.

Changing patterns in attitudinal data, such as in partisan attachments, may manifest either party decomposition or party realignment, as was demonstrated by our hypothetical example of the Democratic-to-Republican identification switcher. It may therefore be difficult methodologically to separate the two processes, especially when the evidence is not clearcut. For instance, Figure 1 does not reveal the sharp breaking point we would expect if realignment had occurred, but in Figure 2 the downward trend in the size of the stable partisan group is broken sharply in 1964, only to start up again in 1968. The 1964 election stands out, but it deviates from a trend rather than reversing it, so that even this distinctiveness does not seem sufficient evidence of realignment. Furthermore, even if we accept the argument that a "realigning era" is a more useful theoretical concept than that of a "realigning election" (Campbell, 1966b), we still cannot find positive proof of realignment, since the trend in Figure 2 extends across too long a time span even for the concept of a "realigning era." Consequently, although these data do not rule out the possibility of realignment within this twenty-year period, they do tentatively suggest that party decomposition has occurred. We shall, however, encounter evidence of realignment below.

Despite the possible party decomposition in this period, partisan change has not been great. Accordingly, the thrust of this section is to reaffirm the stability of party identifications among Americans. Nevertheless, changes in identifications have occurred, and stability and meaningful change can be reconciled parsimoniously by introducing the concept of party image, to which we now turn.

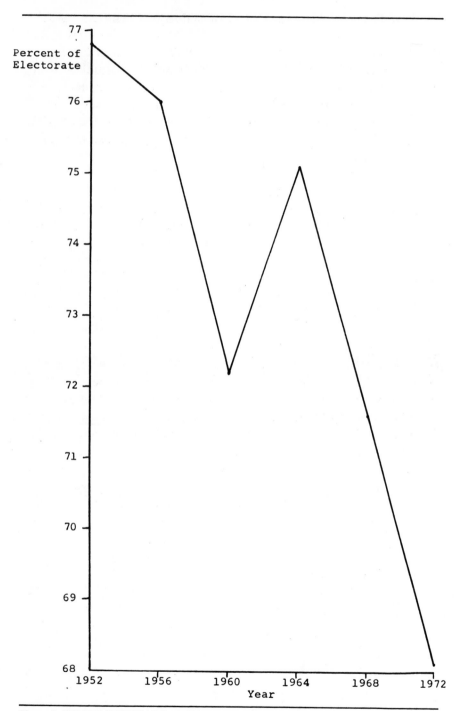

Figure 2: STABLE PARTISANS AS PERCENT OF ELECTORATE

IV. PARTY IMAGE AND STABILITY AND CHANGE
IN PARTY IDENTIFICATIONS

The stability of party identifications and the changes in identifications which do occur are both related to individual party images. When these images serve to reinforce party identification, stability in identification is observed. When images are in conflict with identification, identifications are much more likely to be altered. The data in Table 4 document these conclusions.

Table 4 presents the relationship between patterns of party identification stability (and change) and party image for each of the six presidential election years under consideration. For any given year, the table presents the percentage of individuals with a given past identification who have retained it and of those who have changed it, by party image. Present Independents have been excluded, so that columns often total less than 100%. In 1952, for instance, among those with a past Democratic identification, 98.0% of the strongly pro-Democratic party image-holders (DD) had a present Democratic party identification, and 0.4% had a present Republican party identification; and among those with a past Republican party identification, 13.6% of the neutral image-holders (N) had a present Democratic party identification, and 72.7% had a present Republican identification.

Among individuals with past Democratic identifications, the more pro-Democratic the party image, the greater the likelihood that present identification will be Democratic. A corresponding tendency prevails among individuals with past Republican identification. About 95% of individuals with past Democratic identifications who also have strong pro-Democratic party images will have present Democratic identifications, and there is a precise parallel in the case of individuals with past Republican identifications. The role of party image in inducing stability of identification is apparent.

When party image is not so strongly directed toward the party with which one identified in the past, there is a smaller likelihood that one will retain that past identification. In fact, the more one's party image favors the party with which one did *not* identify in the past, the more likely is one to convert to that party in the present. That is, among individuals *with past Democratic identifications who have strongly pro-Republican party images,* only one third or less still identify with the Democratic Party. This is to be compared with the 95% or higher figures of *past Democratic identifiers with strongly*

Table 4. THE RELATIONSHIP BETWEEN PATTERNS OF PARTY IDENTIFICATION AND PARTY IMAGE, BY YEAR (in percentages)[a]

Year	Present Party Identification[b]	Past Party Identification[b]									
		Democratic					Republican				
		Party Image[c]					Party Image[c]				
		DD	D	N	R	RR	DD	D	N	R	RR
1952	Democratic	98.0	93.0	80.0	60.4	35.6	85.2	58.7	25.0	12.0	5.3
	Republican	0.4	6.1	16.2	36.8	61.4	14.8	36.5	71.4	84.8	92.5
	(N)	(244)	(345)	(130)	(144)	(101)	(27)	(63)	(56)	(158)	(187)
1956	Democratic	100.0	92.9	73.3	41.7	7.7	86.7	50.7	11.1	4.3	0.0
	Republican	0.0	4.6	17.0	52.5	90.4	13.3	43.3	84.6	94.3	98.5
	(N)	(233)	(366)	(165)	(120)	(52)	(30)	(67)	(117)	(230)	(133)
1960	Democratic	100.0	92.2	73.8	32.4	29.8	94.9	58.4	13.6	8.6	0.0
	Republican	0.0	5.7	18.2	56.1	61.7	3.4	31.7	72.7	91.1	100.0
	(N)	(198)	(424)	(187)	(139)	(47)	(59)	(101)	(110)	(269)	(150)
1964	Democratic	98.4	94.5	86.6	57.3	14.3	91.4	67.4	24.8	7.5	2.6
	Republican	1.6	4.1	11.6	37.6	85.7	8.6	27.5	70.6	90.6	97.4
	(N)	(550)	(1,118)	(560)	(295)	(105)	(81)	(316)	(327)	(477)	(228)
1968	Democratic	96.5	96.1	78.9	54.4	25.3	100.0	62.0	26.8	12.0	3.4
	Republican	1.2	1.9	13.0	38.2	68.0	0.0	34.7	69.5	86.5	96.6
	(N)	(268)	(621)	(399)	(351)	(150)	(37)	(121)	(164)	(326)	(234)
1972	Democratic	98.7	93.5	75.9	55.4	35.3	85.7	62.1	9.8	5.3	2.4
	Republican	1.3	2.8	8.0	39.1	64.7	14.3	24.1	82.6	91.2	97.6
	(N)	(76)	(214)	(174)	(92)	(17)	(7)	(29)	(92)	(115)	(41)

a. Entries are percentages of party-image categories with present party identification as given.
b. Independent Democrats coded as Democrats; Independent Republicans coded as Republicans; Independents excluded from table so columns do not total 100.0%.
c. Key: DD = Strongly Pro-Democratic; D = Mildly Pro-Democratic; N = Neutral; R = Mildly Pro-Republican; RR = Strongly Pro-Republican.

pro-Democratic images who identify in the present with the Democratic Party (compare columns 1 and 5 in Table 4). Similarly, among past Republican identifiers who have strongly pro-Democratic party images, very few identify with the Republican Party in the present—no more than 14.8% (1952) and as few as 0.0% (1968). These figures should be compared with the 92.5% or higher figures of past Republicans with strongly pro-Republican party images who still identify in the present with the Republican Party (compare columns 6 and 10). The role of party image in inducing changes in party identification is also apparent.

When extreme positive images are projected by the party with which one identified in the past, an individual is very likely to retain his past identification. Thus, extreme images *consistent* with past identifications are conducive to stable identifications. At the same time, when extreme positive images are projected by the party one did *not* identify with in the past, an individual is very likely to forsake this past identification. Thus, extreme positive images *inconsistent* with past identifications are conducive to changing identifications.

If we return to the data of Table 1, we can "postdict"[12] present party identification from past identification with fairly good success because of the general stability in identifications among Americans. That is to say, past Democrats are very likely to be present Democrats and past Republicans are very likely to be present Republicans. If we were to predict that present identification would be the same as past identification, the errors we would make are the cases which appear in the nonmodal cells of each column in Table 1: among past Democratic identifiers, the present identifications of individuals who actually became present Independents or present Republicans would have been predicted incorrectly; among past Republican identifiers, the identifications of present Independents and present Democratic identifiers would have been predicted incorrectly. The general stability of identifications leads to predictive success, but despite this success we can improve on our predictions by considering present party images.

If we ignore past Independents, for whom information is incomplete, then the question is whether or not we can better predict present identification with the use of the party image construct in addition to past identification. Within the categories of past identification given in Table 4, we have seen that party image is strongly related to present party identification. In Table 4, within each category of party image, cases that are in nonmodal present party identification cells constitute errors as before in our efforts to predict present identifications. When we use party-image categories for these predictions of present party identification, the number of errors is reduced sharply for every year, in fact by as much as 33.2% in 1960, as compared to predictions made only on the basis of past identification.

It is important to realize that we are not comparing directly the ability of past identification and the ability of present party image to predict present identification. Our theoretical thrust, according to Sellers's (1965) argument, is whether past identifications change in response to party images. In other words, do party images play an intervening role which is crucial in the transformation of past identifications to present? It is therefore appropriate to examine the predictive ability of party image while controlling for past party identification. The data of Table 5 let us evaluate the predictive ability of the party-image construct.

Table 5. ERRORS IN PREDICTING PRESENT PARTY IDENTIFICATION FROM PAST PARTY IDENTIFICATION, WITH AND WITHOUT THE INTERVENING VARIABLE OF PARTY IMAGE, AND FROM PARTY IMAGE ALONE, BY YEAR

	Year					
	1952	*1956*	*1960*	*1964*	*1968*	*1972*
1. Total predictions: N of past Democratic and Republican identifiers	1455	1503	1684	4057	2661	855
2. N of errors predicting present identification from past identification only	294	285	389	811	607	164
3. Errors as % of total predictions: (2)/(1)	20.2	19.0	23.1	20.0	22.8	19.2
4. N of errors predicting present identification from party image, controlling for past Democratic and Republican identification	235	202	260	543	473	143
5. Reduction in errors: (4)−(2)	59	83	129	268	124	21
6. % reduction in errors: (5)/(2)	20.1	29.1	33.2	33.0	22.1	12.8
7. Total predictions: N of present Democratic and Republican identifiers[a]	1729	1690	1864	4561	3049	1342
8. N of errors predicting present identification from party image only	401	419	471	1118	897	453
9. Errors as % of total predictions: (8)/(7)	23.2	24.8	25.2	24.5	29.4	33.8

a. Number of usable cases for item (7) is considerably greater than for item (1).

Knowing only past party identification, we can expect to be wrong in approximately 20% of our predictions (row 3 of Table 5). However, if we are given past party identification and present aprty image, our predictions of present party identification will involve considerably fewer errors, ranging from a high reduction in error of 33.2% to a low of 12.8% in 1960 and 1972, respectively (row 6). In other words, we increase our ability to predict from past party identification to present if we include the apparently intervening variable of party image.[13]

The predictive power of party image in combination with past identification, although consistently greater than past party identification alone, is itself variable. Figure 3 traces the percent reduction in errors over time. An inverted U-shape is obvious. The transition role of party image seems to have been greatest in 1960 and 1964 but has declined sharply since 1964. It is difficult to interpret these data, but if we return to Sellers's argument, we may be able to make sense of them. In the critical role that party image is said to have in transforming party identification, the impact of party image varies over time. Before a realignment begins, party image apparently would have very little impact. In the midst of realignment, its impact would be great. As the forces producing realignment ebb, as realignment ebbs, as the critical issues producing realignment are resolved, the impact of party image would also decline. Consequently, the picture in Figure 3 is consistent with the argument that an electoral realignment occurred within this twenty-year period, and that it occurred around 1964.

This is not to say that Figure 3 alone proves that a realignment occurred. Figure 3 only traces the ability of party image to predict present party identification: the peak in 1960-1964 does not mean that more identification changes took place in this four-year period. However, we have already encountered evidence relevant to this discussion. We have noted that 1964 marked a high point in Republican to Democratic and in Republican to non-Republican conversions, and a low point in Democratic to Republican conversions (see Table 2). Furthermore, despite the fact that a high proportion of voters was classified as stable partisans in 1964 (74.1%), at the same time, the proportion of stable Republicans reached a low point (21.1%) for this twenty-year period (see Table 3).

It is difficult to separate the idiosyncratic and theoretically less interesting aspects of the 1964 election from those aspects that

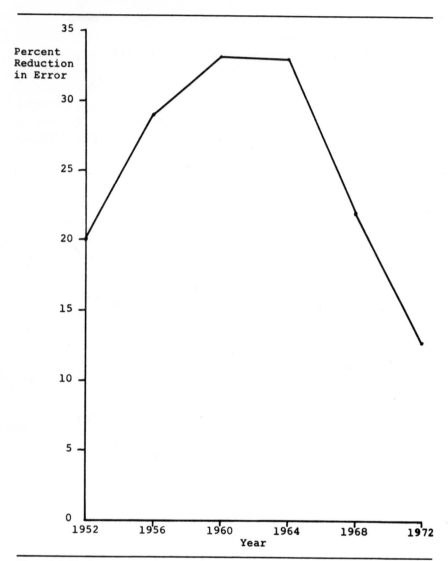

Figure 3: PERCENT REDUCTION IN ERROR IN PREDICTING PRESENT PARTY
IDENTIFICATION FROM PARTY IMAGE, CONTROLLING FOR PAST
DEMOCRATIC AND REPUBLICAN IDENTIFICATION (see Table 5)

manifest forces of underlying, durable social and electoral change.
Burnham (1968), for one, argues that realignment-like phenomena
occurred in 1964, producing social groupings which resembled those
of 1896. Pomper (1970) and Campbell (1966c) both note the
abnormally high conversion rate in 1964 of former Republicans to
Democratic identifications. Yet the highly negative personal appeal

of the Republican candidate cannot be discounted (see Converse et al., 1965), and it is difficult to know whether conversions, through party image or otherwise, were more the result of the idiosyncratic candidate factor than of other, more interesting, theoretical matters. Nevertheless, the evidence provides indirect support for the contention that 1964 was a critical election, to complement the argument that party decomposition has occurred.

It is also important to realize that Tables 4 and 5 display a significant and substantively important interaction between party image and party identification. In predicting present identification from party image, controlling for past identification, we improve our predictive abilities beyond what they would be if we were to predict present identification on the basis of past identification alone. But we also improve them beyond what they would be if we were to predict present identification on the basis only of present party image, as Table 5 shows. The propensity of strongly pro-Democratic image-holders for identification with the Democratic Party is higher than that of pro-Republican image-holders, but specifying past party identification serves also to specify this tendency: the likelihood of strongly pro-Democratic image-holders to be currently identified with the Democratic Party is greater for past Democratic identifiers than for past Republican identifiers.

Let us briefly return to the role of party image in inducing stability or change in party identifications. The data of Table 4 would offer conclusive evidence of this role if we were able to demonstrate that present party image had in fact been developed before present party identifications were acquired. Unfortunately, the survey instruments used by the Survey Research Center (which furnished the data for this paper) do not ask respondents when they developed their present party images, when they came to like or dislike the parties to the extent that they do now. It is possible that present identifications in some cases have caused individuals to develop the images we have measured here; in other words, individuals may rationalize present party identifications by adopting images consistent with identifications. However, the patterns of data in Table 4 strongly suggest that our interpretation of the crucial role of party image is correct. If present identifications had, in fact, been acquired before present party images had been developed, we certainly would expect images and identifications to be associated, as indeed they are. But the apparent interaction of present identification, party image, and past identification, which is evident in Table

4, is not easily explained under the assumption that present identifications precede present images. Why should we find the consistency of image and past identification among stable identifiers, or the inconsistency of image and past identification among unstable identifiers?

Furthermore, the argument that present party images are rationalizations of present party identifications can be tentatively rejected on other grounds. It is difficult methodologically to determine causal relationships between attitudinal and behavioral dimensions when both are measured at the same time and when consistency is observed (Page and Brody, 1972). For instance, scholars have noted the difficulty in determining whether opinion on issues causes one's vote or whether individuals rationalize their votes by forcing their opinions to fit their voting preference (see also Kovenock et al., 1970; Brody and Page, 1972; and Kirkpatrick, 1970). In addition, scholars have found actual instances of rationalization (Berelson et al., 1954; Brody and Page, 1972). However, on occasion they have also concluded that rationalization is not likely (Kovenock et al., 1970; Page and Brody, 1972: 454). Furthermore, even if we can never completely rule out the rationalization hypothesis when we observe consistency, we can at least reject that hypothesis in the absence of consistency (Page and Brody, 1972: 452-453). In Table 4, many individuals do in fact possess present party images which conflict with present party identifications. For these individuals, at least, images have not been rationalized; and this finding suggests that rationalization among the remaining individuals in Table 4 is less likely. The data of Table 4 would be consistent with the rationalization hypothesis only if we were to insist that among all individuals who have changed party identifications, some rationalize *past* and others *present* identifications with present images. While such a complex structure of rationalization is possible, its complexity argues against its acceptability. Consequently, the data of Table 4 do seem to demonstrate the crucial intervening role of party images (as Sellers described it) in transforming past identifications to new identifications.

Given the short-term nature of issues and the long-term trends of the role of party image in Table 4, we might tentatively conclude that the party-image construct, rather than its substantive components, accounts for party identification stability and change. That is, those issues, events, and candidates—or even other unnamed forces—which alter and mold party images would seem less important for changing or maintaining party identifications than the general predisposition they create on the part of an individual toward the parties, that is, the extent to which an individual likes or dislikes the parties. A preliminary examination of the role of key issue components of the party-image construct has shown these issues to be less important than the overall party-image index in affecting political behavior (see Trilling, 1974a; 1974c). That is, the specific likes and dislikes people have about the parties are less important than the overall affect which is measured by the party-image index.

V. PARTY IMAGE AND THE AMOUNT OF PARTISAN CHANGE

The role of party image in inducing stability or change is striking, but it is possible to probe this role even further by constructing a measure of the amount of partisan change. If we assign interger values to the party identification categories (1 = Democratic, 2 = Independent, 3 = Republican) and subtract past identification scores from present identification scores, we obtain an Index of Partisan Change, which provides a rough measure of how far individuals have moved in their partisan attachments between their past identification and their present identification. Obviously, individuals who have not changed affiliations will have a change score of 0, which is desirable. This measure, however, neither distinguishes between changes from Democratic to Independent and changes from Independent to Republican,[14] nor assigns scores to individuals who were not included in Table 1. Nevertheless, some tentative distinctions appear when we cross-tabulate this partisan change schore by party-image scores.

We have noted that party image is conducive both to stability and to change in party identification. When images favor the party with which one identified in the past, one is likely to retain that identification in the present. When images favor the party with which one did not identify in the past, one is likely to alter identification so that present identification is consistent with party image. Not surprisingly, party image is also related to the amount of change in party identification.

Table 6 presents cross-tabulations of the index of partisan change by party image, for each year.[15] As we read across for any year, some clear patterns emerge. First, most individuals, whatever their party image, are scored zero on the partisan change measure; in other

Table 6. CROSS-TABULATIONS OF THE INDEX OF PARTISAN CHANGE
BY PARTY IMAGE, BY YEAR (in percentages)[a]

Index of Partisan Change[b]	1952 Party Image[c]					1956 Party Image[c]				
	DD	*D*	*N*	*R*	*RR*	*DD*	*D*	*N*	*R*	*RR*
−2 R→D	8.4	8.5	3.9	5.8	3.4	10.0	7.2	3.5	2.6	0.0
−1 R→I, I→D	0.0	0.7	0.6	1.5	1.4	0.0	0.8	1.3	0.8	1.1
0 R→R, D→D, I→I	89.8	85.3	88.2	75.3	73.2	90.0	86.4	83.3	78.4	73.1
+1 D→I, I→R	1.5	0.7	1.4	1.2	1.0	0.0	1.9	4.3	1.8	0.5
+2 D→R	0.4	4.8	5.9	16.2	21.0	0.0	3.6	7.5	16.4	25.3
N	275	434	355	328	295	259	472	371	384	186
			$\gamma = .361$					$\gamma = .484$		

	1960 Party Image[c]					1964 Party Image[c]				
	DD	*D*	*N*	*R*	*RR*	*DD*	*D*	*N*	*R*	*RR*
−2 R→D	20.7	10.5	3.5	5.4	0.0	11.5	14.3	7.3	4.3	1.8
−1 R→I, I→D	0.4	1.8	3.5	0.2	0.0	0.0	1.1	1.3	1.1	0.0
0 R→R, D→D, I→I	79.0	81.9	81.6	72.2	83.3	87.1	80.5	84.7	79.3	71.7
+1 D→I, I→R	0.0	1.6	3.5	3.8	2.0	0.0	1.0	0.9	1.8	0.0
+2 D→R	0.0	4.3	7.9	18.4	14.6	1.4	3.1	5.8	13.4	26.5
N	271	564	430	424	198	644	1,487	1,115	828	339
			$\gamma = .470$					$\gamma = .414$		

	1968 Party Image[c]					1972 Party Image[c]				
	DD	*D*	*N*	*R*	*RR*	*DD*	*D*	*N*	*R*	*RR*
−2 R→D	12.1	9.6	6.3	5.3	2.0	6.5	6.3	2.5	2.4	1.5
−1 R→I, I→D	0.0	0.5	0.9	0.7	0.0	6.5	9.4	4.2	5.2	1.5
0 R→R, D→D, I→I	85.0	86.8	80.8	72.1	70.1	85.9	78.7	77.8	69.1	74.2
+1 D→I, I→R	2.0	1.5	4.6	3.6	2.5	0.0	3.5	11.5	8.8	6.1
+2 D→R	1.0	1.5	7.5	18.3	25.4	1.1	2.1	3.9	14.5	16.7
N	307	778	697	731	402	92	286	356	249	66
			$\gamma = .450$					$\gamma = .381$		

a. Entries are the percentages of each category of party image with the given Index of Partisan Change score.
b. Index of Partisan Change computed by subtracting past party identification from present party identification. Coding: Republican (R) = 3; Independent (I) = 2; Democratic (D) = 1. Independent Republicans and Independent Democrats coded as partisans, not as Independents. Past identification is listed to the left of present identification.
c. Key: DD = Strongly Pro-Democratic; D = Mildly Pro-Democratic; N = Neutral; R = Mildly Pro-Republican; RR = Strongly Pro-Republican.

words, they retain the same partisan attachment or nonattachment they recall having had in the past, and this is consistent with the great stability we have already noted (see the middle row for all of the years in Table 6). Second, among these psychological stand-patters, stability is greatest among strongly pro-Democratic image-holders. With the exception of 1960, the more pro-Democratic the party image, the greater the proportion of individuals who recall no partisan change. Third, the more pro-Republican the image, the greater the proportion of individuals who show a pro-Republican identification shift. This trend is especially evident in the bottom row for each year, in which the proportion of switchers from a Democratic to a Republican party identification rises dramatically as we read across from the most pro-Democratic party image column (DD) to the most pro-Republican party image column (RR). Consequently, in noting that pro-Republican image-holders were less stable in their party identifications, we now see that the reason for this greater instability is a definite movement to Republican partisan attachments. Fourth, there is also a trend for the proportion of switchers toward Democratic identifications to increase as party image moves from most strongly pro-Republican to most strongly pro-Democratic. Finally, however, the pull of party image among pro-Democratic switchers is clearly weaker than among pro-Republican image-holders. Throughout this twenty-year period, a much greater proportion of strongly pro-Republican than of strongly pro-Democratic image-holders has been comprised of individuals who report having switched party identifications to the party which projects the positive image they possess.

In 1960, the impact of party image in affecting change to Democratic identifications was much greater than at any other time in this period. In 1972, it was the weakest. Thus, while party image fostered pro-Democratic conversion in 1960, it was unable to produce a normal share of converts in 1972. The 1972 election stands out in another respect, as well. In 1972, the impact of party image on pro-Republican conversions was also the smallest in this twenty-year period. In 1972, the electorate was least stable in its party identification; a low of 76.5% reported no change in attachments. Despite or perhaps because of the greater movement in 1972, the movement was less related to party image than for any other year in this period.

We have seen that the data of Table 4 are consistent with the theory that party image induces change or stability in partisan attachments. To this we can now add that the data of Table 6 are consistent with the theory that party image affects the amount of change in identification.

VI. PATTERNS OF PARTISAN ATTACHMENTS

Having documented the apparent role of party image in fostering stability and change in party identification and in affecting the amount of partisan change, we can now examine specific patterns of partisan attachments over time. If party image completely determined present party identifications, then all individuals with a given party-image score would have the same party identifications, but this is clearly not so. It is the interactive pattern of party image with past party identification that produces present identification, and the importance of this interaction warrants further examination.

Matthews and Prothro (1966a: 392-396) reported that patterns of stability and change in party identification from 1960 to 1964 were strongly related to party images among Southerners. By classifying individuals by pattern of party identification (past-present), Matthews and Prothro (1966a: 393) showed that switchers from a Republican to a Democratic identification had the most pro-Democratic mean party-image score and those from a Democratic to a Republican identification the most pro-Republican of all switchers. Table 7 presents mean party-image scores for groups of party identification switchers and stand-patters, separating groups of individuals who were assigned the same Index of Partisan Change score in Table 6 despite their different patterns of identification.

The stable partisans in Table 7 (D→D and R→R) generally have the most extreme mean party-image scores. Stable Democratic identifiers have the most pro-Democratic, and stable Republican identifiers have the most pro-Republican mean party-image score. Stability and extreme party images are thus related once again. Among switchers, those who moved farther in their identifications (R→D, D→R) have more extreme mean party-image scores than other switchers (R→I, D→I).

Consequently, two general points emerge. First, with regard to mean party-image scores, there is a constant rank ordering of five categories into which can be placed the seven patterns of partisan attachment: (1) stable Democrats; (2) converts to Democratic identification; (3) converted and stable Independents; (4) converts to

Table 7. MEAN PARTY-IMAGE SCORES OF STABLE AND CHANGING
PARTY IDENTIFIERS, BY YEAR[a]

Year	Pattern of Stable and Changing Party Identification[b]							Entire Electorate
	D→D	R→D	D→I	I→I	R→I	D→R	R→R	
1952	−2.09	−1.03	+0.32	+0.71	+2.29	+2.67	+3.30	−0.01
(N)	(787)	(103)	(19)	(63)	(14)	(158)	(374)	(1,783)
1956	−2.39	−2.21	−0.03	−0.11	+0.85	+2.03	+2.07	−0.41
(N)	(738)	(83)	(33)	(97)	(14)	(155)	(480)	(1,759)
1960	−2.15	−2.36	+0.55	−0.66	−0.63	+1.45	+2.33	−0.35
(N)	(786)	(153)	(44)	(113)	(27)	(165)	(509)	(1,928)
1964	−1.98	−1.60	+0.23	−0.10	−0.13	+1.76	+1.85	−0.61
(N)	(2,267)	(410)	(40)	(259)	(40)	(321)	(979)	(4,551)
1968	−1.40	−1.18	+0.58	+0.33	+0.33	+2.59	+2.55	+0.16
(N)	(1,390)	(203)	(86)	(203)	(15)	(303)	(664)	(3,056)
1972	−1.35	−1.08	−0.02	+0.01	−0.07	+1.43	+1.58	−0.19
(N)	(464)	(40)	(41)	(108)	(15)	(68)	(227)	(1,361)

a. Party image ranges from −10 (most strongly pro-Democratic) to +10 (most strongly pro-Republican) except for 1972, when it ranges from −6 to +6.
b. Past party identification is listed to the left of the arrow, present party identification to the right of the arrow. Key: R = Republican; I = Independent; D = Democratic. Independent Democrats and Independent Republicans are coded as partisans, not as Independents.

Republican identification; and (5) stable Republicans. These groups have, respectively, the least pro-Republican to the most pro-Republican mean party-image scores. Not surprisingly, the least precision to this rank ordering occurs when assigning classifications to the three groups of category 3: Democrats turned Independents (D→I), Republicans turned Independents (R→I), and stable Independents (I→I). The greater volatility of Independents has been well documented (Campbell et al., 1960: 143-145; Campbell, 1966a) and again seems to manifest itself here.

Second, a "strain toward consistency" (Lane and Sears, 1964: 44-53; Kirkpatrick, 1970) apparently operates on these two attitudinal dimensions. Mean party-image scores are very much in line with *present* party identifications. This is especially evident in Figure 4, which plots the data of Table 7 over time. In Figure 4, the seven patterns of partisan attachment separate themselves into three sets, according to *present* identification. The two present Democratic identification groups (D→D, R→D) are together at the pro-Democratic party image end of the continuum; the three present Independent groups (D→I, R→I, I→I) are together in the middle; and the present Republican identification groups (D→R, R→R) are

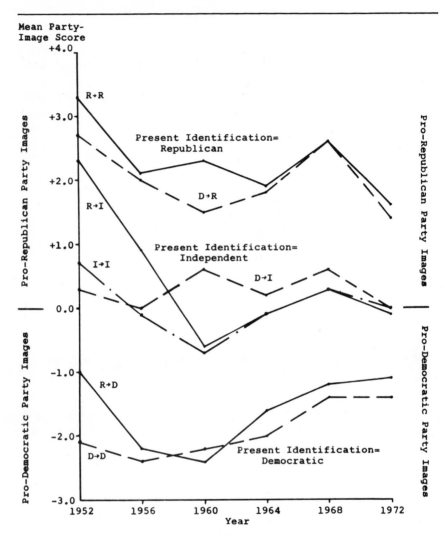

Figure 4: **MEAN PARTY-IMAGE SCORES OF PATTERNS OF PARTISAN**
ATTACHMENT, BY YEAR

together at the pro-Republican end of the continuum. The pictorial display in Figure 4 reveals the striking relationship between party image and present party identification: the consistency which individuals attain, consciously or unconsciously, in party image and present party identification.

We have argued that the reasonable interpretation of this

consistency is that present identifications are made to conform with present party images, rather than images with identifications. Applying this logic again, we are led to conclude that Figure 4 reveals strong evidence of the role of party image in producing present identifications, either by maintaining past identification consistent with present image, or by altering past identification to make present identification consistent with present image.

VII. PARTY IMAGE AND THE VOTE

The ramifications of party image for partisan stability and change are considerable. The final impact of party image can be seen in its apparent ability to affect the voting preference of individuals whose party identifications it has converted. Table 8 examines voting preferences of image-holders who have had their identifications converted. With only one exception, individuals whose identifications apparently have been converted by extreme images are more loyal in their voting than party identifiers generally. Individuals who were past Republican identifiers but now possess strongly pro-Democratic party images and identify with the Democratic Party (column 2) are more likely to vote Democratic than all present Democratic identifiers (column 1). Individuals who were past Democratic identifiers but now possess strongly pro-Republican party images and identify with the Republican Party (column 12) are more likely to vote Republican than all present Republican identifiers (column 7). This is all the more remarkable given the high Republican voting rates of Republican identifiers.

Thus, party images seem to convert individual identifications when past identifications are inconsistent with present images. In so doing, images seem to create a set of converts whose fidelity cannot be surpassed. (The figures in columns 2 and 12 are close to or equal to 100%.) In other words, among extreme image-holders there are individuals about whom we might justly say, "There is none so fanatical as the convert." Furthermore, we see that the more extreme the party image of these converts, the greater the likelihood that they will vote for the party with which they currently identify (read from column 6 to column 2 or from column 8 to column 12). When individuals change their party identification because of strong party images, their fanatical voting support thus distinguishes them not only from present party identifiers generally, but also from changers

Table 8. THE IMPACT OF PARTY IMAGE ON VOTING PREFERENCES OF CONVERTED PARTISAN IDENTIFIERS, BY YEAR

Year	% Voting Democratic among All Present Democratic Identifiers	% Voting Democratic among Present Democratic Identifiers with Past Republican Identification, by Party Image[a]					% Voting Republican among All Present Republican Identifiers	% Voting Republican among Present Republican Identifiers with Past Democratic Identification, by Party Image[a]				
		DD	D	N	R	RR		DD	D	N	R	RR
1952	70.5	100.0	89.3	44.0	0.0	0.0	95.7	0.0	76.9	100.0	95.6	100.0
(N)	(654)	(18)	(28)	(9)	(11)	(10)	(460)	(1)	(13)	(16)	(45)	(57)
1956	73.7	95.8	77.8	70.0	12.5	100.0	95.7	b	92.3	95.0	100.0	100.0
(N)	(634)	(24)	(27)	(10)	(8)	(2)	(511)		(13)	(20)	(55)	(44)
1960	81.8	77.8	95.0	57.1	17.6	b	92.2	b	66.7	100.0	98.6	92.0
(N)	(719)	(45)	(40)	(7)	(17)		(565)		(15)	(31)	(74)	(25)
1964	89.3	100.0	98.5	95.5	36.4	50.0	73.5	0.0	32.6	42.4	75.8	93.1
(N)	(1,997)	(74)	(196)	(66)	(33)	(6)	(1,116)	(6)	(46)	(59)	(99)	(87)
1968	67.2	92.0	66.7	46.2	17.2	100.0	86.3	0.0	60.0	95.8	94.1	95.7
(N)	(1,088)	(25)	(57)	(26)	(29)	(6)	(768)	(1)	(10)	(48)	(102)	(92)
1972	57.4	100.0	53.3	0.0	0.0	0.0	97.2	b	100.0	91.7	100.0	100.0
(N)	(494)	(4)	(15)	(4)	(5)	(1)	(394)		(4)	(12)	(33)	(11)

a. Key: DD = Strongly Pro-Democratic; D = Mildly Pro-Democratic; N = Neutral; R = Mildly Pro-Republican; RR = Strongly Pro-Republican.
b. No respective identifiers on whom to base a percent.

in general, such as the one we discussed earlier, who behaves in a more inconsistent fashion.

Finally, among individuals for whom party images do not reinforce present identifications (columns 5, 6, 8, and 9), voting support for the party one presently identifies with is severely reduced. When party image reinforces present identification, it serves to fortify voting loyalty; when the image conflicts with the identification, it serves to weaken voting loyalty.[16]

VIII. CONCLUSION

The data presented here are consistent with Sellers's (1965) theory that party images play a crucial role in the transformation of party identifications. When party images serve to reinforce past identifications, identifications are stable, but when they conflict with past identifications, identifications are likely to be altered. Thus, there is a systematic pattern to stability and change in identification, and a parsimonious theory—that of the role of party image—seems able to account for such diverse behavior as stable and unstable partisanship. Party images also seem to affect the amount of partisan change and the voting preference of individuals who have experienced change.

Now that so much has been claimed for the concept of party image, it is important to reiterate that party image interacts with party identification and that the impact of images is clearly affected by past party identification. This finding of interaction enhances the validity of the concept. Attitudinal forces which operate on electoral behavior frequently interact in a similar fashion (Campbell et al., 1960: 128-145; RePass, 1971). It would therefore seem that party images deserve further empirical study so that their theoretical role might be refined.

We have also encountered softer evidence that this twenty-year period was marked by the process of party decomposition and the occurrence of party realignment (the latter in 1964). These conclusions must certainly remain tentative until harder, less ambiguous data become available. Nevertheless, they also deserve further study, for they suggest that the ability of political parties to link electorate and government has declined even as new social groupings demand governmental resolution of those issues which prompted realignment. It is difficult to speculate about the significance for American politics of the coexistence of forces producing decomposition and

Table 9. MOST FREQUENT REASONS FOR LIKING AND DISLIKING THE DEMOCRATIC AND REPUBLICAN PARTIES, FIRST RESPONSE ONLY, FOR EACH YEAR (in percentages)[a]

	Year					
	1952	*1956*	*1960*	*1964*	*1968*	*1972*
Responses Favoring the Democratic Party						
Like the Democratic Party because:						
1. It promotes good times for average people[b]	25.8	18.6	20.7	14.6	13.0	17.1
2. It stands for higher wages.[c]	4.6	---	---	---	---	---
3. It's my traditional preference.[d]	3.7	6.0	6.5	8.5	9.0	3.4
4. I just like it.[e]	---	---	---	3.3	---	---
Dislike the Republican Party because:						
1. It causes bad times for average people and stands for business interests.[f]	19.0	12.1	10.2	10.4	6.6	13.1
2. of Goldwater.[g]	---	---	---	6.2	---	---
3. I just don't like them.[h]	---	---	---	3.3	---	---
4. It's too much like the Democratic Party.[i]	---	---	---	---	5.0	---
Responses Favoring the Republican Party						
Like the Republican Party because:						
1. of Eisenhower.[j]	4.7	13.2	---	---	---	---
2. It's time for a change.[k]	4.8	---	---	---	3.3	---
3. It's the party of peace.[l]	---	4.7	5.2	---	---	---
4. It's conservative.[m]	---	---	4.0	8.7	5.2	4.3
5. It's my traditional preference.[n]	---	---	3.9	4.0	3.1	---
6. It will spend less.[o]	---	---	---	---	3.9	---
7. of Nixon.[p]	---	---	---	---	---	3.5
Dislike the Democratic Party because:						
1. of corruption.[q]	7.5	---	---	---	---	---
2. It will spend too much.[r]	6.4	---	4.7	3.4	5.0	---
3. Taxes are too high.[s]	5.4	---	---	---	---	---
4. of Stevenson.[t]	---	3.1	---	---	---	---
5. It's the war party.[u]	---	4.0	3.4	---	---	---
6. of its campaign.[v]	---	5.6	---	---	---	---
7. of its civil rights stand.[w]	---	---	---	3.4	---	---
8. It's too much like the Republican Party.[x]	---	---	---	---	4.0	---
9. of Vietnam.[y]	---	---	---	---	4.5	---
10. of McGovern.[z]	---	---	---	---	---	5.8
11. It's too liberal.[a]	---	---	---	---	---	3.7
N	1,899	1,762	1,954	4,658	3,100	1,372

a. Entries are percentage offering respective responses. ICPR Codebook response category Master Codes are given in notes b through a'. Where more than one response category is combined to compute the table entries, the frequencies for individual response categories are also given in notes b through a'. To be included in table, at least *3.0%* of sample had to be coded in ICPR Master Code Category.
b. 1952: 353 (7.2%), 711 (6.2%), 712 (11.4%); 1956: 353 (3.0%), 711 (8.5%), 712 (9.1%); 1960: 350 (4.0%), 710 (16.7%); 1964: 713; 1968: 711 (7.1%), 712 (5.9%); 1972: 1,205 (14.0%), 1,233 (3.1%). c. 1952: 370. d. 1952-1968: 800; 1972: 101. e. 1964: 900.
f. 1952: 351 (5.0%), 355 (4.9%), 633 (9.1%); 1956, 1960: 633; 1964: 633 (7.3%), 713 (3.1%); 1968: 633; 1972: 1,209. g. 1964: 40. h. 1964: 900. i. 1968: 204. j. 1952, 1956: 10. k. 1952, 1968: 913. l. 1956, 1960: 581. m. 1960: 282; 1964: 231 (3.0%), 280 (5.7%) 1968: 280; 1972: 816. n. 1960-1968: 800. o. 1968: 120. p. 1972: 32. q. 1952: 111. r. 1952, 1960-1968: 130. s. 1952: 348. t. 1956: 50. u. 1956, 1960: 581. v. 1956: 841. w. 1964: 410. x. 1968: 204. y. 1968: 582. z. 1972: 8. a'. 1972: 815.

forces producing realignment, especially in light of the increased cynicism among Americans (Miller, 1972; 1974). It is likely, however, that party images will reveal perceptions of the parties' ability to perform the linkage function and to resolve contemporary issues. Party images may also reveal the extent to which political parties continue to receive the support of American citizens (on support, see Dennis, 1966; 1974). By briefly examining the issue components of party images for this twenty-year period, we can extrapolate and speculate about the future impact of party images on electoral behavior.[17]

The issue components of party images refer to the specific responses to the four items used for the party-image index; in other words, the issue components of party images are revealed through the specific likes and dislikes of Americans with reference to their political parties. The frequencies of first responses to these four items are presented in Table 9. In order to be included in the table, a response had to be offered by at least 3% of the sample. As Table 9 reveals, very few responses were even this common.

Certain key trends appear in the data of Table 9. First, the most prominent substantive references are to issues and political phenomena which have structured American politics since the New Deal. In Burnham's (1970) description of realignment, the crises which prompt realignment create opposing factions and coalitions which persist throughout the duration of the party system formed by realignment. Furthermore, the critical issues which prompt realignment define the political agenda for the duration of the emergent party system. In response to questions about what people like and dislike about the Democratic and Republican parties, from 1952 through 1972, the single most frequent kind of response involves the class distinctions formed as part of the realignment of the 1930s. The most popular reason for liking the Democratic Party remains that it is seen as the party for the common man, working class, or poor man, that it promotes "Good times for the Average Man." The most common reason for disliking the Republican Party is that it is seen as the party of the Depression and of Big Business and Wall Street. The proportion of respondents who offer some aspect of this theme as their first reason for liking the Democratic Party has remained high throughout this twenty-year period—between 13% and 26% (see Table 9)—although it has declined somewhat. It is important to realize that even in 1972, when candidate image and more specific issues seemingly dominated the American political arena, this New

Deal theme still constituted the most basic element of favorable Democratic party images.

No single theme identifies or defines the Republican Party in a favorable light over this twenty-year period to the extent that the "Good times for the Average Man" theme defines favor toward the Democratic Party. The most consistent pro-Republican themes —each considerably less common than the "Good times for the Average Man" theme—are the perceptions that the Republican Party is conservative, that the Republican Party is the peace party, and that the Democrats would (or do) spend too much when in office. More transitory issues tend to benefit the Republican Party throughout this twenty-year period (for example, Vietnam in 1968); but no single, dominant theme persists, as it does for the Democrats, which can provide a hard core of favorable party images.

It becomes obvious very quickly when analyzing these data that few issues intrude on the images of many Americans at the same time. This suggests that the "normal events" of American politics are often unable to penetrate these images very far, or at least to penetrate many of them. Combined with the finding above that the economic well-being theme has persisted since the Depression (or as measured by our data, at least since 1952), we are led to the speculative hypothesis that the party images of citizens reveal most of all the underlying themes of the prevalent coalitional conflict, that these themes persist in the images of citizens so long as the political agenda of the prevalent party system has relevance for the citizenry, and that few other issues can intrude on the party images of large numbers of Americans at any one time.

Many other issues do appear among the responses to the open-ended questions eliciting likes and dislikes about the two parties, including those issues one might regard as "important." Included among these issues are Vietnam, race (civil rights), and government corruption (in 1952). Consequently, it is clear that issues of a short-term nature can intrude on the party images of Americans, but it is equally clear that to do so, such issues must be very important and even then will not penetrate the images of many Americans at the same time. None of these substantive issues is mentioned by as many as one-tenth of the electorate as a reason for liking or disliking either party. (This excludes references to the candidates themselves, which did reach 13.2% in 1956 for Eisenhower.)

In Table 9, it is also clear that references to the "good times" theme declined from 1952 through 1968. Consequently, if party images manifest the underlying themes of prevalent coalitional conflict, then apparently these themes were becoming less relevant as American politics approached the 1970s. Because we have also noted the party decomposition which has characterized this twenty-year period, it is interesting to speculate that these two trends are in some way related. Are parties less relevant to citizens because the issues they sought to resolve, or perhaps still talk about resolving, no longer motivate the public?

The decline of the "good times" theme through 1968 tended to diminish the Democratic Party's defining attribute. Even in 1972, however, this theme had been reaffirmed, either by the nature of economic conditions, by the Democratic Party itself, or by the candidacy of George McGovern. At the time this essay is written (September 1974), one can speculate that present high rates of inflation will serve to fortify this traditional Democratic theme. Recent reports that Americans consider inflation the single most important domestic problem suggest future political success for the Democrats, not just because a Republican presently occupies the White House, but especially because such economic matters have ever since 1932 defined Democratic success. The advances the Republican Party had been making in its party image—the relative gain it had achieved because of substantive issues since 1964 (see Table 9)—are severely threatened by the Republican's old nemesis, the image of Republicans creating "bad times for average people."

A final caveat is in order. The relationship between party decomposition and the declining salience in Table 9 of the "good times" theme is not clear. Furthermore, the impact of the economic and welfare component of party image on voting has continued to decline (Trilling, 1974c). Consequently, decling support for the American party system (Dennis, 1974) and apparent party decomposition (Burnham, 1965; 1970), especially among post-Watergate voters, may prevent voters from translating the present inflationary crisis into party images. I myself am inclined to think that a continued economic crisis would in fact serve to redefine American politics along the traditional New Deal lines, that voters would eventually make this translation, and that the Democratic Party would stand to gain by the process.

NOTES

1. For the most part, scholars have not studied the direct impact opinions on issues have on party identifications, but recent efforts have turned their attention to this investigation. See Goldberg (1966), Jackson (1974) and Kovenock et al. (1970).

2. More precisely, " . . . identification is a function of the proportion of a person's life he has been associated with the group" (Campbell et al., 1960: 163).

3. John Meisel (1973: 67) writes that the concept of party identification "may be almost inapplicable in Canada . . . party identification seems to be as volatile in Canada as the vote itself." Consequently, Meisel seeks "a more stable measure of the long-term component of the vote, in Converse's sense" [Converse (1966)]. Meisel suggests that "Party images . . . may give us just such a measure. It could, where necessary, assume some of the explanatory role now performed by Party Identification. . . ." When party identification is less volatile, for instance in the United States, its long-term influence on the vote would be greater than where it is more volatile, thus suggesting a "medium-term" influence for party image.

4. The actual questionnaire items used for the party-image index are as follows:

(1) Is there anything in particular that you like about the Democratic Party? What is that?

(2) Is there anything in particular that you don't like about the Democratic Party? What is that?

(3) Is there anything in particular that you like about the Republican Party? What is that?

(4) Is there anything in particular that you don't like about the Republican Party? What is that?

These items appear, respectively, as the following variables in the Inter-University Consortium for Political Research Codebooks:

1952: v18, v19, v20, v21
1956: v15, v16, v17, v18
1960: v20, v21, v22, v23
1964: v21, v22, v23, v24
1968: v28, v29, v30, v31
1972: v31, v33, v35, v37

To increase the number of cases available for analysis, weighting schemes were used when available. All data reported in this paper rely on valid cross-sectional samples of the following sizes:

1952: N = 1,899 (no weighting)
1956: N = 1,762 (no weighting)
1960: N = 1,954 (weighted from 1,181)
1964: N = 4,658 (weighted from 1,834)
1968: N = 3,100 (weighted from 1,673)
1972: N = 1,372 (no weighting)

Finally, data were made available by the Inter-University Consortium for Political Research, which bears no responsibility for the analysis.

5. In 1972, the Survey Research Center/Center for Political Studies recorded only three responses to each of the vour variables used for the party-image index. Preliminary analysis suggests that the impact of party image for individuals and in the aggregate may be underestimated by this index in 1972. Recording only three responses serves to restrict the

range and artificially cluster the 1972 distributions. The precollapsed index in 1972 ranges from −6 to +6 and was collapsed in the following fashion: −6 to −4; −3 to −1; 0; +1 to +3; +4 to +6.

6. For a discussion of the party-image construct over time, see Trilling (1975).

7. To ascertain past party identification, Republicans and Democrats were asked, "Was there ever a time when you thought of yourself as a (R) (D) rather than (D) (R)?" Independents leaning toward the Republican or Democratic Party (coded as partisans in this study) were asked, "Was there ever a time when you thought of yourself as closer to the (R) (D) party instead of the (D) (R) party?" Independents were asked, "Was there ever a time when you thought of yourself as a Democrat or a Republican? Which party was that?" These items appear as the following variables in the Inter-University Consortim for Political Research Codebooks:

1952: v60, v65
1956: v89
1960: v92
1964: v147
1968: v121
1972: v143, v144, v145, v148, v149, v150

The 1952 and 1972 studies elicited this information in a slightly more complicated manner, and only the 1972 study permitted the determination of whether present partisans were once Independents.

8. Except in 1972, present identifiers were not asked if they once were Independents. It is possible to determine, however, how many present Independents were also past Independents. Thus, the numbers of cases for the top and bottom cells of the Independents column in Table 1 are unknown, so percents for the column are not computed. The marginals for present party identifiers in Table 1 correspond fairly well to the frequencies for the entire sample, even though Table 1 excludes individuals for whom complete information is not available. In 1972, surprisingly since data are more complete, the proportion of Independents in Table 1 (15.7%) exceeds the proportion within the entire sample (12.4%). In Table 3 estimates for the entire population rely on the more complete information in the entire sample, rather than on the data of Table 1, whenever possible.

9. Stable identifiers are defined for the purposes of this paper as individuals whose present party identification is the same as recalled past identification, i.e., individuals who report not having changed identifications. Stable partisans are stable Democratic and stable Republican identifiers; stable Independents report never having been closer to either the Democratic or Republican parties. Past-present patterns of identification will be represented by two sets of identification symbols (D = Democratic, R = Republican, I = Independents) attached by an arrow. Past identification will always be given to the left of the arrow and present identification to the right. The arrow will be used, for convenience, even for stable identifiers. Thus, I→D represents a past Independent presently identifying with the Democratic Party, and R→R represents a stable Republican identifier.

10. Ladd and Hadley (1973) and Ladd et al. (1971) claim that a realignment has occurred in the South and discuss the realigning potential of the racial issue as a threat to the present middle class character of Democratic Party support.

11. The reader should note that I have coded Independents who acknowledge feeling closer to one of the two major parties as partisans, not as Independents.

12. Technically, the predictions discussed in the text are after the fact, or "postdictions," but they will be referred to as predictions for convenience.

13. The procedures utilized here resemble those underlying some "Proportional Reduction of Error" measures developed by statisticians. See, for instance, Goodman and Kruskal (1954).

14. Screiber (1971) speaks of Independence as a halfway house for Democrats in the process of changing identifications, so these numerical assignments may not be so arbitrary.

15. Space does not permit a complete discussion of the behavior of this Index of Partisan Change. Over time regional and racial differences do appear. Racial differences, particularly, have been striking since 1964, with Blacks much more likely to switch toward the Democratic Party than Whites.

16. For a discussion of the interactive impact of image and identification on the vote, see Trilling (1975).

17. The following remarks draw heavily on my recent examination of the issue components of party images. See Trilling (1974c), Stokes et al. (1958), and Matthews and Prothro (1964; 1966a and 1966b).

REFERENCES

ABNEY, F. G. (1969) "Partisan realignment in a one-party system: the case of Mississippi." Journal of Politics 31: 1102-1106.

BECK, P. A. (1974) "Partisan stability and change in the American South: 1952-1972." Delivered at the Annual Meeting of the American Political Science Association, Palmer House Hotel, Chicago, Illinois, August 29-September 2.

BERELSON, B., P. F. LAZARSFELD, and W. N. McPHEE (1954) Voting. Chicago: University of Chicago Press.

BRODY, R. A. and B. I. PAGE (1972) "Comment: the assessment of policy voting." American Political Science Review 66: 450-458.

BOYD, R. W. (1972) "Popular control of public policy: a normal vote analysis of the 1968 election." American Political Science Review 66: 429-449.

BURNHAM, W. D. (1970) Critical Elections and the Mainsprings of American Politics. New York: Norton.

––– (1968) "American voting behavior and the 1968 election." Midwest Journal of Political Science 12: 1-40.

––– (1965) "The changing shape of the American political universe." American Political Science Review 59: 7-28.

––– (1964) "The Alabama senatorial election of 1962: return of inter-party competition." Journal of Politics 26: 798-829.

CAMPBELL, A. (1966a) "Surge and decline: a study of electoral change," pp. 40-62 in A. Campbell, P. E. Converse, W. E. Miller, and D. E. Stokes, Elections and the Political Order. New York: Wiley.

––– (1966b) "A classification of presidential elections," pp. 63-77 in A. Campbell, P. E. Converse, W. E. Miller, and D. E. Stokes, Elections and the Political Order. New York: Wiley.

––– (1966c) "Interpreting the presidential victory," pp. 256-282 in M. C. Cummings, Jr. (ed.) The National Election of 1964. Washington, D.C.: The Brookings Institution.

CAMPBELL, A., P. E. CONVERSE, W. E. MILLER, and D. E. STOKES (1960) The American Voter. New York: Wiley.

CONVERSE, P. E. (1972) "Change in the American electorate," pp. 263-337 in A. Campbell and P. E. Converse (eds.) The Human Meaning of Social Change. New York: Russell Sage Foundation.

––– (1966) "The concept of a normal vote," pp. 9-39 in A. Campbell, P. E. Converse, W. E. Miller, and D. E. Stokes, Elections and the Political Order. New York: Wiley.

CONVERSE, P. E., A. R. CLAUSEN, and W. E. MILLER (1965) "Electoral myth and reality." American Political Science Review 59: 321-336.

CONVERSE, P. E., W. E. MILLER, J. RUSK, and A. C. WOLFE (1969) "Continuity and change in American politics: parties and issues in the 1968 election." American Political Science Review 63: 1083-1105.

CRITTENDEN, J. (1962) "Aging and party affiliation." Public Opinion Quarterly 26: 648-657.

CUTLER, N. (1974) "Aging and generation in politics," pp. 440-462 in A. R. Wilcox (ed.) Public Opinion and Political Attitudes. New York: Wiley.

——— (1969) "Generation, maturation, and party affiliation." Public Opinion Quarterly 33: 583-588.

DENNIS, J. (1974) "Trends in public support for the political party system." Delivered at the Annual Meeting of the American Political Science Association, Palmer House Hotel, Chicago, Illinois, August 29-September 2.

——— (1966) "Support for the party system by the mass public." American Political Science Review 60: 600-615.

DeVRIES, W. and V. L. TARRANCE (1972) The Ticket-Splitter: A New Force in American Politics. Grand Rapids, Michigan: William B. Eerdmans.

DREYER, E. C. (1973) "Change and stability in party identifications." Journal of Politics 35: 712-722.

GOLDBERG, A. (1966) "Discerning a causal pattern among data on voting behavior." American Political Science Review 60: 913-922.

GOODMAN, L. A. and W. H. KRUSKAL (1954) "Measures of association for cross-classifications." Journal of the American Statistical Association 49: 732-764.

Inter-University Consortium for Political Research (1972) The 1972 Election Study–Codebook. Ann Arbor: ICPR.

——— (1968) The 1968 Election Study–Codebook. Ann Arbor: ICPR.

——— (1964) The 1964 Election Study–Codebook. Ann Arbor: ICPR.

——— (1960) The 1960 Election Study–Codebook. Ann Arbor: ICPR.

——— (1956) The 1956 Election Study–Codebook. Ann Arbor: ICPR.

——— (1952) The 1952 Election Study–Codebook. Ann Arbor: ICPR.

JACKSON, J. E. (1974) "Issues, party choices, and presidential votes." Delivered at the Annual Meeting of the American Political Science Association, Palmer House Hotel, Chicago, Illinois, August 29-September 2.

KEY, V. O., Jr. (1961) Public Opinion and American Democracy. New York: Knopf.

——— 1959) "Secular realignment and the party system." Journal of Politics 21: 198-210.

——— (1955) "A theory of critical elections." Journal of Politics 17: 3-18.

KIRKPATRICK, S. A. (1970) "Political attitudes and behavior: some consequences of attitudinal ordering." Midwest Journal of Political Science 14: 1-24.

KOVENOCK, D. M., P. L. BEARDSLEY, and J. W. PROTHRO (1970) "Status, party, ideology, issues, and candidate choice: a preliminary theory-relevant analysis of the 1968 American presidential election." Delivered at Specialist Meeting B:XI ("New Approaches to the Study of Social Structure and Voting Behavior"), Eighth World Congress of the International Political Science Association, Munich, Germany, August 31-September 5.

LADD, E. C., Jr. and C. D. HADLEY (1973) "Party definition and party differentiation." Public Opinion Quarterly 37: 21-34.

——— and L. KING (1971) "A new political realignment?" Public Interest 23 (Spring): 46-63.

LANE, R. E. and D. O. SEARS (1964) Public Opinion. Englewood Cliffs, N.J.: Prentice-Hall.

LIPSET, S. M. (1960) Political Man. Garden City, N.Y.: Doubleday-Anchor.

MATTHEWS, D. R. and J. W. PROTHRO (1966a) Negroes and the New Southern Politics. New York: Harcourt, Brace and World.

——— (1966b) "The concept of party images and its importance for the Southern electorate," pp. 139-174 in M. K. Jennings and L. H. Zeigler (eds.) The Electoral Process. Englewood Cliffs, N.J.: Prentice-Hall.

——— (1964) "Southern images of political parties: an analysis of White and Negro attitudes," pp. 82-111 in A. Leiserson (ed.) The American South in the 1960's. New York: Praeger.

MEISEL, J. (1973) Working Papers on Canadian Politics (enlarged ed.). Montreal: McGill-Queen's University Press.

MILLER, A. H. (1974) "Change in political trust as a function of discontent with authorities and economic policies." Delivered at the Annual Meeting of the American Political Science Association, Palmer House Hotel, Chicago, Illinois, August 29-September 2.

——— (1972) "Political issues and trust in government." Delivered at the Annual Meeting of the American Political Science Association, Washington Hilton Hotel, Washington, D.C., September 5-9.

———, T. A. BROWN, and A. S. RAINE (1973) "Social conflict and political estrangement, 1958-1972." Delivered at the Midwest Political Science Association Convention, Pick-Congress Hotel, Chicago, Illinois, May 3-5.

MILLER, A. H., W. E. MILLER, A. S. RAINE, and T. A. BROWN (1973) "A majority party in disarray: policy polarization in the 1972 election." Delivered at the Annual Meeting of the American Political Science Association, Jung Hotel, New Orleans, Louisiana, September 4-8.

PAGE, B. I. and R. A. BRODY (1972) "Policy voting and the electoral process: the Vietnam War issue." American Political Science Review 66: 979-995.

POMPER, G. M. (1972) "From confusion to clarity: issues and American voters, 1956-1968." American Political Science Review 66: 415-428.

——— (1970) Elections in America. New York: Dodd, Mead.

RePASS, D. E. (1971) "Issue salience and party choice." American Political Science Review 65: 388-400.

SCHREIBER, E. M. (1971) " 'Where the ducks are': Southern strategy versus fourth party." Public Opinion Quarterly 35: 157-167.

SELLERS, C. (1965) "The equilibrium cycle in two-party politics." Public Opinion Quarterly 29: 16-38.

STOKES, D. E. (1966a) "Some dynamic aspects of contests for the presidency." American Political Science Review 60: 19-28.

——— (1966b) "Party loyalty and the likelihood of deviating elections," pp. 125-135 in A. Campbell, P. E. Converse, W. E. Miller, and D. E. Stokes, Elections and the Political Order. New York: Wiley.

———, A. CAMPBELL, and W. MILLER (1958) "Components of electoral decision." American Political Science Review 52: 367-387.

SUNDQUIST, J. L. (1973) The Dynamics of the Party System. Washington, D.C.: The Brookings Institution.

TRILLING, R. J. (1975) "Party image and electoral behavior." American Politics Quarterly 3 (July).

——— (1974a) "Party image, party identification, and partisan realignment." Unpublished manuscript. Duke University.

——— (1974b) "Party image and partisan change, 1952 to 1972." Delivered at the Annual Meeting of the American Political Science Association, Palmer House Hotel, Chicago, Illinois, August 29-September 2.

——— (1974c) "Party images among Americans, 1952 to 1972." Unpublished manuscript. Duke University.

Chapter 3

ISSUES AND PARTY ALIGNMENT

JOHN E. JACKSON

The determinants of American voters' partisan affiliations are receiving increased scrutiny due to the variations in party strength and success observed during the 1960s and early 1970s. The proportion of the electorate identifying with the Republican party has varied from about 30% in 1956, to a low of 25% in 1964, and a subsequent high of 29% in 1970 (Gallup, 1973). Democratic affiliations have followed a somewhat but not completely opposite pattern. These aggregate figures hide even larger fluctuations at the individual level (Key, 1965). A recent paper studying voters' issue preferences, party affiliations, and votes in the 1964 presidential election concluded that party affiliations are largely determined by comparisons between people's own preferences on different issues and their perceptions of the competing parties' policies (Jackson, 1975). Although various social, economic, and geographic variables were also important in explaining party identification, the paper speculated that these variables properly measure the influence of previous party affiliations. Current party affiliations are the result of voters' current evaluations of the issue positions associated with each party and their previous party attachments.

AUTHOR'S NOTE: This research was supported by a grant to Harvard University from Resources for the Future. The author expresses his appreciation to Doug Price for helpful comments and suggestions while absolving him and any others of responsibility for errors, misstatements, and questionable interpretations. The guilt for those is entirely the author's.

The importance of current issue evaluations in determining party affiliations implies that previous party identifications are the result of individuals' preferences on issues important in earlier elections and the parties' stands on those issues. Party identification then is a historical issue variable summarizing voters' and parties' issue positions in past elections. The stability of party membership depends upon the stability of people's positions and the policies associated with each party. Fluctuations or shifts in voters' assessments of the parties will result in fluctuations and shifts in party affiliations.

The proper way to test these assertions, and to examine further the importance of issue evaluations in party choice decisions, is to repeat the study on new data including both a measure of previous party identification and issue evaluation information for a different election. Fortunately such data exist in the 1956-1960 panel study conducted by the Survey Research Center at the University of Michigan (Campbell et al., 1971). Members of the panel interviewed a group of voters before and after the 1956 presidential election and then before and after the 1960 election. (They also included a postelection 1958 survey with which we will not be concerned.) The data contain a clear measure of previous party affiliation, namely that elicited in the 1956 interview. The survey also gives information on people's positions, and their 1960 party affiliations, as well as the required demographic variables. This information makes possible an important further examination of party choice decisions by permitting estimates of the importance of issue evaluations and previous party affiliations in the current party choice. These data also create an opportunity to support or question the previous results about the importance of issues and evaluations in party choice decisions by studying a different election.

I. A MODEL OF PARTY CHOICE

The equation explaining people's party affiliations is drawn from a larger model concerned with people's issue positions, their evaluations of party positions on those issues, and their subsequent voting decisions, as well as individual party identifications. (See Jackson, 1975, for a fuller development of the larger model.) The analysis here concentrates on the party affiliation decision. The basic statistical equation modeling these decisions is shown as equation 1.

$$(1) \qquad P_t = B_1 + B_2E_t + B_3P_{t-1} + e$$

The implication of this model is that the party identifications people exhibit during any one election, P_t, are the result of their previous affiliations, P_{t-1}, plus the effect of their current evaluations of the positions of the parties on various issues, E_t. When we consider the implication that the party affiliation at the previous election is the result of evaluations during that election as well as the affiliation at the second previous election, and so on back, we can see how the model implies that party affiliation at point of time is the result of previous issue considerations. As such it is primarily a historical issue and evaluation variable summarizing people's positions and perceived party stands on past issues in previous elections.

The coefficient B_2 measures how much adjustment takes place each election while B_3 measures the stability of party identification regardless of issues. If B_2 is zero and B_3 is close to one, then party affiliation at time t is simply affiliation at time t−1 plus any random variance associated with people's behavior, their responses to the question, or with the structure of the question itself. Alternatively, a B_2 close to one and a B_3 near zero imply that party affiliations are reconsidered at each election, and stability in these affiliations arises only because people maintain the same position on various issues and perceive the party positions as being the same in each election. Values of B_2 between zero and one reflect increasing amounts of adjustment during each campaign while the reverse is true of the values for B_3.

The structure of equation 1 is presumably applicable to all individuals, although the partisan stability indicated by the coefficients B_2 and B_3 may not be the same for all voters. One important variation is that we can expect the stability of one's party identification to increase over time (Converse, 1969; Nie et al. 1975). This implies that, for each individual, B_2 decreases and B_3 increases with age. The restructured model incorporating this effect is shown in equation 2:

$$(2) \qquad P_t = B_1 + (B_2 + B_4\text{Age})E_t + (B_3 + B_5\text{Age})P_{t-1} + e$$

The equation is estimated by including two additional variables. One is Age times current evaluation and provides an estimate for B_4, and the second is Age times previous party affiliation, which estimates B_5. In the restructured model, the effect of current evaluations on current party affiliation is a linear function of age, and we expect B_4 to be negative. Conversely, we expect B_5 to be positive, which makes the effect of past affiliation an increasing function of age.

Knowing the appropriate values for these coefficients is important because of their implications for partisan stability. The 1964 study estimated a value of 1.00 for B_2, but this estimate is unreliable because no past party affiliation variable was available and the specification did not permit evaluation and party influences to vary with age. The panel data and the specification of the model in equation 2 should remedy these deficiencies.

II. THE 1956-1960 PANEL DATA

The SRC 1956-1960 panel study provides better data with which to assess the magnitude of the influences in this model of party choice. The information in these surveys can be coded into the variables required for estimating the coefficients in the party choice equation.

PARTY AFFILIATION

The 1956 and 1960 surveys requested the party identifications of people identifying with a party, and the party leanings, if any, of independents. We construct three separate party variables for each year from these responses. The first, P_{56} and P_{60}, are scored as 1.0, 0.75, 0.50, 0.25, and 0.00 for strong Democrats, weak Democrats, all independents (and other nonidentifiers), weak Republicans, and strong Republicans. The second party variables, P_{56}^* and P_{60}^*, resemble the previous ones save that independents are scored as 0.375, 0.50, and 0.625 for Republican-leaning, nonleaning, and Democratic-leaning independents, respectively. Finally, separate variables for independents, Ind_{56} and Ind_{60}, are constructed which are 1.0 for Democratic leaners, 0.50 for nonleaners, and 0.0 for Republican leaners. These variables provide the information we need for current and past party identifications.

ISSUE EVALUATIONS

In 1960 respondents were asked nine specific issue questions of the form, "The government ought to help people get doctors and hospital care at low cost." The response choices were Strongly Agree, Agree, Disagree, Strongly Disagree, and Not Sure or No Opinion. Similar questions referred to the federal government's policy in the areas of private power and housing, aid to education, federally guaranteed jobs, school integration, fair employment practices, foreign aid, troops stationed overseas, and isolation. (See Campbell et al., 1971, for the precise questions.) People were then asked which party is more likely to follow a given policy, such as provide health care at low cost. Evaluations for each issue are constructed from these two questions by comparing persons' positions with their perceptions of which party was likely to pursue a given policy. If the person agreed with the statement and felt that the Democrats were likely to follow that policy, *or* if the person was opposed to the statement and felt that the Republicans were likely to do what the statement outlines, the Democrats were assumed to be closer to the respondent's issue position. The opposite of these positions and perceptions is interpreted as meaning the Republicans were closer to the person's position. If the person did not have a position on an issue or if no difference was perceived in the parties' positions, then the person was presumed to be indifferent between the parties on that issue.

The coding of the evaluation variables also takes into account whether the respondent strongly agreed or disagreed with the issue statement. If the Democrats are inferred to be closer, the evaluation variable is coded as 1.00 if the person gave a strongly agree or disagree answer and 0.75 if the weaker response was given. Similarly, if the Republicans are closer to the person's position, the evaluation variable is 0.00 if the person gave a strongly agree or disagree response and 0.25 for a weaker answer. If the person was indifferent on that issue, either because of no expressed opinion or because of no perceived difference in the parties, the evaluation variable was coded as 0.50. Table 1 shows this coding scheme.

Table 1. CODING SCHEME FOR ISSUE EVALUATIONS

Response to Issue Question	Party Most Likely to Follow Policy In Question		
	Democrats	*No Difference*	*Republicans*
Strongly agree	1.00	0.50	0.00
Agree	0.75	0.50	0.25
No opinion	0.50	0.50	0.50
Disagree	0.25	0.50	0.75
Strongly disagree	0.00	0.50	1.00

A tenth evaluation variable is included in the study. The survey asked people if they thought their families would be financially better off if one party or the other won the election, and if so, which one. The three pro-Democratic responses are coded as 1.00, 0.83, and 0.67 with one being the strongest Democratic response. Similarly the three pro-Republican responses are coded as 0.00, 0.17, and 0.33 with zero being the strongest response. People who felt that it made no difference to them financially which party won are scored as 0.50.

The ten separate issue evaluations are aggregated into a single evaluation variable for the purpose of estimating equation 2. The aggregation is done by averaging respondents' evaluations on all issues where one of the parties is preferred. If the person is assessed as being indifferent on all ten issues, the variable is scored as 0.50. This scheme effectively gives an equal weight to all issues where the person both has a position *and* perceives a difference in the parties' positions; it gives no weight to issues on which the person has no evaluation. The values of this evaluation variable can range from 0.00 (pro-Republican) to 1.00 (pro-Democratic) for people who strongly agreed or disagreed with all the relevant issue statements. For those who merely agreed or disagreed with each statement, but not strongly, the range of the evaluation variable is 0.25 to 0.75.

ESTIMATING THE PARTY AFFILIATION EQUATIONS

The model represented by equation 2 is estimated separately for voters indicating a party affiliation in at least one of the two elections and for those identifying themselves as independents in both 1956 and 1960. (Nonvoters in 1960 are excluded from the analysis.) Two equations are estimated for party identifiers, one for each of the alternative party affiliation variables. The equation for independents substitutes the measures of independents' preferences, Ind_{56} and Ind_{60} for the party affiliation variables in equation 2.

The first consideration in estimating equation 2 is that, although current party affiliation is not simultaneously related to issue evaluations or to previous party affiliation, the model is not likely to be recursive. Previous party identification, by simple extension of our model, is the result of prior issue evaluations, party identification, and random effects, as shown in equation 2. The random effects denoted by e_1, represent excluded influences such as other issues, stochastic effects unrelated to political considerations such as the effects of family relationships, and any measurement errors as might be introduced by the categorical nature of the party affiliation question. It seems reasonable to assume these stochastic effects are randomly distributed across the individuals in the sample; however, for each individual, these effects are unlikely to be independent from one election to the next. As long as the error term in the implicit equation for lagged party affiliation is correlated with the error term in the equation for current party identification, the model is nonrecursive.

The same problem exists with the issue evaluation variable. There are a variety of reasons the error terms in the equations explaining issue evaluations and party affiliations are correlated. These correlations result from party identification's influence on people's own issue positions and their perceptions of the party positions, and from errors in measuring issue evaluations. The model's nonrecursivity results in biased coefficient estimates if the issue evaluation and previous party affiliation variables are treated as exogenous or predetermined and the model estimated with ordinary least squares multiple regression.

The appropriate solution for such difficulties is to use an estimating procedure developed for nonrecursive models. In this case we will use two-stage least squares. The first stage estimates the evaluation and previous party affiliation variables as functions of the exogenous demographic variables included in the larger model. The exogenous variables used in this process are all assumed to be related to present or past issue evaluations or to the party affiliation one might have had on entering the political world, and are listed in Table 2. The estimated values for E_t and P_{t-1}, which are presumably purged of the correlated error components, are then used to estimate equation 2.

A second estimation problem is created by the fact that none of the variables in the model are truly interval variables. Party affiliation has five ordinal categories, and each separate issue evaluation has five or six ordinal categories. Although the average of the ten evaluation variables will have more categories, it is wrong to assume that it is an interval variable in the true sense of the word. Such ordinal variables present difficulties for conventional estimation procedures, which have been developed for interval measurements. Unfortunately there are no techniques currently available for handling both nonrecursive models, as we have, and ordinal variables, necessitating a choice of statistical procedure. The possible biases resulting from ignoring the

Table 2. EXOGENOUS VARIABLES INCLUDED IN ESTIMATION OF THE
1960 PARTY AFFILIATION EQUATIONS

Father Democrat
Father independent or not affiliated with a party
Age greater than 50
Age in years
Nonwhite
Catholic
Jew
Central city resident, 1960 (one of 12 largest SMSAs)
Rural resident, 1960
East[a], 1960
South[b], 1960
Union member, 1960
Education level, 1960
College graduate, 1960
Income, 1960
Central city resident, 1956
East[a], 1956
South[b], 1956
Union member, 1956
Income, 1956

a. East defined as New England, New York, New Jersey, Pennsylvania, Delaware, and
West Virginia.
b. South defined as Virginia, North Carolina, South Carolina, Georgia, Florida, Tennessee,
Alabama, Mississippi, Arkansas, Louisiana, and Texas.

nonrecursiveness of the model indicate it is the more severe problem. This assertion, along with results which show the robustness of conventional estimation procedures in the face of noninterval variables (Jackson, 1973), supports the decision to use conventional procedures designed to deal with the nonrecursive nature of the system.

III. THE ESTIMATED MODELS

The estimated models for party identifiers are shown in systems 3 and 4 and for independents in equation 5:

(3) $\quad P_{60} = -0.07 + (1.56 - 0.024\text{Age})E_{60} + (-0.29 + 0.022\text{Age})P_{56}$
$\qquad\qquad (0.03) \ (0.55) \ (0.012) \qquad\qquad (0.57) \ (0.012)$
$\qquad R^2 = 0.60 \text{ (party voters)}$

(4) $\quad P^*_{60} = -0.05 + (1.60 - 0.026\text{Age})E_{60} + (-0.37 + 0.025\text{Age})P^*_{56}$
$\qquad\qquad (0.03) \ (0.54) \ (0.012) \qquad\qquad (0.57) \ (0.012)$
$\qquad R^2 = 0.63 \text{ (party voters)}$

(5) $\quad \text{Ind}_{60} = -0.28 + 0.69E_{60} + 0.77\text{Ind}_{56}$
$\qquad \quad (0.13)\ (0.22) \qquad (0.20)$
$\quad R^2 = 0.06 \text{ (independents)}$

The results for party members strongly confirm the hypotheses about both the effects of evaluations on party affiliations and the reduced propensity to change affiliation with increasing age. The coefficients on the age variables in both equations 3 and 4 indicate that the influence of issue evaluations decreases with age at virtually the same rate with which the influence of past party increases with age. Table 3 shows the estimated evaluation and past party coefficients for different age levels. Voters in their twenties give almost full weight to evaluations and no weight to previous party affiliations in deciding their current identification. Conversely, the over-sixty voters' current affiliations are virtually equal to their identifications in the preceding election, with no weight given to current evaluations. Among older voters, party attachments exert an important stabilizing effect on party membership, reducing the speed of partisan adjustment to changes in issue evaluations to zero. For young voters, this adjustment process is virtually instantaneous, indicating that even though older voters maintain their party affiliations, these affiliations grew out of earlier issue considerations.

The equation for those voters identifying as independents in both elections omits the two age variables. When these variables are included, both have the wrong sign and are statistically quite insignificant. The influence of evaluations increased while the effect of past preferences decreased with age. This is quite contrary to our hypotheses and probably indicates that the age effects associated with party identifiers do not exist among independents. Consequently the equation is estimated with only the evaluation and previous party preference variables. The results suggest that independents' party leanings are about equally influenced by past

Table 3. ESTIMATED PARTY AFFILIATION MODELS BY AGE

| | | Variable | | | |
| | | Evaluation | | Party | |
Age	Equation:	3	4	3	4
21		1.06	1.05	0.17	0.15
30		0.84	0.82	0.37	0.38
40		0.60	0.56	0.59	0.63
50		0.36	0.30	0.81	0.85
60		0.12	0.04	1.03	1.10

leanings and current evaluations; however, the low amount of explained variance suggests that independents' responses to the party preference question are largely random and have very little systematic content.[1] Part of the difficulty in estimating this equation may be attributable to the small sample size. There are only 102 voters who were independents in both elections, leading to quite unreliable coefficients.

A further test of the model proposed in equation 2, as opposed to a model arguing that party identifications are the result of individuals' reference groups and social experiences and possibly issue evaluations, is possible. Equation 4 is reestimated for party identifiers with the social, economic, and geographic variables hypothesized to represent such socialization effects included. The variables are parental party identification, religion, union membership, age, income, region and place of residence. These are the same demographic variables used to explain party affiliation in the 1964 election study (Jackson, 1975). If previous party identification is an intervening variable, as hypothesized in equation 2, the addition of the exogenous variables should neither add to the explanatory power of the model nor be statistically significant. If previous party identification is not an intervening variable and current party identifications are directly related to persons' family backgrounds and current social environments, the lagged party affiliation coefficient should become smaller and statistically less significant.

The results of the reestimation support the inclusion of the lagged party variable and the omission of the social variables. The coefficients on the 1956 party affiliation variables only fell to -0.61 and 0.025 (without the exogenous variables, they are -0.47 and 0.026 for party identifiers), implying a 25% reduction in the influence of previous party affiliations. For example, the influence of past party on the current affiliation of a fifty year old fell from 0.8 to 0.6. All the exogenous demographic and social variables have small coefficients with standard errors as large or larger than the coefficients. The largest coefficient is for father's party affiliation and indicates that having a Democratic rather than a Republican father increases current affiliation by 0.08 in a Democratic direction, a rather small increase. If father's identifications are the only exogenous variables included along with issues and past party, this difference falls to 0.05 while the party coefficients increase to -0.28 and 0.020.

It seems fair to conclude that the results support the model presented in equation 2 and the contention that party affiliations reflect current issues plus the historical influences of issues and the positions of the parties on those issues as represented by the lagged party variable. It should also be pointed out that the issue evaluation coefficients in the reestimated equation are 1.88 and 0.028, indicating slightly larger evaluation influences than those shown in Table 3, further supporting the conclusion about the importance of issue evaluations in party choice decisions.

IV. A SYNTHETIC PREVIOUS PARTY VARIABLE FOR 1964

The results from the panel study indicate that equation 2 is the appropriate party choice model and that it would be worthwhile to synthesize a 1960 party affiliation variable for the 1964 sample of voters to permit estimation of the appropriate 1964 party affiliation equation. Estimation of the proper 1964 equation, even with a synthetic lagged party variable, should provide additional estimates of the influence of issue evaluations and previous party affiliations on party choice decisions and how these influences change with age. If these additional estimates are similar in magnitude to the coefficients in equations 3, 4, and 5, it will corroborate both the validity of the model and the estimated coefficients.

The 1964 equations' lagged party affiliation variables rely on the relationship between party affiliation and the exogenous demographic variables. Equations relating voters' 1960 party affiliations and the leanings of independent voters to the exogenous variables are estimated with the panel data. These equations, shown in Table 4, explain 41% and 29% of the variance in party affiliations and in independents' preferences, respectively, indicating systematic relationships among these variables.

Estimates of 1960 party affiliations for the 1964 sample are generated using the estimated equations in Table 4 and the values of the appropriate variables in the 1964 survey. This procedure assumes that individual social, geographic, and economic variables are stable between elections. If none of the variables were likely to change, for example if there was no regional or metropolitan migration, then we should have accurate estimates of previous party affiliation. Certainly some of the variables, such as race, religion, and possibly education levels are not subject to change. The most likely variable to change in a nonsystematic and uncorrectable manner is income. In this case

Table 4. PARTY AFFILIATION AND INDEPENDENT LEANING EQUATIONS
ESTIMATED WITH 1960 PANEL DATA

Variable	Party Affiliation	Leaning
Constant	0.325 (0.057)[a]	0.165 (0.144)
Father Democrat	0.394 (0.026)	0.245 (0.073)
Father, no party	0.241 (0.029)	0.171 (0.068)
Age >50	−0.017 (0.023)	0.088 (0.063)
Nonwhite	0.179 (0.047)	0.045 (0.127)
Catholic	0.208 (0.028)	0.347 (0.072)
Jewish	0.184 (0.063)	0.387 (0.129)
Central city resident	0.071 (0.035)	−0.079 (0.097)
Rural resident	0.020 (0.024)	−0.066 (0.063)
East	−0.133 (0.026)	−0.137 (0.063)
South	0.116 (0.029)	−0.094 (0.092)
Union	0.122 (0.025)	−0.034 (0.062)
Education level	−0.001 (0.004)	0.018 (0.012)
College graduate	−0.051 (0.042)	0.067 (0.101)
Income	−0.010 (0.003)	−0.025 (0.009)
R^2	0.41	0.29

a. Numbers in parentheses are standard errors.

1964 income is deflated to 1960 prices to make it comparable to 1960 incomes, although concern remains that this deflated income variable accurately measures 1964 respondents' 1960 income.[2]

The 1964 party affiliation equation is then estimated for the voters in that election using this postdicted previous party variable and the 1964 evaluation variable.[3] Again the two-stage least square procedure is used with the same exogenous variables. (Previous party affiliations are not treated exogenously, but since the variables used to predict these values are also the exogenous variables used in the estimation procedure, the values for the lagged party variables used in the second stage of the estimation procedure are the calculated values.)

It is impossible to separate the independents in the 1964 sample into the habitual independents and those who usually identify with a party, as we did with the panel sample, because we only have expression of party preference in 1964. Consequently three separate equations are estimated for the 1964 equations. The first equation pools all voters into one sample, and the asterisked form of the party affiliation variables is used to estimate the party affiliation equation. The sample is then stratified into identifiers and nonidentifiers and separate equations estimated for each group. For independents, the estimated 1960 party preference of independents obtained from the equation in Table 4 is used as the previous party variable and the age variables are omitted, which is consistent with the results from the 1960 models.

The estimated equations for 1964 party affiliations and independent preferences are shown in equations 6-8:

(6) $\quad P^*_{64} = -0.01 + (1.89 - 0.029\text{Age})E_{64} + (-0.85 + 0.029\text{Age})P^*_{60}$
$\qquad$ (0.04) (0.64) (0.013) $\qquad$ (0.65) (0.013)
$\qquad R^2 = 0.18$ (all voters)

(7) $\quad P^*_{64} = -0.06 + (1.60 - 0.022\text{Age})E_{64} + (-0.39 + 0.021\text{Age})P^*_{60}$
$\qquad$ (0.05) (0.51) (0.010) $\qquad$ (0.52) (0.010)
$\qquad R^2 = 0.36$ (party voters)

(8) $\quad \text{Ind}_{64} = 0.08 + 0.76\,E_{64} + 0.11\,\text{Ind}_{60}$
$\qquad$ (0.12) (0.19) $\qquad$ (0.12)
$\qquad R^2 = 0.09$ (independents)

The 1964 results show remarkable similarity to the estimates from the 1960 equations for party identifiers. The influence of evaluations and past party affiliation and the change in these influences with age nearly equal the estimates shown in equations 3 and 4. Most of the differences in the estimated coefficients can easily be attributed to the variance in the estimated coefficients themselves. All the differences are less than one standard error of the appropriate coefficients.

The only estimate that differs markedly from its 1960 estimate is the influence of previous party preference on the current preference of independents. This estimate decreases from 0.77 to 0.10. The difference could be attributable to changed behavior among independents in 1964, who exhibited a marked swing toward the Democrats in that election, as well as to the previously discussed instability of our 1960 results for this group of voters.

The similarity of party identifiers' equations in both elections provides important support for the model of party affiliation in equation 2, for the estimated influence of issue evaluations and past party affiliations on party choice decisions, and for the political implications to be drawn from such a model.

INTERPRETATION OF THE ESTIMATED MODELS

Accurate estimates of the coefficients in the party choice equations are important for the information they provide about how fast party affiliations respond to changes in issue evaluations. In interpreting the model, we will examine party preference changes in different situations. This treatment of the model requires that we interpret the SRC party affiliation variable as an ordinal measure based on some latent continuous party strength variable. This latent variable implicitly varies from strong Republican attachments through very weak or marginal Republican and then Democratic affiliations and finally ending with very strong Democratic identifications. On this implicit scale, zero and one are not the most Republican and Democratic positions. Presumably "true" party attachments scores range below and above these values. Similarly, there also are gradations of attachments associated with each numerical value between zero and one. We have merely assigned values of 0.25 and 0.75 to people indicating other than a strong attachment to their respective parties.[4]

We treat the predicted party affiliation values from our estimated equation as values on this latent party identification scale. For example, someone with a predicted party affiliation of 0.60 will be treated as a weaker Democrat than someone with a predicted score of 0.70. Implicitly, a person with a score of 0.50 is treated as being indifferent between the two parties, although the person may still indicate a very weak affiliation with one party or the other. Consequently, we consider party members with estimated affiliation scores close to 0.50 as being very marginal members of one party or the other.

In interpreting the model, the estimates in equations 4 and 7 are combined to make a composite model for party members. The estimated coefficients are so similar that there seems to be no loss of information in doing this. The equation used for this purpose, which is an unweighted average of the two equations, is

(9) $P_t = -0.05 + (1.60 - 0.024\text{Age})E_t + (-0.38 + 0.023\text{Age})P_{t-1}$

The illustrations are done for both a thirty year old and a fifty year old for the sake of comparison. The first illustrations are strong Democrats ($P_0 = 1$), who now prefer the Republicans on all issues. If the persons feel strongly about each issue so that the new evaluation variables equal zero, the party affiliation of the thirty year old would be 0.26 and that of the fifty year old 0.72, indicating that the younger person had become a weak Republican while the older person had become only a weak Democrat. If evaluations do not change in subsequent elections, the thirty year old is a strong Republican by the next election while the older individual becomes a very marginal Democrat. Even if evaluations do not change, the older person never becomes more than a weak-Republican-leaning independent because of the increasing influence of past affiliation and the declining influence of evaluation with age.

More likely examples might be voters who previously classed themselves as weak Republicans ($P_0 = 0.25$). If new issues arise on which they favor the Democrats, so that each party is favored on some issues, the appropriate evaluation variable might be 0.60. The younger voter has predicted party affiliations of 0.56 and 0.64 in the next two elections, indicating a rapid adjustment of party affiliation to the new evaluations. The fifty-year-old voter, on the other hand, has an expected affiliation of 0.38, or a Republican-leaning independent position, in the first election, becomes a pure independent after three elections, and assumes a stable Democratic leaning position after four elections.

Finally, we can illustrate the results when persons' evaluations fluctuate over several elections. Consider again weak Republicans ($P_0 = 0.25$) whose evaluations over four elections are 0.6, 0.7, 0.4, and 0.3. The resulting party affiliations of the younger person are 0.56, 0.72, 0.57, and 0.45 and those of the older voter are 0.38, 0.48, 0.41, and 0.40. Both voters exhibit fluctuating affiliations with the younger voter showing considerably greater variation as one expects. This voter goes from being a weak Republican, to being a weak Democrat, and back to identifying as a very weak-Republican-leaning independent during the four elections. The older voter, however, never gets any further than being on the Republican side of complete independence and ends up a Republican-leaning independent.

The illustrations highlight the type of movement in party affiliations implied by the estimated equations. In the first case, we see strong Democrats switch party affiliations, or at least leave the party, as the result of a massive reevaluation of the parties' issue positions. Less drastic cases are the weak Republicans' becoming marginal Democrats after moving to evaluations marginally favoring the Democrats. Finally, we illustrated the fluctuating party affiliations of people whose evaluations of the parties fluctuated over several elections. All cases show how affiliations change in response to changes in issue evaluations; how any measure of party affiliation is simply assessing the historical effects of issues, persons' positions on those issues, and finally their perceptions of party positions; and how the stability of party affiliation increases with age.

V. FLUCTUATIONS AND SHIFTS IN PARTISAN AFFILIATION

There are strong implications in these results for how one treats party affiliation in electoral studies and, more important, how one considers party affiliation as a substantive part of the electoral process. The results erode the notion of individual party identification as some predetermined, stable, exogenous variable which exists autonomously at the center of the electoral process. This does not deny that individual party affiliations may be stable over several elections, exert an influence on what positions people take on different issues, and have perceptual effects on voters' evaluations of the parties' and candidates' positions. It does argue, however, that party affiliations are themselves subject to change based upon the positions people take on issues and their evaluations of party positions.

The analysis of the 1964 election (Jackson, 1975) implies that the influence of party affiliation on persons' issue positions is smaller than that of the exogenous social, economic, and geographic variables and is generally limited to issues that are substantively close to the issues central to existing party platforms and coalitions. For example, in 1964 party identification was an important influence on voters' positions on Medicare and federal aid to education, but not on civil rights or foreign policy. Likewise, the same study argued that the perceptual bias of party membership on evaluations is only evident on foreign affairs issues, and is considerably smaller than the effect of persons' issue positions. Thus the effect of issues on party affiliation is much stronger than the effects of party on positions or evaluations. The greater importance of the link from issues to party makes even stronger the case against treating party identification as a stable, predetermined aspect of the electoral process.

The notion of party identification as the stabilizing force in American politics is further undermined by the voting equation estimated for party affiliates in the 1964 election. The equation indicates that voting decisions respond more completely and more quickly to changes in evaluations than do party affiliations and that the responses are independent of age. Issue evaluations have a larger influence on voting decisions than on party affiliations (the evaluation coefficient in the voting equation is about 1.0), and party affiliations have only a minor influence on voting (the coefficient is about 0.30). When the age variables are included in the 1964 voting equation their coefficients are very small and insignificant (less than 0.005), indicating that the importance of party affiliation in voting decisions does not increase with age and that the influence of evaluations is constant across age groups. (Preliminary work with the 1960 voting decisions has yielded coefficients that are very similar to the ones estimated with the 1964 data.) Even though voters' attachment to their party increases with age and becomes less susceptible to change, the 1964 voting results indicate that this stability does not hold for voting decisions. The decisions involved in choosing a president reflect voters' evaluations of the parties and are responsive to individuals' and parties' issue positions.

Considerable attention is currently focused on the stability of party affiliations among the electorate and whether this stability is declining in the 1960s and 1970s (Asher, 1974; Burnham, 1975). Asher analyzes the party identification questions in the panel data used here and concludes there is considerable stability in party membership among panel members. The model here does not contradict that straightforward observation, it merely says that such stability arises from the stability of persons' evaluations of the parties on issues relevant to them.

Asher does not specify or estimate a model explaining party identifications, consequently he cannot provide any conclusions about the basis for the observed stability. One explanation for this stability, of course, is that party affiliation is a stable, predetermined voter characteristic which exists prior to, if not independent of, other political behavior. An alternative explanation, and the one adopted here, is that issue evaluations, which are the determinants of party affiliation, were stable over the time period of the panel.[5] The consequence of stable evaluations is stable party membership. The latter explanation holds out the possibility that if evaluations vary between two or more elections, party affiliations will also vary.

SHORT-RUN FLUCTUATIONS IN AFFILIATION

There are two types of party affiliation changes predicted by this model. There are short-term fluctuations resulting from fluctuations in persons' positions on different issues and variations in their perceptions of the parties' positions or expected performance on these issues. For example, evaluation changes in favor of one party or swings away from the other party to positions of indifference on some issue will alter the strength of persons' party identifications. These alterations may be from strong to weak associations with the same party or possibly from weak to quite normal affiliations (for which no category is included but which is implicit in our treatment of the party variable), or it might actually result in moves from one party to another. However, the magnitudes of the coefficients are such that changes in evaluations on one or two issues or changes from a partisan to an indifferent position on several issues will have a minor effect on most persons' party affiliations during the course of one election, such as a move from a stronger to a weaker affiliation with the same party.

If the evaluation changes are of a short-run nature, so that people return to their previous issue evaluations during the next one or two elections, party affiliations will, in a very short period, return to original levels, and one will have noticed at most a short-term fluctuation in the strength of party affiliations. The best example of such a short-run effect would be a single issue which rises to some prominence during one election and then is gone or of very limited interest by the next election. If one of the parties commands a dominant position on that issue, it will attract the loyalties of a number of voters due to the effects of that issue. However by the next election, when this issue has receded in importance and people no longer base decisions on the parties' positions on that issue, but resort to their evaluations on previously important issues, we can expect party affiliations to return to "normal." Examples of such issues would be charges of corruption against an incumbent administration or displeasure with its handling of a particular issue, such as inflation or unemployment. The same process occurs if one candidate captures or alienates the support of a sizable proportion of the electorate on some issues. If people perceive one candidate as being particularly able to deal with current issues, they will be attracted to that candidate's party while he or she is running or in office. The reverse will hold for candidates perceived as incompetent or unable to handle the issues. This support for one party will dissipate subsequently unless the successor maintains the advantage or disadvantage.

One can easily envision such evaluation fluctuations occurring with each election, although with different magnitudes and with unpredictable patterns during any given time period. This implies that the concept of a "normal" party vote is hard to define explicitly. It is certainly possible to average votes or even to compute some average party affiliation index for a given number of elections; however, this merely converts the series of fluctuations, which are the result of a multitude of specific factors, to the level of stochastic effects, and treats them as random events supposedly distributed about some mean. In fact, they are the natural fluctuations of the electoral process attributable to the short-run rise and fall of issues, of candidate difference, and possibly of exogenous events which raise certain issues and people to prominence. The averaging of these circumstances is in fact creating a statistical artifact which is dependent upon what events and circumstances developed during the course of several elections. It seems preferable to treat party affiliations and voting decisions during individual elections as a result of voters' positions and evaluations on different issues, some of which are relatively unchanged from the previous election (or elections) and some of which are different in each election for a multitude of reasons. This focuses one's attention on what issues were important at each election, the stability of persons' positions on those issues, on their perceptions of party positions, and ultimately on the expected permanence of any changes.

LONG-RUN SHIFTS IN PARTY ALLEGIANCE

In addition to short-run fluctuations in party support, there are also situations that develop into long-run shifts in voter allegiance to one party or the other. If voters' positions on certain issues change, or the positions of the parties change in such a way that voters' evaluations change in a permanent fashion, then over the course of several elections party affiliations will shift and exhibit a new pattern of partisan support which will not reverse itself in subsequent elections. In the examples given above, the younger strong Democrat who came to prefer the Republicans on all issues switched to the Republican party over the course of several elections, and both weak Republicans who favored the Democrats on several issues became marginal Democrats over a similar period. In all of these cases, the change in evaluations remained and was incorporated into the persons' party affiliations, leading to altered party identifications.

If one suspects that such changes are permanent, at least for several elections, the prediction is that party identifications will be permanently altered. Evaluation changes may occur because of altered social, economic, or geographic characteristics. For example, persons with increased income might alter their position on various social welfare programs. Or a change in geographical residence from one region of the country to another or from a central city to the suburbs may cause people to feel differently about various public policies. Such environmental changes are likely to be more or less permanent, as would be the resulting changes in issue positions. Assuming that the party positions on various issues did not change, it is expected that these persons' evaluations on some, but not necessarily all, issues will change. These altered evaluations will lead to altered party affiliations. The extent and magnitude of the change in party identification depends upon how much these persons' positions changed and on how many issues.

Changes in individual voters' positions on various issues will lead to changes in their party affiliations, but large scale realignment is possible only if such changes are quite widespread and systematically distributed among the voters. Such realignments are likely in two important cases. The first is if the party positions on various issues change and the other is if new issues arise which divide the existing party coalitions. If the relative positions of the parties change, such as when one party adopts new positions or nominates a candidate who advocates different positions than previous candidates, it will systematically alter the evaluations of a large number of voters. If the party were to continue to advocate the new positions, we would expect a substantial and permanent realignment of a large proportion of the electorate. Depending upon the policies being advocated relative to the distribution of voters' positions, we could expect switching of voters in both directions. Presumably some voters will be attracted to the party because of its new policies while others will be estranged from the party and move in the direction of the competitor.

A more likely reason for partisan realignment is the rise of new and salient issues which remain part of the issue structure for an extended period of time. If the new issue (or a new set of related issues) divides the parties' supporters, the parties cannot maintain their patterns of support. Some members in each party will agree and others will disagree with whatever positions the parties and candidates adopt, resulting in altered evaluations among party members. The long-run result of these altered evaluations among segments of each party will be restructured parties built on the divisions within the electorate associated with the new issues and the positions adopted by the parties and their candidates.

The 1964 election study (Jackson, 1975) provides tentative illustrations of how this process might evolve. Support both for civil rights programs and for federal efforts to guarantee jobs for those unable to find work differed markedly from support for more traditional social welfare programs such as Medicare and federal aid to education. Civil rights and employment guarantees were more strongly supported by upper class professional and college educated individuals than the more traditional programs. There were also regional shifts in the support of these new programs with southerners more opposed to the new programs while easterners generally supported them more than the old programs. The 1964 analysis also shows that on the civil rights and employment issues persons' issue positions were very important in determining their party evaluations. The implication here is that these two programs tended to split the existing party coalitions, with some previously Republican voters supporting these issues while others opposed them, and similarly for some Democrats. Because each party could not adopt positions that appealed to all existing party members, some reevaluations and eventually some realignment would occur if civil rights and Great Society issues dominated other issues in succeeding elections. To the extent that concern over defense spending and the Vietnam War, the environment, income redistribution, northern segregation issues, or the positions adopted by the Democrats during the 1972 campaign further divided or alienated members of the existing party structures, we would expect further changes in party affiliation within the electorate following the 1968 and 1972 elections.

The extent of any realignment and the amount of time it takes to complete depends upon how the current parties' supporters split on the new issue, the importance of the new issue relative to previous issues, the positions adopted by each party, and the age distribution of the population. The more evenly the new issues divide the existing party coalitions, the greater and the more apparent will be the realignment. The more the new issues dominate the old issues in importance and the greater the proportion of the electorate who perceive a new party taking positions in accord with their own positions, the larger will be the shifts in issue evaluations and the more rapid the resulting changes in party affiliations, as in the case of our young Democrat turned Republican. And the younger the population, the faster the realignment.

Overall evaluations of the parties (and thus party affiliations) will not exhibit large or rapid changes if the new issues must compete with the old for attention and if people maintain their previous evaluations on the older issues, or if voters do not see one of the parties taking stands on the new issues which reflect their own positions. Combinations of conflicting and indifferent evaluations result in overall issue evaluations close to 0.5, which increase the number of voters expressing no or at most a weak attachment to one of the parties. The result of this situation will be a weakening of past party identifications, fewer party identifiers, and considerable fluctuations in aggregate party strength as the relative importance of new and old issues varies and as persons' perceptions of party positions change. Weak or nonexistent party attachments will be most apparent among young voters, who are least anchored to some previous affiliation. Strengthened and realigned parties will emerge when the importance of the new issues permanently dominates that of the old issues and when people begin perceiving party positions reflecting their own positions on the new issues. At this point, voters' evaluations will more definitely favor one party or the other and will lead to stronger expressions of party affiliation. Which groups of voters align with which party depends upon what issues are important, the positions of the members of each group on these issues, and the policies associated with each party.

NOTES

1. This randomness apparently also holds for those voters indicating a party affiliation in 1956 but identifying as independents in 1960. Equation 4 estimated only for party identifiers is

$$P_{60}^* = -0.08 + (1.74 - 0.028\text{Age})E_{60} + (-0.47 + 0.026\text{Age})P_{56}$$

with an $R^2 = 0.66$, which suggests more systematic behavior among party identifiers.

2. For comparative purposes, the 1960 party affiliation variable has a mean of 0.58 in the sample of voters in the panel while the mean of the estimated 1960 party variable for the 1964 voters is 0.61. This difference is best explained by differences in the composition of each sample. The 1964 sample contains more respondents who are black, southern, and who say they have Democratic fathers. All of these characteristics are associated with Democratic affiliations in 1960. The greater proportion of these respondents in the 1964 sample is enough to account for the difference in mean party affiliations.

3. The 1964 evaluation variable is based on seven rather than ten issues. The previous 1964 election study did not exclude indifferent evaluations from the construction of the overall evaluation variable, as does the analysis of the panel data. For the purposes of these estimations, the 1964 evaluation variable is recomputed so its construction is comparable to the 1960 evaluation variable used in estimating equations 3-5.

4. This is the root of the ordinal variable problem mentioned previously. Even though some respondents are assigned a party affiliation score of 0.75 on the basis of their responses to the survey question, they may have different party affiliations if viewed on the implicit true party strength scale.

5. Unfortunately it is not possible to determine the stability of voters' evaluation because the 1956 and 1958 surveys did not ask people which party was most likely to follow the policy presented in the question. People were simply asked which party was most likely to do what they wanted. This question will yield quite a different evaluation variable from the one used here which compares persons' positions with their perceptions of party positions.

REFERENCES

ASHER, H. B. (1974) "Some consequences of measurement error in survey data." American Journal of Political Science (May): 469-485.

BURNHAM, W. D. (1975) "American politics in the 1970s: beyond party," pp. 238-277 in L. Maisel and P. M. Sacks (eds.) Sage Electoral Studies Yearbook, vol. 1. Beverly Hills and London: Sage.

CAMPBELL, A., P. CONVERSE, W. MILLER, and D. STOKES (1971) The SRC American Panel Study. Ann Arbor: Inter-University Consortium for Political Research.

CONVERSE, P. E. (1969) "Of time and partisan stability." Comparative Political Studies (July): 139-171.

Gallup Opinion Index (1973) Report No. 100. Princeton: Public Opinion Press.

JACKSON, J. E. (1975) "Issues, party choices, and presidential voting." American Journal of Political Science (May): 161-185.

––– (1973) "Senate voting: problems of scaling and functional form," in A. S. Goldberg and O. D. Duncan (eds.) Structural Equation Models in the Social Sciences. New York: Seminar Press.

KEY, V. O., Jr. (1965) The Responsible Electorate. Cambridge: Belknap.

NIE, N., S. VERBA, and J. PETROCIK (1975) "The changing American voter." Unpublished manuscript prepared for the Twentieth Century Fund.

Chapter 4

SOCIAL CHANGE AND THE FUTURE OF POLITICAL PARTIES: THE AUSTRALIAN CASE

D A V I D   K E M P

The Australian case provides an unusual opportunity to assess the future of political parties in industrial societies. Australia is, in many respects, almost the "pure" case of an advanced industrial society—if such a thing is possible. Australia is unusual in two respects: it is a society that has come into being entirely since the industrial revolution; it exhibits some of the supposed "typical" characteristics of the advanced industrial society to a marked degree.

European settlement of Australia dates from 1788, and the main migration to the continent commenced in the mid-nineteenth century in response to the discovery of gold. The population drawn to the continent has been remarkably homogeneous linguistically, culturally, and ethnically. Until World War II migration was almost entirely from Britain and Ireland, and the population was almost wholly English-speaking. The country is therefore without an ethnically distinct region such as Quebec in Canada, and without any

AUTHOR'S NOTE: I am indebted to the Yale Political Science Research Library and to the Council for Comparative and European Studies at Yale University for the funding of this research; to the Roper Public Opinion Center for making available the Australian Gallup Surveys; to Professors Aitkin and Kahan for permitting secondary analysis of the data from their 1967 Australian Survey Project (Australian National University) and to the (Roy Morgan) Gallup organization in Australia for its extremely valuable record of Australian public opinion over three decades.

of the feudal remnants that have influenced the politics of the industrial states of Europe: it has no traditional landed aristocracy, no rural peasantry, no traditional culture of deference and ascription.

Economically Australia has been a significant participant in imperial, and later world, markets, and the economy has been based on the investment of private capital and free wage labor. In historical terms there is no region comparable to the South in the United States. It would be difficult to conceive of a society (unless it be New Zealand) more dependent for its form and development on meeting the demands of domestic and international markets.

Culturally Australia has been characterized as egalitarian, achievement-oriented with a universalistic code of norms, and somewhat more collectivist than the United States in its stance toward the economic and social role of the state (Crawford, 1955: 704-727; Forster, 1967: 156-163; Lipset, 1967: 227-230). It appears to be widely accepted among students of Australian society that the pursuit of egalitarian social and economic goals though collectivist techniques in a universalistic culture has been a potent source of that "characteristic talent . . . for bureaucracy" (Davies, 1958: 3) which has made Australia a model of development which would delight students of Weber (Weber, 1968; Encel, 1970). Assessments of the distribution of power in the society vary widely, but it seems indisputable that an early shortage of labor (especially rural labor) laid the basis for an unusually powerful working-class movement. The first Labor Party government came to power in 1904 at the federal level, and 59% of the work force belonged to trade unions in 1968 (Ford, 1970: 120).

In its economic and social structure, Australia seems to provide almost an extreme example of the characteristics of an advanced industrial society:

(1) There has been a steady decline in the proportion of the work force in primary industries and an equally steady increase in the proportion in the tertiary sector. Despite the significance of primary production for Australia's external trade balance, the proportion of the male labor force in agriculture is only about 13%, while the proportion in professional and technical occupations is over 14% (third in the world behind Canada and the United States). Equally significant, the proportion of the male labor force engaged in manufacturing (29.7% in 1961) is substantially less than in West Germany (43.7%), the United Kingdom (39.8%), and Sweden (38.8%), and is similar to that

in the United States and Canada (Taylor and Hudson, 1972: 334, 335, 329). Australia, in "objective" occupational terms, is one of the most "white collar" of the world's industrial societies.

(2) Despite its geographical extent, Australia is possibly also the most urbanized of the world's major industrial countries. According to data recently provided by Kingsley Davis, Australia in 1969 had a smaller proportion of its population living in rural areas (11.5%) than any other industrial country (United States, 24.8%; Great Britain, 20.9%; West Germany, 17.8%; Netherlands, 27.8%; Japan, 16.8%) (Davis, 1969; also Taylor and Hudson, 1972: 219).

(3) Australia may also be the most suburban of industrial societies. In 1966, 85% of the population lived in single detached houses and of these 79% were privately owned or being purchased. To these must be added privately owned apartments. International comparisons are difficult, but in 1968 in the United States 64.3% of occupied dwelling units were owner-occupied. Australian cities take their distinctive character from the vast low-density suburbs which spread around largely residentially empty commercial centers.

(4) Residential mobility appears to be high and comparable to that in the United States. Between the 1966 and 1971 censuses, no less than 45.7% of the population alive at both censuses recorded a change in address, and 15.6% had actually moved between states—a more substantial change in terms of distance and impact on personal relationships than an interstate move in the United States (Census, 1971).

(5) As in other industrial societies, knowledge has become an increasingly significant resource. The 1960s saw a vast expansion in higher secondary and tertiary education, as well as in the production of new knowledge through research (Australian Universities Commission Report, 1972: 10-12). In the 17 years from 1955 to 1972 the proportion of the 17 to 22 age group in universities doubled, and in addition many new institutions of tertiary education were established.

By 1965 (when this expansion was gathering speed), Australia ranked tenth out of 121 countries in the number of students in institutions of higher education, substantially ahead of the major European industrial countries: France, West Germany, and the United Kingdom (Taylor and Hudson, 1972: 229).

(6) Australia has long been, and remains, among the most affluent of countries. The high level of ownership of real property has already been noted. As measured by gross national product per capita in American dollars, Australia during 1960-1965 ranked eighth out of 135 countries (Taylor and Hudson, 1972: 314). Perhaps more

significantly, income and property in Australia have been remarkably evenly distributed relative to other industrial societies. When Lord Bryce visited Australia early in this century, he commented that "the wage earning classes live so much more comfortably than do the like classes in France, Germany or England, as to be up to what is there called a 'middle class' standard" (Bryce, 1921: 186). The *World Handbook* confirms that in equality of income distribution Australia ranks after only the United Kingdom, Sweden, and Israel (Taylor and Hudson, 1972: 264). It should also be noted in this context that Australia has been remarkably fortunate in the stability of its economy. Throughout the post-World War II period unemployment never reached 3.5% of the work force, and for most of the period remained below 2%. Periods of high inflation in the early 1950s and early 1970s enclosed an era of relatively stable prices.

(7) Although the populace has frequently been characterized as "apathetic" in relation to politics, comparatively the judgment must be accepted with caution. Compulsory voting in federal elections since 1924 has ensured turnouts of over 90%, and over 250,000 voters actually belong to political parties (3.8% of the electorate) (Watson, 1973: 364). Using a variety of indicators one study suggests that 30% of the electorate can be classified as "politically active and aware," 37% as a "passive audience," and 33% as "quite indifferent and uninterested" (Aitkin, 1973: 303). Membership in organizations of all kinds, as determined by a secondary analysis of a national survey undertaken in 1967, was higher than in any of the five countries studied by Almond and Verba in 1960, including the United States (60% of respondents belonged to at least one organization, including trade unions [N = 2,054]).

(8) Insofar as the advance of secularism is supposed to be a characteristic of industrial societies, Australia probably fits within the mold. The most extensive study of religious beliefs classifies 52% of the population as "secularist" in terms of belief in God, church attendance, and prayer habits, though only 16% were classified as "consistent secularists" (Mol, 1971).

This recitation of some of the "objective" characteristics of Australian society has been designed to show that Australia has many of the characteristics of a "postindustrial" society. Most, if not all, of these characteristics are becoming more exaggerated over time. The primary question this article discusses is: What are the implications, if any, of these characteristics and trends for the future of political parties in Australia? What, if any, are the lessons of the Australian experience for other advanced industrial countries?

The research on which this article is largely based has been concerned to examine the nature, if any, of the changes that have taken place in the bases of support of the major parties since 1945, and to explain such changes as have occurred. A simple model underlies the research: the electoral support available to political parties is viewed as a function of (1) the structure of social contexts in the society, (2) the extent to which these contexts come to have political meaning for voters, and (3) the extent to which party elites are successful in persuading voters that their political interests are best advanced through support of particular parties. "Social contexts," "political meanings," "political interests" are broad concepts referring essentially to the life situations of voters and the political actions they may believe will improve their chances of realizing their values. This is, of course, the basic model for a sociology of politics. In the present context the interesting questions concern the impact of changes or developments in advanced industrial societies, such as those noted above, for the distribution of political interests. From the viewpoint of political elites, the issue is one of the strategic opportunities (and risks) opened by the process of changes in the structure of the industrial system and accompanying changes (in any) in social structure.

I. SOME THEORIES OF SOCIOPOLITICAL CHANGE IN ADVANCED INDUSTRIAL SOCIETIES

A central theme in many discussions of industrial society over the last quarter century has been the theme of the disappearance of differences between categories of voters within the major cleavage systems. It has been said, for example, that there are increasing similarities between middle- and working-class values, attitudes, and behavior:

> . . . not only has the middle class been increasing in size relative to the working class, but its social standards are permeating the working class more with each passing year . . . as a result, an ever increasing number of people who are objectively manual workers think and act like the middle class. [Lenski, 1963: 48-49]

Similarly many notable differences between rural and urban life are believed to be waning:

Rural-urban differentials in modernised societies have been greatly reduced or even eliminated in many respects. [Larson, 1968: 587]

Again, the trend toward secularism has been seen as dampening the ardor and importance of religious conflict. In short, from one perspective a process of "homogenization" appears to be occurring in Western industrial countries. This is not necessarily to say that all differences are vanishing, but at least those based on the great historic cleavages are. It is from such a perspective that Daniel Bell has recently commented more generally that "the 'social location' of the individual (his social class or other position) no longer determines his life style and his values" (Bell, 1970: 19).

If changes in society of these dimensions are in fact occurring, it is easy to see that they could have profound consequences for existing political organizations and for mass political behavior. Given that political parties in Western democracies have built their support on foundations of class, religious, ethnic, and regional groupings, transformation in the character of these groupings would seem likely, over time, to introduce a new fluidity into political life—leading perhaps to new kinds of appeals, new styles of leadership and authority, new tensions within party organizations, and a new volatility in electoral behavior. The traditional mass-elite alliances might well decay only slowly, but decay they would, in the process opening the door to a new kind of politics. Chief among the processes seen as bringing about these changes are generalized affluence, urbanization and suburbanization, more extensive and immediate private and mass communications and transport, the restructuring of work place and market contexts, and the advent of the high information "knowledgeable society."

Central to the claim that advanced industrial society is producing a new structure of political interests is the conclusion that fundamental changes are occurring in the nature of the class system. The most respectable and persistent of these claims is the assertion of the *embourgeoisement* of the working class. More recently convergence has been approached from the other direction in the claim that postindustrial society is witnessing the radicalization of the technocracy. David Apter has recently tried to encompass these two perspectives in a grand theory of political system change (Apter, 1971).

That working-class politics have become more instrumental—less ideological—in the last twenty-five years has become a commonplace in political discussion, and, despite the "end of ideology" debate, not really controversial in these terms. This has been seen as accompanying a decline in class hostility, most frequently attributed to the increasing affluence of the industrial societies and, presumably, in part to the consequent satisfaction of materialist values (Campbell et al., 1960: 359; Lenski, 1966: 381-382; Marcuse, 1964; Bell, 1970; Lipset, 1972). How deep a transformation in fundamental class interests this affluence has brought about, of course, remains open. Indeed, in light of Lord Bryce's argument that it was precisely the affluence of the working class (in a nondeferential culture) which explained the intensity of class conflict in Australia (Bryce, 1921: 273), the argument resting on affluence alone is by no means self-evidently sound. If Bryce's claim were valid, it would be necessary to postulate, in addition, some absolute level of affluence which provided substantial marginal satisfaction of material values, or a change in the culture. And the question would remain whether any foreseeable economic crisis could bring about a resurgent recognition of differences in class interest.

In addition to the simple fact of increasing material well-being, it has been further argued that structural changes are occurring in mature industrial societies which fundamentally alter the nature of interactions between classes and have the effect of permanently blurring, if not obliterating, class identities and the sense of distinct class interests. Here urbanization, developments in communication, transportation and the mass media, and suburban development have been identified as increasing contact and interaction between classes and other groups, though there seems to be uncertainty about how far the argument should be pushed (Taviss, 1969; Lipset, 1964; Mayer, 1963). Even research that has questioned whether the interaction patterns of industrial society do, indeed, bring the classes into closer contact has found that the extent of contact between classes does appear to be a significant intervening variable in *embourgeoisement* of the working class and alteration in its political identity (Goldthorpe et al., 1969: 159). Whether such increased contact does become significantly more common as the industrial system matures is an empirical, and in principle, resolvable, problem. That such processes have actually taken place in Australia has been asserted, for example, by L. F. Crisp (1971: 187), who has identified the extensive suburban development of the post-World War II era as a key factor in changing class identities in Australia and in the diminution of class hostility. Even if his view could be substantiated, it would still remain to be shown from an interactionist standpoint that Australian suburban development does indeed encourage increased interaction between classes. Theory on the significance of changes in interaction patterns for class identity and political partisanship is supported both by the theory and research on attitude change and "homogeneity effects" (McGuire, 1968: 187-191; Campbell and Alexander, 1965; Putnam, 1966; Segal and Meyer, 1969; Butler and Stokes, 1969: 147-150).

Just how fundamental the reductions in class hostility in advanced industrial societies may be is a matter of keen dispute. Causal theories point in different directions depending on the processes identified as of primary importance. It appears to be an implication of several of these theories that, while current conditions are such as to mute the conflict of interests, there has been no significant change in the underlying bases of class interest and that different elite behaviors, or changing economic or institutional conditions, could revive class conflict as a significant political phenomenon again (Goldthorpe et al., 1969; Dahrendorf, 1959; Stinchcombe, 1965; Hamilton, 1967). The major cross-national study in this area of theory in fact argues that the Anglo-American democracies in particular may be converging toward a class politics founded on some basic structure of class interests, and that this process is furthered by urbanization, secularism, and processes increasing national integration (Alford, 1963 and 1967). That is, the argument runs directly counter to the theory of the effects of structural change advanced above.

The message of these theories for the future of parties is unclear. Alford's theory of sociopolitical development would lead one to expect a relative stability in the division of class support between the parties in countries where class-based parties have come into existence and established their bases of support. Short-term fluctuations there might be, and even reductions in class hostility (depending presumably on social and economic conditions, and elite strategies), but the system of class-based parties should be relatively stable. Under other theories significant decay of class support seems possible in the short or medium term provided institutions for resolving class conflict remain effective (Dahrendorf, 1959) or employers are forced (encouraged) by economic conditions to woo employees.

Logically independent of theories of this kind is another body of work which approaches the class alignment from the other end and argues that the condition of the professional and technical expert in advanced industrial societies is such as to produce increasing alienation from the industrial and bureaucratic system as it is presently organized. Dahrendorf described a position for the professional and technical expert outside the main structure of authority in the industrial economy—a position that might under some circumstances be consistent with opposition to those in authority (1959: 255). Serge Mallet (1963) has argued that advanced technology encourages solidarity between workers, technicians, and operating managers which may be a basis for common action on the part of employees of all kinds. Touraine (1971), in his explanation of the 1968 "May Movement" in France, develops an argument concerning the revolutionary potential of the professionals based on their position in the authority structure of modern French industrial society. In his view the professionals sought "a democratic structure capable of regulating the massive structures that both ensure economic growth and manipulate society" (Touraine, 1971: 314). Again, for the United States, Irving Kristol has recently argued that the greatest challenge to the authority of the existing social institutions comes from the tertiary educated professionals:

> The simple truth is that the professional classes of our more bureaucratised societies are engaged in a class struggle with the business community for status and power. [Kristol, 1972: 75]

The alienation of the professionals and a possible alliance between them and the oppressed working class has sustained the hopes of New Left theorists in recent years. Yet, for the present at least, the truth of the matter appears to be as recently stated by S. M. Lipset:

> Efforts to find a mass base for so-called New Left Groups which reject the established Social Democratic, Communist, and Democratic Parties, all oriented to the electoral system, have failed dramatically in areas as diverse as France, Germany, Italy, Northern Europe and the United States. [Lipset, 1972: 22]

Of course, to the extent that bourgeois instrumentalist notions have gripped the old working class—and perhaps transformed its fundamental nature—this is hardly surprising. The natural allies of the alienated professionals are not the new "middle-class" workers, but the oppressed marginals, as David Apter (1971: 91, 94) has pointed out. But in the advanced industrial society the "oppressed marginals" may not be easy to find—and this seems particularly so for Australia. In such an affluent and relatively egalitarian society, without an obvious lower class, and a well-hidden "poor," the alienated professional or technocrat is likely to feel politically lonely. The existing parties, seeking mass support, are unlikely to offer an easy resting place for such as these. How might such a disaffected section of society express itself electorally? What would the existence of such a section mean for the existing political parties? In the Australian context it is still necessary to ask the logically prior question: Does such a disaffected technocracy exist at all?

II. THE AUSTRALIAN PARTIES

The Australian party system has been characterized as a two-party, two-and-a-half party, three-, four- or five-party system depending on the purposes of the classification. In terms of the opportunity to form governments, politics at the national level in Australia have been dominated by two political groupings: the Australian Labor Party on the one hand, and the alliance of the Liberal Party and the Country Party on the other. A coalition of the Liberal and Country Parties provided the federal government from 1949 to 1972. Since 1972 the Australian Labor Party (A.L.P.) has formed the government.

In terms of the working of the parliamentary institutions, it is necessary to take account of a third party, the Democratic Labor Party, formed in 1955 as a breakaway from the A.L.P. Between 1955 and 1970 the D.L.P. averaged 7.4% of the national vote in House of Representative elections and 8.9% in the Senate. Because of the electoral system for the House of Representatives (preferential voting in single-member constituencies) and the lack of sufficient geographical concentration of support, the D.L.P. failed to win seats in this chamber. It did, however, win seats in the Senate, elected by proportional representation from multimember, statewide constituencies. Between 1970 and 1974 it held 5 of the 60 Senate seats, its peak of representation.

In addition to these parties, the only ones that have won federal parliamentary representation, there have been numerous smaller parties over the post-World War II period. These have included a small Communist Party (and fragments) which averaged 0.5% of the vote from 1955 to 1969, and whose significance lies in its role in the trade union movement rather than in its direct participation in the electoral process. In 1969 a new minor party contested the election for the House of Representatives (and succeeding national elections for the Senate in 1970; the House of Representatives in 1972; the House of Representatives and Senate in 1974), the Australia Party. This party has not yet won as much as 3% of the national vote, but it has polled a much larger proportion in some of the seats it has contested, its largest vote being 17.5% of the formal ballots in a by-election in the Australian Capital Territory in 1970. This party merits consideration both because its preferences have affected the result in some constituencies, and because, it will be argued here, it has considerable significance for understanding the impact of social change on electoral patterns.

These party labels serve to identify the main political elites who have sought mass support through Australia's electoral system. To the extent that the maturing of the industrial system in Australia has brought about changes in the distribution of political interests, the simple model outlined earlier would suggest that electoral success over the longer term would require successful identification of these changes by elites and the crystallization through their efforts of the political meaning of these changes. Such a model, involving both the changing receptivity of electors to political appeals as a result of social change and the capacity of political elites to perceive and maximize their opportunities in light of these changes, raises complex issues of causation which cannot be investigated here. Rather the present analysis seeks to investigate several more restricted but central issues in the study of sociopolitical change: (a) whether there have been any long-term trends in the bases of electoral support of the parties in Australia; (b) whether these trends (and the processes underlying them) permit any evaluation of the relevance of the above theories of sociopolitical change to Australia; and (c) whether these trends have any evident meaning for the future of political parties in Australia, and more generally for political parties in advanced industrial societies. The focus of the present report will be on trends in the class basis of party support in Australia.

III. THE RESEARCH

The research reported in this paper has been based on the secondary analysis of several substantial files of data derived from surveys undertaken in Australia between 1946 and 1974. The largest of these files has been drawn from the collection of Australian (Morgan) Gallup Poll data held by the Roper Public Opinion Center in Williamstown, Massachusetts. A number of surveys from this file were analyzed by the author in the United States. To this has been added analysis of poll results since 1967 published by the Morgan Gallup organization in Australia. A third file containing data for the period 1971-1974 has been (and continues to be) developed by the Australian Sales Research Bureau in conjunction with the Department of Political Science at the University of Melbourne. In 1971-1972 the latter surveys were based on clustered probability samples of Sydney and Melbourne (the two largest cities) but since then have been national samples. Finally some secondary analysis has been performed on a national survey of Australian political attitudes undertaken by Aitkin and Kahan from the Australian National University in 1967. The Gallup samples have been national throughout the period. Between 1946 and 1966 quota sampling methods were used. Since 1966 stratified clustered probability sampling has been employed.

The findings reported here arise from a larger project which seeks to examine the implications for mass electoral behavior of changes in Australian social structure since 1945, using census and electoral statistics as well as survey data.

IV. TRENDS IN CLASS VOTING 1946-1972

In order to provide a basis for the analysis of short-term fluctuations as well as long-term trends in party support, 73 surveys from the Gallup data file and published breakdowns for 1946 through 1972 were analyzed to determine the distribution of class support between the parties at many points of time. For this purpose "class" was defined as the occupational class of the head of the household, categorized into manual and nonmanual occupations. As a measure of the power of occupational class to account for the division of support between the two major political groupings, phi-square was employed. The advantage of this statistic lies in its mathematical equivalence to the square of the product-moment correlation coefficient in the case of dichotomous variables (Alker, 1965: 80-84). It thus provided a readily interpretable measure of changes in the power of class to order the vote over time. Because

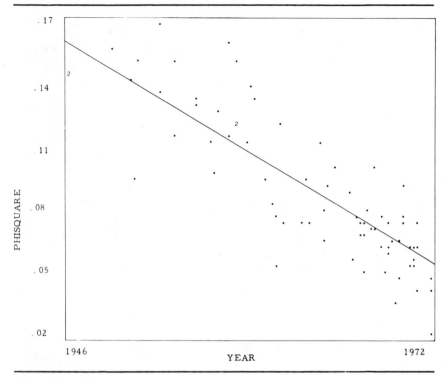

Figure 1: TREND IN CLASS VOTING, 1946-1972

the concern of the present analysis is with long-term trends, the linear least-squares line was plotted for the observations across time, to provide a convenient overall description of the data.

Figure 1 shows the trend in phi-square plotted from late 1946 (the first survey analyzed) to late 1972. Each point indicates the value of phi-square in one survey. Each value of phi-square has been calculated from a two-by-two table, the column categories of which were manual/nonmanual occupational class and the row categories, A.L.P. and L.C.P. preference.

Figure 1 shows that over the quarter century there has been a clear decline in the explanatory power of occupational class as a structural basis for party preferences. The trend is described by the equation

$$T = .16 - .004Y \qquad (r^2 = .73; \text{df}: 71)[1]$$
$$(.0003)$$

where T is the value of phi-square at any point of time;
.16 is the estimated value of phi-square in 1946;
Y is the number of years since 1946.

Farm occupations are excluded, as are D.L.P. and other minor party supporters. For each survey, N is approximately 2,000. In order to control for the possibility of a trend in the proportions of the sample in manual and nonmanual occupations, a second calculation was performed holding these proportions constant by percentaging the data. When this was done, r^2 was reduced from .733 to .728 and B from $-.00426$ to $-.00425$, indicating that the sensitivity of phi-square to changes in the marginals has not been a significant factor with respect to changes in the class makeup of the sample over time. Because we are interested, initially, in the nature of the long-term trend, the trend line calculated by least-square methods is shown. For a variety of reasons the observations fluctuate about the trend line. Sampling error alone would account for some fluctuation, even if the trend line were a perfect representation of the state of the class-voting relationship in the population at any given point in time. However some of this fluctuation will almost certainly be attributable to fluctuation in the actual relationship. In the present context, however, these short-term fluctuations do not concern us.

Over the quarter century the explanatory power of occupational class declined by over two-thirds. The class cleavage has indeed become less and less important as a source of structure in voting preferences in Australia, to a point where only 5% of the variance in party preference is attributable to it. Further, the very high correlation of the plots with the trend line indicates a striking continuity in the trend over time. However, inspection reveals that the observations prior to 1961 fall mainly above the trend line while those after 1961 tend to fall below, indicating that despite the high correlation coefficient the trend has not been consistent over the whole period. Because Alford's data were primarily drawn from the earlier period, the possibility must be considered that his conclusion that there was no clear long-term decline in class voting was valid for the period before 1961 (Alford, 1963: 291), and that the appearance of a trend covering the whole period may be due to a change in the relationship in the last decade and to a weighting of the observations in this period.

Table 1 shows that this was not the case. There was a similar trend in both periods, though somewhat more clearly defined in the second period than in the first. The similarity of the regression coefficients for the two periods, and the lower correlation for each (when compared with the slope and correlation for the whole period), raise

Table 1. COMPARISON OF TRENDS IN CLASS VOTING 1946-1960 AND 1961-1972

	1946-1960	*1961-1972*
Slope (B)	−.002	−.003
Standard error	.00098	.00071
r^2	.14	.31
df	22	47

a problem. How is it that the overall trend, and the correlation of all the observations with the trend, is greater for the whole period than for each subperiod? The reason is that there appears to have been something of a step-down in the level of class voting around 1961, which then became the base line for a continuance of the former trend. When all the observations are taken together, this step is obscured. What caused the step? A working hypothesis is that the economic difficulties of 1960-1961 when unemployment rose to the highest levels for over a decade produced a significantly greater reaction against the L.C.P. government among its nonmanual supporters than among manuals, and the losses of this time were not fully recovered. This hypothesis must await further examination at a later time.

The third and final aspect of Figure 1 to be noted here is that at no time in the last quarter century has occupational class accounted for more than 17% of the variance in party preference, despite the great weight which has been placed upon it in analyses of voting in Australia. Although relative to other variables which have been identified it is a variable of considerable explanatory force, it is clearly only a start in the process of constructing reasonably satisfactory explanations of the structure of voting preferences in the population.

V. THE PROCESS OF DECLINE

MANUAL AND NONMANUAL TRENDS

Given that a decline in class voting has occurred, the next step is to examine the processes which have brought about that decline. One pattern of change suggested above was the probable convergence of the blue-collar workers toward the pattern of preferences of the middle class under the impact of suburbanization and affluence. If this hypothesis is correct, the pattern of convergence in manual/

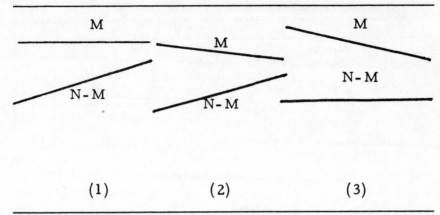

Figure 2: HYPOTHETICAL PATTERNS OF CONVERGENCE IN CLASS PREFERENCES

nonmanual preferences would resemble that in case (3) of Figure 2. In Figure 2 the top line in each case represents the trend in manual support for the Australian Labor Party, the bottom line, the trend in nonmanual support. (1) is the case where a decline in the difference in class patterns of preferences has been brought about by an increase in Labor's proportionate support among nonmanuals combined with a steady level of support among manuals; (2) and (3) both represent cases where the Labor Party's support among blue-collar workers has declined, in (2) toward a rising level of support among white-collar voters, in (3) toward a stable level of white-collar support. As stated above, the case most consistent with the *embourgeoisement* hypothesis (on an assumption of stable elite behavior) is case (3).

Figures 3(a) and 3(b) show the trends over the period in the percent support for the Australian Labor Party among manuals and nonmanuals. The trend lines are described by the equations:

$$M = 72.76 - .41Y \qquad (r^2 = .36; df: 71)$$
$$(.07)$$

$$NM = 31.01 + .26Y \qquad (r^2 = .16; df: 71)$$
$$(.07)$$

Where M is the percent support for the A.L.P. among manuals;
NM is the percent support for the A.L.P. among nonmanuals;
the constant is estimated A.L.P. support in 1946; and
Y is the number of years since 1946.

The opposite signs of the regression coefficients indicate that there has been a convergence toward similar levels of support for the

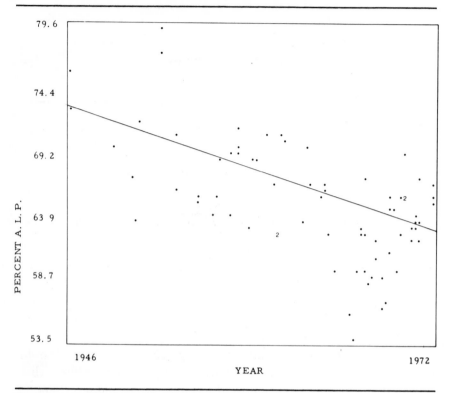

Figure 3(a): TREND IN MANUAL SUPPORT FOR A.L.P., 1946-1972

A.L.P. among both manuals and nonmanuals, the pattern of case (2). However the magnitude of the coefficients indicates that the decline in A.L.P. support among manuals has been considerably steeper than the increase in A.L.P. support among nonmanuals—that the A.L.P.'s loss of support among its blue-collar base has been the most significant element in the declining importance of occupational class for voting patterns.

The correlation coefficients draw attention also to another significant aspect of the pattern of convergence: the observations for the blue-collar workers conform more closely to the overall trend than do the observations for white-collar workers; that is, blue-collar support for the Labor Party has fluctuated much less than white-collar support *about its respective trend*. It is as if the loss of working-class support from Labor has been more inexorable than the gains in white-collar support. Inspection of Figure 3 confirms this. For neither class do fluctuations of support appear to be random: for periods of several years at a time, observations are predominantly

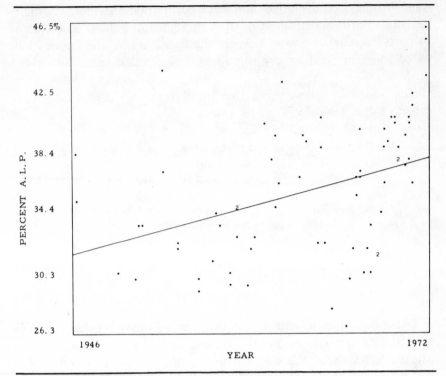

Figure 3(b): TREND IN NONMANUAL SUPPORT FOR A.L.P., 1946-1972

above or predominantly below the trend line. The obvious conclusion from this is that there have been systematic short-term
influences raising or lowering support for Labor in each class.

For the moment, however, the important point is that for
blue-collar workers these short-term movements occur around a
declining trend: each successive short-term fall seems lower than the
previous one, each successive increase (until the early 1970s) failing
to reach the peak of the previous increase. For white-collar voters,
however, the pattern is less clear, observations are more spread, and
fluctuations more severe.

With respect to the nonmanual voters the hypothesis that in
advanced industrial societies the traditional lines of class voting are
blurred by radicalization of the technocracy leads to the prediction
that within the nonmanual class the most rapid gains to the major
"left" party will be among the upper white-collar voters, particularly
the professionals and some sections of the managerial and executive
categories. The data for white-collar voters are available for four
categories within this class: managerial and executive, professional,

small business, and clerical and sales occupations. If the hypothesis has any validity as an identification of significant shifts in the bases of party support, we would expect the trend toward the Labor Party to be most marked among the upper white collars, particularly the professionals.

The equations describing the trend lines for the white-collar categories for 1946-1972 are as follows:

Managerial, executive	$15.07 + .30Y$ $(.09)$	$(r^2 = .13; df: 69)$
Professional	$4.77 + 1.04Y$ $(.15)$	$(r^2 = .41; df: 69)$
Small business	$42.06 - .42Y$ $(.15)$	$(r^2 = .11; df: 69)$
Clerical	$39.14 + .001Y$ $(.08)$	$(r^2 = .00; df: 69)$

Where the constant is estimated percent support for A.L.P. in 1946 and Y is the number of years since 1946.

These equations confirm that there was indeed a striking differentiation in trends within the nonmanual class. Among the two categories which, at the start of the period, gave least support to the A.L.P., managerial and professional, the long-term trend has been toward increasing levels of Labor support. This has been most evidently so among professionals, whose tendency to vote Labor has increased by over 2% every three years, on average. By the end of the period several samples showed professional support for Labor approaching 40%. Moreover, despite the relatively small number of professional respondents in each sample (and hence the possibility of substantial sampling error), the observations correlate relatively well with the trend line, giving yet greater confidence to the assessment. The trend among managers and executives is likewise fairly well defined, though the lower correlation coefficient indicates wider fluctuation about the trend line.

By contrast with the upper white-collar group, the lower nonmanual categories have shown either declining or static levels of support for Labor, with loss being rather more obvious among the smaller category of small businessmen. On inspection of the scatterplots (not reproduced) both these categories, as well as the managerial and professional categories, show the pattern of systematic short-term fluctuation evident in the data for the nonmanual class as a whole.

With these further data in hand, it is possible to define much more precisely the pattern of change in class voting. Among manual workers and among the lower status categories of nonmanuals, there has been a drift toward the more conservative political parties. But among the upper status nonmanuals there has been a decisive gain by Labor. The pattern of convergence 1946-1972 most closely approximates that of case (2) in Figure 2, *but the dividing line is not that between manuals and nonmanuals, but between upper status nonmanuals, on the one hand, and the remainder of the population, on the other.* Long-term trends have occurred in both upper status and lower status support, but the appropriate dividing line has not been provided by a bipolar concept of occupational class. The problem of accounting for a distinctive long-term trend is not confined to blue-collar voters.

The inference might be made from the data represented above that two basic long-term processes have operated with respect to the class basis of mass voting patterns, one process operating on lower middle and working-class voters, the other on upper middle class voters. So as not to prejudge this issue, in the analysis that follows blue collar and lower white collar will be kept distinct, but the possibility of common factors at work must be kept in mind.

URBANIZATION AND SUBURBANIZATION

Robert Alford argued that increasing integration of the networks of communication in a country would only make more obvious the common political interests among members of the same class and encourage mass political action organized on class lines. One process that would have this effect, in his view, was urbanization: the increasing concentration of the population in cities (Alford, 1963: 331; also Lipset et al., 1954: 1136). In this context the high level of urbanization in Australia becomes an important part of the explanation as to why class has been so important in Australian politics. When Alford examined the evidence he had collected, however, he was puzzled to discover that Victoria and New South Wales, the older and more urbanized regions, had *lower* levels of class voting than did other states. One solution he suggested was that "urbanism" was too inclusive a concept, and that while it might legitimately be used to distinguish between nations, it might not be adequate for analysis within nations. This led him to a very significant qualification to his argument which may well lead away from his general conclusion that the countries in his study might be converging toward a structurally based level of class conflict. The qualification was that urban areas are centers of innovation, and the ideologies spawned there spread to the rest of the country. In the past, he hypothesized, cities may have been centers of class conflict and traditions of class voting spread from there to the rest of the country; but as these traditional identifications break down under the "rationalizing" impact of industrialism, it is possible that the level of class voting in cities might fall toward the "structurally" based level (Alford, 1963: 329-332). The notion of "structural" levels of class voting is perhaps a dubious one, but the concession that there may be processes at work within cities reducing levels of class conflict below traditional levels is an important concession, for the argument then shifts to the nature of these processes and the likely extent of their impact. For Alford, these processes appear to have an intellectual component (he refers to "ideologies," "rationalizing forces"), though stemming from the development of the industrial system. But if they are "structural" (i.e., involving changes in patterns of class interactions), then it makes little sense to refer to "structural limits" of class conflict as being fairly stable, while at the same time conceding the presence of structural change.

As part of an attempt to investigate the hypothesis that change in the structure of residential contexts within the metropolitan areas has been a major cause of the movements of blue-collar support, data produced as part of a national survey of political attitudes in 1967 was submitted to secondary analysis. The responses of voters from households whose head was in a blue-collar occupation were examined to determine the effect of residential context on blue-collar voting patterns. The first step in this analysis offered some support for explanations stressing the suburban context. It was found that voters from blue-collar households were significantly more likely to support the major conservative party in the new outer suburban areas than in the older working-class suburbs. Table 2 shows this effect clearly.

By further secondary analysis of the data, it was possible to throw some light on the processes that might explain this relationship. In view of the hypothesis that the difference results from the "middle classing" effects of residence in the new outer suburbs, it might be inferred that, if the respondent's own (subjective) sense of social class were held constant, the difference between the voting habits of blue-collar respondents in the two contexts would disappear. The

Table 2. PARTY SUPPORT OF BLUE-COLLAR VOTERS BY RESIDENTIAL CONTEXT

	Inner Suburban	Outer Suburban	
Liberal	22.2	36.2	df 3
Labor	55.6	51.2	$X^2 = 9.33$
D.L.P.	5.1	3.1	
Other	17.2	9.4	$p < .05$
Total	100.2	99.9	
N =	99	287	

best that can be said about Table 3 is that it is not inconsistent with this being the case.

Table 3 shows the distribution of support between the two major parties among blue-collar workers, controlled both for the respondent's residential context and the respondent's own sense of his social class position. There are no statistically significant differences in the allocation of support between the major parties by suburb, once the respondent's subjectively perceived class is taken into account. But although it lacks significance, there is nevertheless an association between residence and vote which should caution against accepting the conclusion that suburban residence operates through subjective class perceptions in influencing the vote, until the relationship has been examined with larger samples. Table 3 does, however, provide illumination of the role of subjective class perceptions in voting behavior. Comparing respondents' answers within suburban contexts according to their subjective class, it does appear that subjective class perceptions are related (at a statistically significant level) to party support among voters from blue-collar households, in both kinds of suburban context. Recalling that "objectively" Australia is one of

Table 3. DISTRIBUTION OF PARTY SUPPORT AMONG BLUE-COLLAR VOTERS BY RESIDENTIAL CONTEXT AND SUBJECTIVE CLASS

	Subjective Class			
	Working		Middle	
	Inner Suburban	Outer Suburban	Inner Suburban	Outer Suburban
Liberal	20	33	50	53
Labor	80	67	50	47
Total	100	100	100	100
N	55	136	20	104
	$X^2 = 3.24$		$X^2 = 0.06$	
	$p < .10$ NS		$p < .80$ NS	

the most white collar of nations, and that "subjectively" a substantially larger proportion of the electorate identifies itself as middle class in Australia than in Britain or the United States (Broom et al., 1968: 220), this finding is of considerable potential importance in assessing the *embourgeoisement* hypothesis for Australia. If it could be demonstrated that there has been a marked change in the balance of class perceptions in the electorate over time, the outlines of a mechanism inducing the working class to shift allegiances in a context of static appeals from the Labor Party elites can be seen. It would then remain to examine the sources of changes in subjective class perceptions and the processes that link these perceptions to support for a particular political party.

Surveys of Australian political attitudes have only rarely asked respondents to identify their own social class, and such national data as exist relate only to the period since 1961. There is therefore no direct means of establishing changes in the distribution of subjective class perceptions over a substantial period of time. An alternative approach may be made to the problem, however, by questions in the 1967 survey designed to tap both the respondent's own sense of class and his assessment of his parents' social class. By comparing responses to these two questions, it is possible to examine how far respondents had a sense of upward social mobility across generations. The pattern of responses leaves little doubt that the 1967 sample had a clear sense of upward social mobility. Whereas 60% of respondents (N = 2,054) identified their parents as working class, only 42% identified themselves as working class (Aitkin and Kahan, 1967). Many respondents who saw themselves as coming from working-class families now viewed themselves as middle class, and this self-perception is, as we have seen, related to the tendency of blue-collar workers to support the more conservative political parties.

Without attempting to examine the content and meaning of subjective class assessments, the above analysis leads to the conclusion that there has, at this level of conscious perception, been a "middle classing" of the population in Australia. Although the changes in metropolitan residential patterns may have played a role in this, it is scarcely possible to assert, in view of Table 3 that this process can account for the change. There is, however, evidence that the pattern of suburban development has played some role in the change. Table 4 shows that a subjective sense of upward mobility among blue-collar voters may be more prevalent in the outer suburban than in the old inner city areas. Even more striking is the

Table 4. SUBJECTIVE SOCIAL MOBILITY AMONG BLUE-COLLAR VOTERS BY RESIDENTIAL CONTEXT

	Residential Context	
	Inner Suburban	Outer Suburban
Middle class in both generations	16	20
Upwardly mobile	14	24
Working class in both generations	59	50
Downwardly mobile	11	6
Total	100	100
N =	92	265
$X^2 = 6.61$	df. 3	p < .05

comparison in the distribution of class perceptions among "objectively" white-collar voters between suburban areas (Table 5). White-collar residents in the new suburbs are much more likely than those in inner suburbs to see themselves as either having been middle class over two generations, or having moved into the middle class from working-class parents. The tables do not establish, of course, that the suburban environment has caused, or even encouraged this sense of rising social status. It is a prevalent phenomenon regardless of context. Nevertheless, although many of the outer suburban areas in "objective" terms are predominantly peopled by voters from blue-collar households, only a minority in these areas think of themselves as working class.

Insofar as the theory of homogeneity effects accounts for voting behavior, the new suburbs may well provide a potent environment for depressing the Labor vote among the blue-collar voters, despite their "objectively" working-class character. Table 6 provides some evidence for the existence of such an "outer suburban effect" even

Table 5. SUBJECTIVE SOCIAL MOBILITY AMONG WHITE-COLLAR VOTERS BY RESIDENTIAL CONTEXT

	Residential Context	
	Inner Suburban	Outer Suburban
Middle class in both generations	29	45
Upwardly mobile	19	34
Working class in both generations	38	19
Downwardly mobile	14	2
Total	100	100
N =	48	201
$X^2 = 22.8$	df. 3	p < .001

Table 6. PARTY SUPPORT OF BLUE-COLLAR VOTERS FROM TWO-GENERATION WORKING-CLASS FAMILIES, BY RESIDENTIAL CONTEXT

	Residential Context	
	Inner Suburban	*Outer Suburban*
Liberal	13	30
Labor	72	59
D.L.P.	4	4
Other	11	7
Total	100	100
N =	54	133

$$X^2 = 5.51 \quad df. 1 \quad p < .02$$

(calculated for Liberal and Labor categories only)

among blue-collar voters who, in their own eyes, are two-generation working class. The evidence so far cited leaves open the nature of the process producing this effect; the theory of homogeneity effects may provide the answer, but it is possible that some other process is at work. Whatever the explanation, the effect itself is unmistakable, and it lends support to the notion that changes in the structure of residential contexts within the metropolitan areas may well have been an element in the political *embourgoisement* of the blue-collar voters in Australia. It remains to be investigated how "deep" the transformation of the blue-collar voter has been in terms of life-style and sociopolitical attitudes. But at the level of the voter's own sense of social position, the *embourgeoisement* of a significant portion of the Australian working class is established.

The phenomenon of working-class upward mobility, plausibly seen as at least partially resulting from structural changes in urban contexts, has presented a challenge to the Australian Labor Party. Not merely has this transformation required new kinds of electoral appeals, but in the longer term it may seem to present a challenge to the very structure of the party itself. The Australian Labor Party remains one of the five major Labor parties in the world (Labor parties being distinguished from Social Democratic parties by the direct affiliation of trade unions) (Rawson, 1969: 313). The great power that this form of organization confers on bureaucratic trade-union elites in the internal management of the party would seem to be at odds with the desire of influential sections of the party to provide an adequate representation for the blue-collar "middle class." In 1972 the party returned to government after twenty years in opposition led by the most middle class leader in its history on its most middle-class platform. The constituencies that provided its majority were the outer suburban seats around the cities of Sydney and Melbourne. The debate within the party which preceded this appeal was prolonged and bitter and has not been terminated by the return of the party to power (Overacker, 1968: 44-138; Oakes and Solomon, 1973; Oakes, 1973).

VI. UPPER-MIDDLE-CLASS TRENDS AND THE KNOWLEDGEABLE SOCIETY

So far the evidence indicates that there was a long-term decline in Labor Party support among blue-collar voters from 1946 to 1972 and that this accompanied a subjective *embourgoisement* of the working-class electorate, which demonstrably increased the tendency for blue-collar voters to support the more conservative political parties. It also established that the Labor Party made substantial gains among upper- (but not lower-) middle-class voters over the same period. The most marked increase in support occurred among voters in professional occupations. In this section of the paper evidence will be examined bearing on the thesis that this movement of support reflects a growing disaffection of the most highly educated "technocrats" from the established social and political order. Once again it is obviously not possible in this paper to complete all the links of the causal chain necessary to establish such a theory. Rather the inquiry will be whether the available evidence is consistent with the theory, or tends to disconfirm it.

Surveys of political attitudes in Australia in recent years have produced a growing amount of evidence that the most highly educated voters are, as a category, the most skeptical of existing governmental, economic, and social institutions and most receptive to changes in normative codes. It is our intention to review this evidence more fully elsewhere; however, one finding may conveniently be cited here in support of this proposition. In February 1974 a national survey of political attitudes conducted by the Australian Sales Research Bureau in conjunction with the Melbourne University Department of Political Science asked respondents how much faith they had in various institutions, including governments, legal justice, and the church. In each case those respondents with university education were least likely to have faith in the institution. Table 7 reports the mean response for each category of respondent by

Table 7. FAITH IN INSTITUTIONS BY EDUCATION*

			Level of Education			
	University	Other Tertiary	Trade Qualifi- cations	Complete Secondary	Some Secondary	Primary
Governments	2.42	2.28	2.33	2.36	2.35	2.37
Legal justice	2.04	1.87	1.95	1.89	1.91	1.96
The church	2.51	2.18	2.22	2.04	1.95	1.90
N =	168	188	220	471	590	350

*Respondents were asked how much faith they had in the institutions listed. Responses were scored on a four-point scale, with 4 equal to no faith at all, and 1, a great deal of faith. High means indicates a relatively low level of faith.

SOURCE: A.S.R.B. Survey 12, February 1974.

education. In the case of governments and legal justice, it may be noted that the second most skeptical category consisted of those with primary education. Are these perhaps closest to being the "marginals" of Apter's (1971: 78-79) theory? In these two cases again the category with most faith were those with "other tertiary" education. Since the mid-1960s substantial resources have been devoted to the development of Colleges of Advanced Education to provide alternative tertiary degrees to the universities. It is possible (though this remains to be established) that students in these institutions (and the other nondegree tertiary training colleges which preceded them) have been disproportionately drawn from the upwardly mobile working class, that section of the society making self-conscious inroads into the middle class and perhaps most instrumentally satisfied with the existing order.

Other surveys have shown that a majority of those with tertiary education are likely to believe that the Crown is "not very important" for Australia (1967 Australian National University survey data); that the university educated are the category most likely to believe that "big business" has too much power in Australia (A.S.R.B., 1971), and the category most likely to believe that young men were entitled to refuse to register for service in the war in Vietnam, contrary to the law (a relationship which held across all age groups except those over sixty years of age) (A.S.R.B., 1972). Such references can do no more here than raise the possibility of some level of disaffection among the most highly educated voters.

If some characteristic of university education (or some associated factor) has the effect of increasing discontent with the existing organization of society, the question arises whether this effect is one observable only toward the end of the period under consideration, or whether there is evidence of its impact at an earlier time. Unfortunately education has not provided a common classification for respondents in opinion surveys in Australia, and so there are very few data available with which to answer this question. However respondents were classified by education in a Gallup survey of 1961, and Table 8 presents the results of an analysis of the relation between education and party support in that year, broken down by nonfarm occupational class. The table reveals an intriguing pattern. Within the nonmanual stratum, respondents with tertiary education are somewhat less likely to support the Liberal and Country Party government than are respondents with secondary education only. By contrast, within the manual stratum, the probability of supporting the Liberal and Country Party government increases consistently with education. Interpreting this finding as supporting the hypothesis of the effects of higher education requires us to regard a vote for the Australian Labor Party as in some sense a "protest" vote against the existing order. If we are prepared to make this assumption, then Table 8 supports the view that higher education among blue-collar workers increases support for the status quo, whereas among white-collar voters it may be more likely to increase discontent. The effect appears the more marked if the comparison is made, not between those nonmanuals with secondary and those with tertiary education, but across classes. Whereas at primary and secondary levels of education the likelihood of supporting the L.C.P. government *doubles* between occupational classes, only a relatively small increase in L.C.P. support occurs at the tertiary level of education.

Despite the possible effect of some factor associated with university education in reducing support for the more conservative parties among white-collar nonfarm voters (a finding supported by the 1967 A.N.U. study), in 1961 the Liberal and Country Party

Table 8. PARTY SUPPORT BY EDUCATIONAL LEVEL BY OCCUPATIONAL CLASS

	Manual			Nonmanual		
	Primary	*Secondary*	*Tertiary*	*Primary*	*Secondary*	*Tertiary*
L.C.P.	21.8	30.6	52.4	42.3	64.0	59.2
A.L.P.	73.9	64.0	38.1	53.8	29.6	35.0
D.L.P.	4.2	5.4	9.5	3.8	6.4	5.8
Total	99.9	100.0	100.0	99.9	100.0	100.0
N =	380	578	21	130	622	120

SOURCE: Gallup Survey 154, December 1961.

government was still receiving majority support from those with tertiary education in nonfarm occupations. During the next thirteen years, this situation was dramatically altered. The rapid slide away from the conservative parties among the upper-middle class becomes a substantial alienation when the university educated are considered. A national survey in February 1974 showed that, not merely was this category now offering more support to the Labor Party than to the L.C.P., but what is even more significant, it may have been less favorable to the L.C.P. than the lower stratum of blue-collar workers, as seen in Table 9. To an astonishing degree the symptoms of disaffection evident in the surveys of political attitudes have been paralleled by a substantial alienation among this category from the more conservative political parties. By 1974 the university educated had become as little inclined to support the parties most identified with the established order as voters at the bottom of the occupational class structure.

The comparison between the university educated and the lower-blue-collar voters in Table 9 nevertheless reveals a key difference. The voters with university education are much more inclined to support minor parties than are the lower-blue-collar voters. And in early 1974 the minor party that had most significantly attracted their attention was the Australia Party. From being yet one more minor party the Australia Party may have a significance as yet unsuspected by most observers of Australian parties. It may be bidding to become the party of the most disaffected portions of the technocratic elite. This view is supported both by its unusual pattern of electoral support, and by the nature of its membership and their perceptions of politics. As such, it may be both the symptom and the beneficiary of a momentous sociopolitical change.

Table 9. COMPARISON OF DIVISION OF PARTY SUPPORT, UNIVERSITY EDUCATED AND LOWER-BLUE-COLLAR VOTERS, 1974

	University Educated	*Lower-Blue-Collar*
Liberal	31.6	32.0
Country	3.8	4.3
A.L.P.	40.3	54.6
D.L.P.	1.6	0.9
Australia	15.7	1.0
Other	1.3	0.3
Not established	5.7	7.0
Total	100.0	100.1
N =	159	238

SOURCE: A.S.R.B. Survey 12, February 1974.

VII. THE AUSTRALIA PARTY

The Australia Party traces its origins back to 1966, to a protest against the war in Vietnam. On October 22, 1966, one Gordon Barton, a Sydney businessman, placed an advertisement in the *Sydney Morning Herald* in the form of "An Open Letter to the President of United States of America." Barton's letter challenged the representativeness of the Australian government's policy on the war. It drew an immediate response from several hundred people, and in early November 1966 a group known as the Liberal Reform Group was formed to contest the forthcoming federal election. It stood candidates in 12 New South Wales seats and 19 Victorian seats. It purported to differ from the Liberal Party solely in its policy on Vietnam. Despite a very brief campaign, the L.R.G. averaged 4.5% in the seats it contested in N.S.W. and gained 6% in three of these. Its performance in Victoria was comparable. Apparently encouraged by this performance, the group decided to stay in existence after the election and broaden its objectives.

Liberal Reform intends to stay in existence as a permanent political organization. It intends to stand for liberal humanitarian, and anti-authoritarian principles, in society and government. [Barton, 1967]

Changing its name to the Australian Reform Movement, the organization stood candidates in the 1967 Senate election in New South Wales and Victoria, but polled only 2.3% of the vote in N.S.W. and 0.7% in Victoria (Weaver, 1973: 9). The basis of its support at this time is not clear, but a comment of Barton's following this election suggested that at that time it was capitalizing on disaffection from the government over Vietnam, especially among the university educated:

At present we have the support of many people in the Universities, but we have a long way to go to get our message through to farmers and factory workers. [*The Australian,* Nov. 27, 1967]

There was little evidence of much activity from the A.R.M. in the eighteen months following the Senate election, but in July 1969 it emerged as a new organization, the Australia Party, with a previously independent Senator (Senator Turnbull) as its national convenor. It has been suggested that at this point many of the original members of the L.R.G. dropped out, believing the movement had become "tarnished" by political maneuvering (Weaver, 1973: 8). At the same time it was joined by a number of members of a defunct organization called the Australian Party which had also been formed in 1966 as an expression of discontent with the lack of a satisfactory alternative among the major parties. For the 1969 House of Representatives election, the Australia Party established an organization in all states, endorsed candidates in 37 constituencies, and published a national platform with a comprehensive set of policies (McPherson and Whitington, 1973: 89). Its policies emphasized an independent foreign policy (including withdrawal from the A.N.Z.U.S. pact with the United States), economic growth, increased educational expend- iture, legalization of abortion and homosexuality, removal of restrictions on public comment by public servants, and encourage- ment of worker involvement in industry. Its internal organization stressed lack of hierachy (Blackshield, 1972). The party won less than 1% of the total national vote, but polled markedly better in some seats. In the middle-class seats of Berowra and Bennelong in Sydney, it gained over 5% of the vote. From that time its fortunes improved. In a by-election in the heavily white-collar Australian Capital Territory in 1970, the Australia Party candidate polled 17.5% of the vote. In the New South Wales state elections in February 1971, the Australia Party averaged 8.04% of the vote in the 14 seats it contested (Weaver, 1973: 12).

The Australia Party's membership continued to increase and by the time of the 1972 House of Representatives election was approximately 3,000, nationwide. It contested 58 seats in all states on a revised platform which pushed foreign policy and defense into the background and emphasized health, education, conservation and the environment, and social welfare. It won only 2.42% of the national vote, but polled 11.02% in the A.C.T. and over 6% in about 10 seats (Weaver, 1973: 14-15).

Despite the Australia Party's objective of becoming a nonsectional party, *its support in the electorate as a whole has been strongly weighted toward those with higher education.* Table 10 shows this clearly. It presents data for Australia Party support aggregated from 10 surveys for the years 1971-1974. Such an aggregated analysis is necessary because of the small number of Australia Party voters picked up in any one survey. The table shows that in each of the three periods analyzed the largest single block of support for the Australia Party came from those with university education, and that approximately 50% of the Australia Party's support came from

Table 10. AUSTRALIA PARTY SUPPORT BY EDUCATION

	1971	*1972*	*1973-1974*
University	30.6	27.0	32.6
Other tertiary	24.5	16.3	18.2
Trade qualifications	14.3	9.2	8.8
Complete secondary	14.3	24.1	21.0
Some secondary/primary	16.3	23.4	19.3
Total	100.0	100.0	99.9
N =	49	141	181

SOURCE: A.S.R.B. Surveys March, August, November 1971 (Sydney, Melbourne samples); March, June (Sydney, Melbourne samples); October, November (marginal electorates sample) 1972; May, September (national samples) 1973; February 1974 (national sample).

voters with tertiary education, although only 7.2% of the population over 15 had tertiary qualifications in 1971.

What was true of the Australia Party's electoral support was even more true of its membership. Two studies based on samples of the Australia Party's membership confirm the extent to which the party has recruited from "the middle-income, tertiary-educated, 'egghead,' and professional class; it is not a party of upper-income business entrepreneurs" (Blackshield, 1972: 41; Stephens, 1971; Weaver, 1973). Table 11 based on data collected by Stephens, shows a weighting in the occupational structure of the membership toward the educational and research institutions, despite the tiny fraction of

Table 11. OCCUPATIONS OF AUSTRALIA PARTY MEMBERS, 1971

	Percent
School and university teachers Scientists, engineers, architects Library, research, and technical	33.3
Accountants, etc. Doctors, lawyers Clergy, social work, welfare, nursing	14.4
Executive and managerial staff Media, advertising, public realms	9.9
Sales and clerical Skilled and unskilled workers Primary producers	14.4
Housewives Students Pensioners, retired	27.9
N =	112

SOURCE: Blackshield (1972).

Table 12. EDUCATION OF AUSTRALIA PARTY MEMBERS, 1973

	Percent
Postgraduate qualifications	7.2
University	31.9
Other tertiary	17.4
Trade qualifications	5.8
Completed secondary	23.2
Some secondary	8.7
Primary	1.4
Not established	4.3
Total	99.9
N =	69

the total electorate which these voters comprise. Table 12, based on a small random sample of the Victorian membership in 1973, shows that over 50% of the membership had some tertiary education. Far from being a nonsectional party, the Australia Party was probably the most highly selective in its appeal of all the political parties. Indeed, Stephen's sample included no business owners, whether large or small (Weaver, 1973).

Not merely is the party's membership weighted toward the technocracy, but it is also markedly less religious than the general population. Among members who claim a religious denomination, the party is heavily Protestant. Catholics, who comprised 27% of the population at the 1971 census, made up only 7% of the party's membership in 1973. Nonbelief is widespread among party members. Whereas surveys suggest that approximately 7% of the adult population are atheists, agnostics, or have no religion, 39% of the Australia Party sample fell into this category (Weaver, 1973: App. II, 12).

The claim that the Australia Party represents a disaffected portion of the "knowledge elite" requires not merely evidence as to its bases of support. The demonstration also requires evidence that the potential crisis of authority noted above has some meaning in the Australia Party context. Two pieces of evidence in particular offer support to this view. One is the Australia Party's internal structure, and in particular its emphasis on participatory democracy. This emphasis finds expression in a number of features of the party's constitution. The chief executive officer of the party is described as a "convenor" rather than president or chairman, to symbolize his role of assisting the membership to make its own decisions rather than acting on its behalf (Australia Party [Vic.], Constitution, Rules Sec.

2[i]). The executive's functions are specified as "routine organization and administration" and the right to make "necessary emergency decisions." Any matter may be put to the membership for decision by ballot either at the instigation of the executive, a general meeting, or of 2% of the membership, or 20 members, whichever is the greater, petitioning the executive in writing. The party rejects hierarchical principles of organization which it believes characterize other political parties and other institutions. It carries its emphasis on participatory democracy over into a belief in a reorganization of industry along participatory lines.

Further evidence of the party's role in bringing together disaffected member's of the technocracy was provided by Weaver's study. Weaver asked her sample the following question:

> Some people say that modern industrial society has run into a dead end in its development, and that there are going to have to be some rather revolutionary changes before things get better. Do you agree with this?

Agreement with this sentiment was expressed by 53.6% of the respondents, and a further 11.6% said they did not agree but did feel that a change of emphasis in the society was needed (Weaver, 1973: App. II, 7). The significance of the finding is highlighted by the fact that five of Weaver's respondents were "horrified at even the use of the word 'revolutionary' in relation to themselves and did not answer for this reason." Over half the respondents were not only not "horrified" but quite willing to accept the term.

It would perhaps be easy to see the Australia Party, in light of its origins, as bringing together simply those who had become disaffected with the political system over the Vietnam War. Whether or not the Vietnam War provided a catalyst for a crisis of authority among some members of the technocratic elite, Weaver's evidence does not support the view that the party is merely a symptom of Vietnam and its effects. Over 80% of Weaver's sample had joined since 1971, by which time Vietnam had begun to decline as a political issue, and over 72% had joined in 1972 and 1973 (Weaver, 1973: 7). Indeed, there is some evidence of a change in the membership of the party around 1971-1972 and an increasingly radical stance in some of its policies (Minogue, 1972); however, this change appears to have been in personnel rather than in the bases of the party's support. When asked why they joined the party, only three members of Weaver's sample mentioned Vietnam.

The response of the party's members to the question above suggests a high level of disaffection with the existing social order, and in this it presents us with a paradox concerning the nature of the Australia Party. If a very large body of members are indeed as disaffected as this response indicates, is there any felt sense of discomfort in working through a political party—surely a very "traditional" type of institution—whose use perhaps indicates some acceptance of the existing political order? There *is* some evidence that members do perceive this paradox, and attempt to resolve it in one of several ways. One technique used to justify the Australia Party is to stress the extent to which its organization differentiates it from the other political parties. A second technique is to emphasize the "amateurism" of the party, compared to the compromising professionalism of the other parties. One leaflet, for example, described the party as "THE NON-POLITICAL PARTY . . . made up of . . . people sick of party politics" (Blackshield, 1972: 47). A third, though related technique, is to see the party's objective as differing from those of the other political parties. Weaver asked her sample to choose between several statements describing a possible role for the Australia Party in Australia. Only 27.4% saw the Australia Party's aim as eventually to govern in its own right. The largest single category (34.8%) saw its main purpose as demonstrating a new kind of politics. That is, for many of its members the party is expressive rather than instrumental, a protest rather than an immediate claim to power (Weaver, 1973: App. II, 9).

Not merely is there an ambivalence within the Australia Party concerning its role in the Australian political system, but there is also some evidence of ambivalence in its attitude toward the desirable organization of institutional authority. One of the problems for an organization seeking broad participation of members is to define a role for leadership. This problem has constantly plagued the Australian Labor Party, influenced as it is by notions of "solidarity" and "mass control" current in the labor movement. It is also a problem in the Australia Party and one over which its members are divided. When asked whether the leadership of the party should be strengthened to take more of the decisions as membership grows, almost half the membership said that it should, a fifth said it should not, and a further fifth claimed that this did not make sense given the structure of the party. A quarter of the sample of members believed that the role of one individual, Gordon Barton, was very important or essential to the continued success of the party, and a fifth pictured the most desirable qualities of a politician as ambition, ruthlessness, or strength. These responses suggest an uneasy diversity in orientations toward leadership within the party which may well lead to internal conflict at a later stage.

Although there are elements of New Left ideas in the Australia Party it would not be regarded either by its members, by the public, or by self-conscious members of the New Left as being a new-left party. While its members may be prepared in private to commit themselves to the view that some "rather revolutionary changes" are needed in society, the party's public stance has been less than revolutionary. Its Victorian constitution, for example, commits it to "lawful activity," and its policies have implied the desirability of peaceful reform. Perhaps it is this characteristic that has enabled it to make a broader public appeal than new-left movements elsewhere. Nevertheless, both its membership and its electoral support reflect a narrow base of support, not one that would ever support a mass political movement. The hope of Barton, expressed in 1967, that the party might find support among farmers and workers has remained a hope without any degree of realization in practice. In its failure to expand its base of support, the party expresses the frustration of the disaffected technocracy: the existing parties must make too broad an appeal and are too diverse to adequately express its discontents; a party that can provide a voice for this disaffection is too small to win power.

VIII. FINDINGS

The main findings of the research reported here may be summarized as follows:

(1) There has been a marked weakening in the class bases of support of the major parties in Australia from 1946 through 1972.

(2) This decline is proximately caused by (a) a steady drift away from the Labor Party among blue-collar voters and (b) a movement away from the Liberal and Country Parties among upper white-collar voters. These findings are consistent with both the thesis of the *embourgeoisement* of the working class and the radicalization of the technocracy. They may, however, have other explanations.

(3) The new suburban contexts do appear to be associated with a conservative political effect, but this is despite—rather than because

of—their "objective" class compositions, and it is not clearly an effect that has worked through changing voters' perceptions of their social class.

(4) There is evidence of dissatisfaction with the established parties among a portion of the technocratic elite, especially since 1966-1967, and of a searching among this group for a new political expression. At present the Australia Party appears to provide an organized party expression of this discontent, drawing both its electoral support and its members disproportionately from this section. This is fully consistent with theories postulating a radicalization of the technocrats, and this is supported by an analysis of the political attitudes of this section. The processes behind this radicalization remain to be studied, and until this is done it is impossible to predict how far this radicalization may extend through the technocratic elite. The experience of the Australia Party offers no support to the view that radical worker-technocracy electoral alliances are possible.

IX. CONCLUSIONS

Firm conclusions about the effects of social change on mass electoral behavior, and hence on the fates of political parties, suffer a methodological difficulty: the perceived behavior of the party elites in a reasonable model of the process is without a satisfactory measure. The response of the elite to social change must be at least as crucial as the social change itself; yet there is, as yet, no convenient measure of elite responses. A detailed examination of the content of speeches by party leaders over time, and perceptions of these (and the actions out of which they arise) would help bridge the yawning theoretical-empirical chasm. So far impressions and the subjective reports of observers must suffice.

The drift of working-class support from the Labor Party occurred during a period of intense factionalism within the Labor movement, during which the party leaders did not hesitate to make appeals to traditional working-class loyalties. In fact, the principal debate within the party over election strategy during the 1960s can be readily represented as a debate over the necessity for new appeals to meet the results of social change, though the precise nature of this change remained ill-defined and controversial (Overacker, 1968). A situation in which Labor Party elites refuse to alter their electoral appeals and in which the party suffers a steady drift of support from its traditional electoral base is fully consistent with the *embour-*

geoisement thesis. So is the recovery of some support among this base after 1967 with a change in the party leadership and the adoption of a more "middle class" electoral appeal. What is presently lacking is an adequate theoretical account of the nature of this change and the processes behind it backed by the results of empirical research. As we have seen, the simple explanation of the blue-collar drift away from Labor through the "middle classing" effects of the new suburbs is only partly supported by the data available, and if it is to be sustained, requires further elaboration of the elements involved in the process and of the nature of the "middle classing" supposed to be taking place.

Equally striking has been the long-term drift away from the major conservative political parties among the upper middle class and particularly the university educated. Over most of the period studied this drift can hardly be attributed to the appeal of the A.L.P. as an alternative repository of middle-class support, in light of the above argument concerning movements in blue-collar support. It is more plausible to interpret it as sign of growing discontent with the conservative political parties and the very recent data on the distribution of party support among the university educated suggests that this discontent has developed into substantial alienation. The process of blue-collar change and elite response outlined above suggests, however, that to the extent that the Labor Party elite strives to present an acceptable "middle class" alternative to the Liberal and Country Parties, it may attract back the "middle class" workers, but prove unacceptable to the technocracy. Such a context would probably lead us to predict exactly what seems to have happened: a search by the most disaffected among the "knowledge elite" for a new political expression outside the existing major parties.

So clearly do Australian trends seem to support the theories of sociopolitical change in advanced industrial societies based on observations in other countries, and outlined at the start of this paper, that a word of caution is perhaps in order. So far there has been no research into attitudes toward the Labor Party among the disaffected tertiary educated. We do not know whether it is the "middle classness" of the new Labor Party which reduces its support among this section of the electorate, or whether it is the remnants of old "left" factions in the trade unions, or both. Nor is the depth and meaning of the disaffection among this section well explored. As in the case of the link between social change and blue-collar Labor

Party support, there are key links in the causal chain which have not yet been subjected to close examination. Despite these qualifications, however, the general pattern of movements in electoral support is so plausibly an expression of countermovements of blue-collar *embourgeoisement* and upper white-collar radicalization that Australia has claims to be seen as offering the strongest support to these theories. In the "pure" case they may well be valid.

NOTE

1. In this, and the equations which follow, the standard error of the B coefficient is placed in parentheses beneath the coefficient.

REFERENCES

AITKIN, D. (1973) "Electoral behaviour," pp. 301-314 in H. Mayer and H. Nelson (eds.) Australian Politics: A Third Reader. Melbourne: Cheshire.

––– and M. KAHAN (1973) "Australia," in R. Rose (ed.) Electoral Behavior: A Comparative Handbook. New York: Free Press.

––– (1967) Australian Survey Project, Wave 1, September October 1967, Codebook.

ALKER, H. (1965) Mathematics and Politics. New York: Macmillan.

ALFORD, R. R. (1967) Class Voting in the Anglo-American Political Systems and Voter Alignments. New York: Free Press.

––– (1963) Party and Society. Chicago: Rand McNally.

APTER, D. (1971) Choice and the Politics of Allocation. New Haven: Yale University Press.

Australia Party, Victorian Branch, Constitution, Rules Sec. 2(i).

Australian Sales Research Bureau 1971-1974, Survey Tabulations.

Australian Universities Commission Report (1972).

BARTON, G. (1967) "Liberal reform: what is its future?" Comment (Sydney) 1, 6 (March): 13-14.

BELL, D. (1970) "The cultural contradictions of capitalism." The Public Interest 21 (Fall): 16-43.

BLACKSHIELD, T. (1972) "The Australia Party." Current Affairs Bulletin (Sydney, July).

BROOM, L., F. L. JONES, and J. ZUBRZYCKI (1968) "Social stratification in Australia," in J. A. Jackson (ed.) Social Stratification. Cambridge: Cambridge University Press.

BRYCE, J. (1921) Modern Democracies. Vol. II. London: Macmillan.

BUTLER, D. and D. STOKES (1969) Political Change in Britain: Forces Shaping Electoral Choice. New York: St. Martin's Press.

CAMPBELL, A., P. E. CONVERSE, W. E. MILLER, and D. E. STOKES (1960) The American Voter. New York: Wiley.

CAMPBELL, E. Q. and C. N. ALEXANDER (1965) "Structural effects and interpersonal relationships." American Journal of Sociology 71: 284-289.

Census (1971) Bureau of Census and Statistics, 1971 Census of Population and Housing, Bulletin 1, Part 9, Table 8.

CRAWFORD, R. M. (1955) "The Australian national character: myth and reality." Journal of World History 2: 704-727.

CRISP, L. F. (1971) Australian National Government. Melbourne: Longmans.

DAHRENDORF, R. (1959) Class and Class Conflict in Industrial Society. Stanford: Stanford University Press.

DAVIES, A. F. (1958) Australian Democracy. Melbourne: Longmans.

DAVIS, K. (1969) World Urbanisation 1959-1970. Vol. 1: Basic Data for Cities, Countries and Regions. Population Monograph Series No. 4, Berkeley Institute of International Studies.

ENCEL, S. (1970) Equality and Authority. Melbourne: Cheshire.

FORD, G. W. (1970) "Work," pp. 84-145 in A. F. Davies and S. Encel (eds.) Australian Society, A Sociological Introduction. Melbourne: Cheshire.

FORSTER, J. (1967) "The Australasian character." Annals of the American Academy of Political and Social Sciences (March): 156-163.

Gallup Survey, Australian Public Opinion Polls, (Morgan) Gallup.

GOLDTHORPE, J. H., D. LOCKWOOD, F. BECHHOFER, and J. PLATT (1969) The Affluent Worker in the Class Structure. Cambridge: Cambridge University Press.

HAMILTON, R. F. (1967) Affluence and the French Worker in the Fourth Republic. Princeton: Princeton University Press.

KRISTOL, I. (1972) "About equality," Quadrant (December): 75.

LARSON, O. F. (1968) "Rural society," in D. Sills (ed.) The International Encyclopaedia of the Social Sciences. New York: Free Press.

LENSKI, G. E. (1966) Power and Privilege: A Theory of Social Stratification. New York: McGraw Hill.

——— (1963) The Religious Factor: A Sociological Study of Religious Impact on Politics, Economics and Family Life. New York: Doubleday.

LIPSET, S. M. (1972) "Ideology and no end." Encounter (December): 17-22.

——— (1967) The First New Nation. New York: Doubleday.

——— (1964) "The changing class structure of contemporary European politics." Daedalus 63, 1.

———, P. F. LAZARSFELD, A. H. BARTON, and J. J. LINZ (1954) The psychology of voting," in G. Lindzey (ed.) The Handbook of Social Psychology, Vol. 2. Reading, Mass.: Addison-Wesley.

MALLET, S. (1963) La Nouvelle Classe Ouvriere. Paris.

MARCUSE, H. (1964) One Dimensional Man. Boston: Beacon Press.

MAYER, K. (1963) "The changing shape of the American class structure." Social Research 30.

MINOGUE, D. (1972) "The Peter Pan of politics." The Australian, Wednesday, April 19.

MOL, H. (1971) Religion in Australia. Melbourne: Nelson.

McGUIRE, W. J. (1968) "The nature of attitudes and attitude change," in pp. 187-191 in G. Lindzey and L. Aronson (eds.) The Handbook of Social Psychology, vol. 3. Reading, Mass.: Addison-Wesley.

McPHERSON, F. and R. WHITINGTON (1973) "The Australia Party's campaign," pp. 88-96 in H. Mayer (ed.) Labor to Power. Sydney: Angus and Robertson.

OAKES, L. (1973) Whitlam PM: A Biography. Sydney: Angus and Robertson.

——— and D. SOLOMON (1973) The Making of an Australian Prime Minister. Melbourne: Cheshire.

OVERACKER, L. (1968) Australian Parties in a Changing Society: 1945-1967. Melbourne: Cheshire.

PUTNAM, R. D. (1966) "Political attitudes and the local community." American Political Science Review 60: 640-654.

RAWSON, D. W. (1969) "The life span of Labor parties." Political Studies (September): 313-333.

SEGAL, D. R. and M. W. MEYER (1969) "The social context of political partisanship," pp. 217-232 in M. Dogan and S. Rokkan (eds.) Quantitative Ecological Analysis in the Social Sciences. Cambridge: MIT Press.

STEPHENS, D. (1971) "The Australia Party in Australian politics." B.A. (honors) thesis. Monash University.

STINCHCOMBE, A. L. (1965) "Organised dependency relations and social stratification," in J. March (ed.) Handbook of Organizations. Chicago: Rand McNally.

TAVISS, I. (1969) "Change in the form of alienation: the 1900's vs. the 1950's." American Sociological Review 34.

TAYLOR, C. K. and M. C. HUDSON (1972) World Handbook of Political and Social Indicators. 2nd ed. New Haven: Yale University Press.

TOURAINE, A. (1971) The May Movement. Translated by Leonard Mayhew. New York: Random House.

WATSON, L. (1973) "The party machines," pp. 339-365 in H. Mayer and H. Nelson (eds.) Australian Politics: A Third Reader. Melbourne: Cheshire.

WEBER, M. (1968) Economy and Society: An Outline of Interpretative Sociology. Edited by G. Roth and C. Wittich. New York: Bedminster.

WEAVER, E. (1973) "The study of various personality styles of members of the Australia Party, and the influence they have on the party's character." B.A. (honors) thesis. University of Melbourne.

Chapter 5

CONSERVATIVE SUCCESS IN LIBERAL NEW YORK: SOME DETERMINANTS OF CONSERVATIVE PARTY SUPPORT

JOHN J. GARGAN

I. MINOR PARTIES AND AMERICAN POLITICS

Throughout American history the emergence of national or state-level minor party movements has been a manifestation of discontent with the existing political order on the part of a segment of the electorate. The underlying causes of these discontents have been several: economic deprivation, sectional rivalries, "periphery oriented revolts against a cosmopolitan center" (Burnham, 1970: 31). The size of the discontented segment of the electorate has also varied. On occasion it has been large enough to enable the minor party to capture state and local offices or, at the national level, to prevent major-party presidential candidates from gaining an absolute majority of the vote. In one-party states the principal competition faced by the dominant party has often been that deployed by a third party which itself, in many instances, had broken from the majority (Price, 1970: 89).

At the micro-level of analysis, a minor party candidacy may stimulate important individual decisions and responses. It is important to note that the factors eliciting these decisions or responses may take different forms for particular segments of the population. Voting for a deviant candidate, like participation in deviant social movements, is a means of satisfying a variety of social and psychological needs (Rohter, 1969: 196-199). The appeal of a George Wallace, for example, was sufficiently great to bring to the polls a number of traditional nonvoters (Lipset and Raab, 1969).

For those who are regular voters, the decision to support a minor party candidate is equally significant. As students of electoral behavior have amply demonstrated, at least in presidential elections until relatively recently, under "normal" conditions party identification, and especially the strength of that identification, determines the vote of most individuals; a minority of the electorate defects from the party line in response to the short-term influences of a particular campaign (Converse, 1966). Available evidence suggests that at subnational levels party identification and such factors as incumbency of the candidate are powerful determinants of voting. Consequently, the movement to a third or fourth party, rather than simply to the other major party, represents an important departure from normality. Insofar as the third party vote is ideological or issue oriented, as opposed to candidate oriented, another aspect of nonnormality is evidenced (Converse et al., 1969), the general tendency being for the voter to misperceive his party's position on an issue when it differs from his own. Many voters have either no strong opinion on issues or, when the issues are not of long standing but of recent origin, are unable to draw partisan implications from their opinions (Campbell et al., 1960; Converse, 1964).

Minor party movements are also significant at the macro-system level of analysis. Such movements have often preceded major adjustments in the party system (Ladd, 1970; MacRae and Meldrum, 1960) and, during periods of critical realignment, as Key (1958: 308) and others (Burnham, 1970) have pointed out, have provided a mechanism for the "reshuffling of voters between the major parties." The reshuffling thesis would seem to assume that significant numbers of discontented voters perceive the major party to which they are shifting as being somehow different in terms of issues, ideology, candidate types, or group benefits from the party they are leaving. When the major parties are not so viewed, the minor party, rather than being simply transitory, may continue in existence and play an ongoing "blackmail" role aimed at altering one or both of the major parties. In commenting upon the development of new parties, Anthony Downs (1957: 127) distinguishes between those that have as their basic goal the winning of elections and those "designed to influence already existent parties." The latter (such as the States' Rights Party of 1948, the Wallace movement, or New York State's

Liberal and Conservative parties) tend to be "future oriented, since their purpose is to alter the choices offered to voters by the extant parties at some future date" (Downs, 1957: 128, 131).

The continued existence of a future-oriented minor party greatly complicates decision making by major party leaders. In considering alternative political strategies, they must anticipate counterpolicies or reactions of not only the other major party but also of the minor party. Where the electoral system permits the minor party to regularly display its strength (on a separate ballot line, for example), the problems of the major party leaders are compounded. This is particularly true when major party divisions are close. If minor party elites can opt to endorse a major candidate or to run a candidate (and thereby sharply limit the chances of the major party closest to the minor party), their influence becomes especially great.

To students of elections and electoral behavior, then, third party candidacies and movements are important events for analysis. The kinds of questions asked and the conclusions reached are obviously related to the student's theoretical interests and the availability of appropriate data. With survey and poll materials it is possible to consider the relationship between third party support and such factors as sense of political efficacy and status anxieties, or the perceived instrumental and/or expressive motives underlying such support.

Without individual level attitudinal data, one cannot infer that votes cast for minor party candidates are in fact protest votes, manifestations of discontent, or even the votes of individuals in transition from one major party to another. The extent to which such votes actually represent a sense of frustration with the existing political order is, to some degree, situational. The Jewish garment worker in New York City who votes for a Liberal Party candidate may be simply responding to a sense of ethnic identity or following the lead of a respected union leader. Southerners voting for Wallace were doing so within a context generally supportive of the act and, therefore, behaving normally; the Northern Wallace voter lacked, in most instances, this kind of support and was casting more of a radical or protest vote (Burnham and Sprague, 1970). Therefore, when only aggregate data are available, as is generally true of pre-1930s elections and nearly all contemporary state and local elections, individual level based hypotheses cannot be tested directly. It is possible, nevertheless, with aggregate data, to identify the types of places and the characteristics of those places which correlate with minor party votes. As cases in point, the studies by Soares and Hamblin (1967) on left voting in Chile and Burnham and Sprague (1970) on Wallace voting in Pennsylvania have employed aggregate data and multiplicative models in a most sophisticated manner to demonstrate the interactions between ecological variables and voting patterns.[1]

II. THE RESEARCH SITE

This paper examines patterns of minor party voting in selected New York State elections in recent years. Through aggregate data analysis, the sources and distribution of support for the Conservative Party are considered and the ecological and political variables associated with it are described. Finally, some of the consequences of minor party voting for the state political system are suggested.

The choice of the 1960s as a time period and New York State as a research site are relevant from several perspectives. In New York, as elsewhere, the latter half of the decade was marked by widespread social and political unrest. A number of the issues that were, or were alleged to be, at large in the society were central to the state's politics during these years.[2] These would include, at least, a questioning of the capability of political systems to respond to the aspirations of social groupings, whether they be blacks seeking justice or blue-collar ethnics hoping to ward off perceived social, political, economic, and residential threats from blacks. Involved too were conflicts between central cities, their suburbs, and state government over the allocation of funds for education and other services. And the issues that defined intraparty politics at the national level—new politics versus the old, reformers versus bosses, independent candidacies versus support for party primary victors—were reflected in New York's party organizations.[3]

Also for technical reasons New York State is a relevant research site. Through time the state's election law has been sufficiently flexible to permit minor parties to gain their own separate lines on state and local ballots. From the vantage of the mass electorate, this has provided a structural mechanism for exercising a protest vote; it has also enabled minor party elites to demonstrate the extent of their electoral support even when endorsing major party candidates.

Minor parties are not recent phenomena in New York politics. During the nineteenth and twentieth centuries, voters in the state have regularly confronted ballots listing a number of candidates for important and unimportant offices. (In the 28 gubernatorial elections between 1900 and 1970, the modal number of separate candidates was six; only in the 1946 election were there two candidates.) In the more recent past, since 1962, New Yorkers have been able to vote for both left- and right-oriented minor parties of some significance. Organized earliest was the party of the left which has appeared on the ballot as either the American Labor Party (1936-1952) or the Liberal Party (1944-present).[4]

The Conservative Party which first ran statewide candidates in 1962 was founded by a small group of New York City metropolitan area Republicans disenchanted with what they claimed to be the undue liberalism of then Governor Nelson Rockefeller and U.S. Senator Jacob Javits.[5] Since 1962 the Conservatives have evidenced significant political clout, despite opposition from both Republican and Democratic party leaders.[6] From a nucleus of activists in 1962, some form of Conservative Party apparatus was created in nearly every county of the state over a relatively short period of time.[7] The party has adopted a mixed strategy in its approach to electoral politics. Conservatives have run as third or fourth party candidates for local office in a number of communities. Where Republican or Democratic candidates have been adjudged acceptable, they have received the party's endorsement. For statewide offices the Conservatives, from 1962 until 1972, put forth their own candidates, the most notable to date being U.S. Senator James Buckley. Richard Nixon, in 1972, and Malcolm Wilson, in 1974, were the first Republican presidential and gubernatorial candidates to receive official Conservative endorsement.[8]

III. CONSERVATIVE PARTY SUPPORT AND
TRADITIONAL PATTERNS OF NEW YORK STATE POLITICS

A summary of Conservative voting strength is provided in Table 1. For five elections since 1962, the table reports percentage of the total vote, mean county vote, and coefficient of variability for the statewide offices of governor, U.S. senator, attorney general, and comptroller.

Overall, Table 1 indicates a growth in the Conservative vote during the eight years. The increases are most striking, of course, in voting for the office of U.S. senator. The 38.8% of the vote received by James Buckley in 1970 brought victory to the Conservatives. But in

Table 1. BASIC STATISTICS FOR CONSERVATIVE PARTY CANDIDATES FOR
SELECTED STATEWIDE OFFICES, 1962-1970 (percentage of major party
vote, mean, and coefficient of variability)

Year	Governor	Senator	Attorney General	Comptroller
1962				
%MPV[a]	2.5	2.0	1.8	1.8
$\bar{X}$[b]	2.3	1.6	1.4	1.5
C.V.[c]	.7	.6	.6	.6
1964				
%MPV		3.0		
$\bar{X}$		1.5		
C.V.		1.0		
1966				
%MPV	8.5		5.7	5.8
$\bar{X}$	6.1		3.3	3.4
C.V.	.6		.8	.8
1968				
%MPV		17.4		
$\bar{X}$		13.3		
C.V.		.5		
1970				
%MPV	7.4	38.8	7.4	8.0
$\bar{X}$	7.7	37.7	5.6	5.7
C.V.	.4	.2	.5	.6

a. Conservative percentage of major party vote. Major party vote is defined by vote for
Republican, Democratic, Liberal, and Conservative candidates.
b. Mean Conservative percentages over 62 counties.
c. Coefficient of variability.

several respects the 1970 election was a deviant case. It was a widely
publicized contest in which an articulate Conservative, supported by
Republican Vice President Spiro Agnew, confronted a liberal
Republican (Charles Goodell) and a liberal Democrat (Richard
Ottinger).

Much more revealing with regard to the impact of the Conservative
Party on New York electoral politics are the data reported in Table 1
for the offices other than U.S. senator. In no instance have the
Conservative candidates for governor, attorney general, or comptroller been of the stature of a James Buckley nor have they received
the media attention or campaign support he received in 1970.[9]
Nonetheless, with the sole exception of the gubernatorial vote
between 1966 and 1970, the Conservative percentage of the total as
well as the mean vote has consistently increased. This would suggest
that through time there has been some expansion of the geographic
base of the party's support. The general decline in the coefficient of

variability, particularly in the cases of governor and senator, demonstrates that the voters in all types of counties are responding increasingly alike to Conservative candidates.

A basic question to be raised in analyses of any minor party relates to the nature of its constituency, from what segments of the population or regions of the system does it draw votes? On occasion, third party movements have represented bolts from one of the parties in a two party system. Conceivably, such a third party might draw all of its electoral support from the parent party and, through time, replace it as a major party. Assuming no other sources of change, in such cases the independent variables which explained the distribution of the old major party vote would be equally predictive of the new. If, on the other hand, the third party won adherents from discontented elements in both major parties and, in effect, defined a new cleavage structure in the political system, a different set of explanatory variables would be required.

The association between Conservative support in the 1960s and 1970 and traditional patterns of New York politics has been traced by relating the party's votes to two sets of variables. The first involve major party voting in recent elections; the second, a number of items defining cleavages stemming from the New Deal era.

Table 2 contains zero order correlations between county level vote for the Conservative Party in seven gubernatorial and senatorial elections, and the Republican vote for governor, senator, and president since 1950. The last row in the matrix shows correlations between Conservative support and county mean Republican gubernatorial vote, 1938-1954, a measure of the pre-Rockefeller Republican strength.

Conclusions from the figures in Table 2 are perhaps best drawn from the weakness of the correlations, rather than from their strength. The lack of strong correlations in the first three columns of the table is due, in part, to the minimal Conservative vote in 1962 and 1964. But the weakness of the correlations continues in the last four elections where there is considerably more variance to be explained. Some searching is necessary to find relationships of any magnitude; of the 147 correlations reported, only 10 exceed .50; none are as high as .80. And except for the association between 1970 Conservative Senate and 1964 Republican President, all of the correlations above .50 are on the Republican-Liberal Senate rows for 1968 and 1970.[10] Clearly, if one seeks to explain Conservative voting, he does not look to a county's past Republican record for assistance.

Table 2. MINOR-MAJOR PARTY ELECTORAL INTERCORRELATIONS:
CONSERVATIVE (1962-1970) VERSUS REPUBLICAN (1950-1972)

	Conservative						
Republican	*Gov. 1962*	*Sen. 1962*	*Sen. 1964*	*Gov. 1966*	*Sen. 1968*	*Gov. 1970*	*Sen. 1970*
Gov. 1950	.16	.08	−.28	−.06	−.07	.37	.32
Sen. 1950	.05	−.07	−.40	−.18	−.21	.34	.22
Pres. 1952	.10	.00	−.34	−.12	−.17	.33	.27
Sen. 1952	.09	−.02	−.23	−.11	−.05	.23	.26
Gov. 1954	.12	−.02	−.43	−.15	−.19	.39	.24
Pres. 1956	.12	.07	−.21	−.07	−.08	.30	.26
Sen. 1956	.09	−.02	−.36	−.15	−.17	.32	.28
Gov. 1958	.11	.02	−.34	−.09	−.15	.35	.29
Sen. 1958	.07	−.06	−.44	−.14	−.24	.38	.23
Pres. 1960	.10	.02	−.31	−.08	−.12	.35	.33
Gov. 1962	−.13	−.13	−.27	−.20	−.17	.12	.27
Sen. 1962	−.04	−.06	−.27	−.14	−.18	.15	.23
Pres. 1964	.22	.35	.23	.34	.33	.39	.67
Sen. 1964	−.03	−.11	−.37	−.14	−.23	.33	.23
Gov. 1966	−.35	−.29	−.30	−.41	−.32	−.14	.03
Pres. 1968	.07	−.03	−.30	−.13	−.14	.30	.32
Sen. 1968[a]	−.47	−.56	−.63	−.58	−.74	−.15	−.31
Gov. 1970	−.03	.05	.10	−.11	.14	−.23	.41
Sen. 1970[a]	−.38	−.57	−.73	−.62	−.75	−.19	−.67
Pres. 1972	.11	−.09	−.41	−.20	−.41	.33	.27
X 1938-1954[b]	.12	−.01	−.40	−.12	−.19	.39	.27

a. In 1968 and 1970 the Liberal Party endorsed Republican candidates for U.S. Senate.
The correlations reported for those years are based on the combined Republican-Liberal
vote.
b. Mean county Republican percentage of vote for governor, 1938-1954.

The correlations in Table 2 are, with few exceptions, weak; they
are also inconsistent in direction. Conservative voting in all elections
correlates positively only with the Goldwater 1964 vote, and
negatively only with the 1968 and 1970 Senate elections. Note that
the columns for 1966 and 1970 gubernatorial and 1968 and 1970
senatorial elections approach being mirror images of each other. Even
though these pairs of elections involved the same Conservative
candidates for the same offices, apparently different responses were
elicited from the electorate. Not only would one hesitate to predict
Conservative voting from major party voting, he might even be
cautious about doing some from Conservative returns from immediate past elections.[11]

In their study of Pennsylvania politics, Burnham and Sprague
(1970) imaginatively employed five variables to operationalize
cleavages in that state's politics dating from the 1930s:

(1) Percent county population with foreign parents, 1960.

(2) Percent county population registered Democratic, 1960.

(3) Percent population, nonwhite, 1960.

(4) Percent population high school graduate, 1960.

(5) Percent population rural farm, 1960.

For the present study these variables, updated to include 1970 census data for more recent elections,[12] were regressed on the county percentage of the vote received by Republican, Democratic, and Conservative candidates for four major offices in each statewide election since 1962. Table 3 contains the resulting squared multiple correlation coefficients.

Almost without exception, the R^2 reported for the Conservative vote is substantially less than that of either the Republican or Democratic candidates for the same office; in several instances the total variance explained by the New Deal cleavage variables for the Republican and Democrat vote exceeds the Conservative by a ratio of more than two to one. Only in the 1964 Senate race (when the party received 3% of the vote) did the Conservative R^2 reach .50. The single instance where the Conservative explained variance equaled that of one of the major parties was 1968 when the R^2 for both the Conservative and Democratic candidates was a modest .39. Even in 1970 when, at the levels of Republican elites and mass electorate, James Buckley was perceived as the real (if not official) party candidate, less than a quarter of the variance in the Conservative vote is explained by the five predictor variables; 58% of the variance in the Republican line vote for Charles Goodell, the official (if not perceived) party candidate, is so explained.

Despite the substantial demographic, social, and economic changes

Table 3. PREDICTIVE CAPABILITY OF NEW DEAL CLEAVAGE VARIABLES FOR REPUBLICAN, DEMOCRATIC, AND CONSERVATIVE LINE VOTING, 1962-1970

	R^2											
	Governor			*U.S. Senate*			*Attorney General*			*Comptroller*		
Year	Rep.	Dem.	Con.	Rep.	Dem.	Con.	Rep.	Dem.	Con.	Rep.	Dem.	Con.
1962	.66	.63	.10	.67	.58	.24	.70	.60	.15	.83	.77	.14
1964				.73	.60	.54						
1966	.40	.42	.32				.77	.57	.38	.81	.67	.42
1968				.74	.39	.39						
1970	.31	.34	.15	.58	.61	.22	.81	.58	.26	.80	.51	.36

that have occurred in New York State over the past forty years, the indicators of New Deal cleavages continue to "explain" patterns of support for Republican and Democratic candidates, other than those for governor, reasonably well.[13] Regarding Conservative candidates, however, the figures in Table 3 tend to confirm the findings drawn from Table 2. Indeed, the data in the two tables reflect slightly different ways of viewing the same reality. That is, at least across the 62 counties that define the universe of the analysis, Conservative voting in statewide elections is not congruent with the standard profile of New York politics.

IV. DEFINING A POSSIBLE NEW CLEAVAGE BASE

Attempts to define a set of variables that maximize description of the contextual base of Conservative support involve basic problems. Existing literature on recent third parties, aside from that relating to George Wallace's presidential aspirations, is not considerable. And while much work has been done on radical right wing social and political movements (Bell, 1963; Lipset and Raab, 1970), its relevance to any analysis of Conservative Party voting is not overwhelming. On any ideological continuum the Conservatives rank well to the left of such groups as the John Birch Society. Candidates supported by the party have taken positions (e.g., opposition to civilian control of city police review boards, increased welfare spending, and pornography; support for harsh penalties for drug dealers and strong military action in Vietnam) which, though conservative in comparison with the views of the major Republican or Democratic party spokesmen of recent years, are certainly well within the broad mainstream of national and New York State politics. Schoenberger found that Conservatives did not differ significantly from Republican party identifiers on measures of authoritarianism, misanthropy, support for civil liberties, or perceptions of the dangers of Communism. The Conservatives in Schoenberger's sample tended to be of relatively high social and economic status and resided in the suburbs. Conservatives did differ from Republicans, according to Schoenberger (1969: 295), in that the former were:

> bound together politically by a consistent and highly salient opposition to the modern welfare and regulatory role of the federal government,

combined with a solid hostility to the perceived power and influence of labor unions.

Allowing for the problem of fitting the Conservatives between the Democrats and Republicans on the one hand and the radical right on the other, it is possible to draw upon a number of general concepts and factors relating more specifically to New York politics that suggest several county characteristics which might better explain Conservative support than the New Deal cleavages. Four types of variables have been considered:

I. *Population concentration and change characteristics:* (a) percent population urban; (b) percent population rural farm; (c) percent increase in population (1950-1960); (d) percent increase in population (1960-1970); (e) percent population migration to county; (f) percent work force employed outside county of residence.

II. *Population social characteristics:* (a) percent population Negro; (b) percent population foreign stock; (c) percent children grades 1-12 in private schools; (d) median family income; (e) percent families with incomes less than $3,000; (f) percent families with incomes greater than $10,000; (g) percent population lower middle class [100 − (e + f)]; (h) percent work force white collar; (i) percent work force in manufacturing.

III. *Population political characteristics:* (a) percent Republican total enrollment, 1960; (b) percent Democrat total enrollment, 1960; (c) percent Republican total enrollment, 1970; (d) percent Democrat total enrollment, 1970; (e) percent Independent total enrollment, 1960; (f) percent Independent total enrollment, 1970; (g) percent increase Independent enrollment, 1960-1970.

IV. *Public sector growth characteristics:* (a) percent increase in total property taxes, 1962-1967; (b) percent increase in total property taxes, 1967-1972; (c) percent increase in total nonproperty taxes, 1962-1967; (d) percent increase in total nonproperty taxes, 1967-1972; (e) percent increase in total expenditures, 1962-1967; (f) percent increase in total expenditures, 1967-1972.

A frequently cited aggregate relationship is that between rate of population change and community support for right wing movements (Lipset and Raab, 1970; McNall, 1969; Lipset, 1963). Rate of population change is generally assumed to be an indicator of social instability or disorganization. As a community undergoes rapid growth, any of at least three effects may be produced: (a) for long-term community residents, established networks of social relationships are disrupted; (b) for newcomers, the movement into the growing community is a traumatic experience involving coping with an unfamiliar environment; (c) for both oldtimers and new-comers, the results are equally difficult given the nearly inevitable social disorganization resulting from the process of population change (Wolfinger and Greenstein, 1969: 77-78). These effects, it has been argued, lead certain personality types from the subpopulations of old or new residents, or from the entire community population, to search out the intellectual and moral certainty offered by right wing movements. In one of the few published studies on the Conservative Party, Feigert (1973) has found that social change variables are better predictors than static variables and suggests that Conservative voting is a symptom of social stress in the population.

Given the findings from other studies, one would hypothesize a positive relationship between Conservative support and indicators of population change (Ic and d). Because population growth in New York, as elsewhere, has been a suburban phenomenon, positive correlations would also be expected with the two characteristics of suburbia (Ie and f).

Because the areas of rapid growth tend also to be major centers of population concentration, another correlation may be posited. From 1962 on, Conservative leaders devoted greatest attention to recruiting party workers and candidates in New York's major metropolitan areas. If the mass electorate has responded to Conservative organizational activities, a positive relationship should exist between Conservative voting and percent population urban (Ia).

Political conflict in the 1960s centered on a number of domestic concerns which have been grouped under the general rubric, "The Social Issue" (Scammon and Wattenberg, 1970). Involved were questions of public morality, life-styles, racial confrontation and the thrust of domestic policies. Since 1962, the "Social Issue" has received considerable attention from the Conservative Party. In its policy statements and in the rhetoric of its candidates for statewide and local office, conservative positions on the general issue and its specific components have been clearly enunciated.

While relevant to much of the public, the "Social Issue" has been assumed to be more salient to certain subgroupings of the electorate.

Thus, for example, some segments of the old Roosevelt coalition were alleged to be especially susceptible to the appeals of conservatively oriented leaders. Among these segments were Catholics from particular ethnic cultures, those employed in blue-collar occupations, and those with marginally middle-class incomes. If counties with large groupings of voters with these characteristics were responding positively to Conservative blandishments, positive correlations should exist between Conservative voting and ethnicity (IIb), Catholicism (IIc), lower middle-class income (IIg), and blue-collar occupations (IIi). Similarly, because blacks and the poor were usually the implicit targets of conservative criticisms, negative correlations would be expected for variables IIa and IIe.

The tendency of the affluent and those in more prestigious occupations to be more Republican than Democrat and to be more conservative than liberal in issue orientation has been long recognized in voting research. The "Social Issue" notwithstanding, one would expect considerable support for Conservative candidates from communities with high income populations. This expectation would be particularly true if the Conservative claim—that the policies advocated by New York Republican and Democratic leaders were essentially the same—was widely shared by the mass public. Assuming this perception, positive correlations would be predicted between Conservative voting and variables IIf (percent families with incomes greater than $10,000) and IIh (percent work force white collar).

The importance of party identification as vote determinant is very much related to the strength of that identification; however, major developments of the past decade have been the amount of split-ticket voting and the growth in the number of voters designating themselves independents (DeVries and Tarrance, 1972; Burnham, 1969). If the Conservatives are in fact relating to voters for whom party labels and issues associated with those labels are increasingly irrelevant, one would expect a positive relationship between Conservative voting and measures of independence. The percentage of a county's total electorate failing to enroll with any political party (IIIe and f) has been used as such a measure. To determine whether areas growing in the number of independents were supportive of Conservatives, the percent increase in non-party identifiers (IIIg) has also been correlated with Conservative voting.

Among the defining characteristics of Schoenberger's sample of Conservatives was their opposition to governmental economic regulation and welfare programs. Few matters have been more heatedly argued in New York politics during recent years than those related to levels of state taxation and spending. Though without any apparent success, Democratic politicians have regularly criticized former Governor Rockefeller's support for new and expanded taxes, within the state legislature Rockefeller on occasion faced opposition to the size of his budget requests from elements in his own party.

Lacking survey data, it is not possible to determine how New York voters have perceived tax-spending issues. And in this study it has not been possible to disaggregate state spending or taxation to county units of analysis. However, county level data on property and nonproperty taxes (IVa, b, c, and d) and total expenditures (IVe and f) have been employed as indicators of public sector activity. Opposition to such activity, and expansion of the activities, from centers of Conservative strength should be reflected in positive correlations.

The zero order correlations between the four sets of community characteristics and Conservative voting in gubernatorial and senatorial elections are indicated in Table 4.

Even when aggregate units as large as counties are used, inferences can be made about the contextual characteristics associated with Conservative Party voting. In some instances the inferences are decidedly negative. Thus, despite the range of variables considered, for certain elections the correlations are virtually nonexistent. In the 1962 gubernatorial election (when Conservatives gained but 2.5% of the vote), not a single correlation reaches even .40; and in the 1970 gubernatorial (when they received 7.4% of the vote), the only correlation to reach .40 was percentage of families earning under $3,000 per year.

Overall, the variables that correlate with any strength and common direction are those related to urbanization, rate of population change, family income levels, and property tax increase. The specific variables that correlated with Conservative voting at .40 or greater in at least half of the elections are shown in Table 5.

Conservative candidates for governor and U.S. Senate have tended to make their best showings in counties that are urban, are experiencing population growth, have relatively affluent families, have work forces that are white collar and employed outside the county in which they live, and increased property taxes between 1962 and 1967. The candidates tended to do most poorly in counties with rural farm populations and low incomes.

Table 4. CONSERVATIVE GUBERNATORIAL AND SENATORIAL VOTING (1962-1970)
VERSUS SELECTED CHARACTERISTICS OF NEW YORK COUNTIES
(zero order correlations)

	Conservative						
Variable	Gov. 1962	Sen. 1962	Sen. 1964	Gov. 1966	Sen. 1968	Gov. 1970	Sen. 1970
I. Population Concentration and Change Characteristics							
a	.16	.29	.52	.46	.46	−.10	.07
b	−.10	.28	−.52	−.40	−.47	.12	−.18
c	.22	.41	.48	.52	.48	.30	.44
d	.20	.37	.50	.55	.56	.35	.59
e	.22	.37	.34	.52	.55	.33	.60
f	.15	.39	.65	.44	.43	.15	.27
II. Population Social Characteristics							
a	−.04	.18	.44	.30	.25	−.23	−.10
b	.04	.31	.70	.28	.32	.23	−.03
c	.02	.19	.50	.37	.31	−.09	.00
d	.27	.39	.61	.59	.54	.26	.47
e	−.29	−.47	−.56	−.47	−.42	−.40	−.48
f	.25	.51	.63	.54	.48	.28	.42
g	.00	−.19	−.29	−.53	−.47	−.23	−.38
h	.21	.42	.60	.45	.55	−.13	.24
i	.07	−.08	−.23	−.10	−.23	.28	−.08
III. Population Political Characteristics							
a	.09	−.12	−.55	−.22	−.33	.39	.09
b	−.11	.06	.49	.25	.22	−.38	−.18
c	.01	−.24	−.65	−.36	−.42	.29	.01
d	−.08	.10	.48	.33	.22	−.32	−.18
e	.02	.14	.26	.00	.28	−.10	.15
f	.08	.20	.30	.03	.30	−.06	.20
g	.03	−.04	−.14	−.07	−.15	.10	.00
IV. Public Sector Growth Characteristics							
a	.20	.51	.77	.64	.69	.12	.49
b	−.02	−.01	−.06	−.09	−.12	−.06	−.10
c	.00	−.02	−.08	.03	.02	−.03	.03
d	.01	.03	.06	.15	.04	.16	.02
e	.14	.11	.02	.17	.11	.29	.18
f	.06	.27	.61	.43	.37	−.21	.37

Relationships between variables chosen to tap the "Social Issue" publics of the 1960s and Conservative voting proved to be inconclusive. Correlations of any strength between that voting and size of Negro or ethnic stock populations were found only in the 1964 election, and these were undoubtedly manifestations of urban, rather than social group, support for the Conservatives. The lower middle-class indicator associated moderately well in 1966 (−.53) and 1968 (−.47), but in the opposite direction of that hypothesized.[14]

Table 5. VARIABLES CORRELATED WITH CONSERVATIVE VOTING

Variable	Number of Elections Correlations Exceeded .40	Direction
Percent increase in population (1950-1960)	5 of 7	Positive
Percent increase in population (1960-1970)	4 of 7	Positive
Median family income	4 of 7	Positive
Percent families with incomes less than $3,000	6 of 7	Negative
Percent families with incomes greater than $10,000	5 of 7	Positive
Percent work force white collar	4 of 7	Positive
Percent increase in total property taxes (1962-1967)	5 of 7	Positive

Excepting the 1964 Senate election, the measures of party enrollment reaffirm the findings of Table 2, the absence of any
relationship between Conservative and Republican or Democratic
party support. Nor was independent enrollment, in either its static or
dynamic state, of any consequence in describing Conservative
support.

The findings from the simple correlations reported in Table 4 are a
mixed blessing. At least for New York State's 62 counties they
suggest little confirmation for widely publicized accounts that the
Conservatives were drawing blocs of white, blue-collar ethnics from
the Democratic Party. Alternatively, the data do suggest a confirmation at the macro-level of Schoenberger's micro-level findings. The
most supportive context for Conservative voting has been suburban,
white collar, upper income. The relationship between Conservative
voting and increase in property taxes 1962-1967 indicates, too, a
rational electoral response to what is probably, from the perspective
of the voter, the most obvious evidence of governmental activity.[15]

The rapid growth of the Conservative Party in one of the
historically most liberal states is to be explained, at least in part, by
the attractiveness of its candidates and issue positions to an upper
income, suburbanized population. For this segment of the electorate
the issues, the personalities and the party labels of the New Deal
years are increasingly irrelevant. When the predictive capability of
what might be labeled the New Conservative cleavage variables[16] is
compared with that of the New Deal cleavage variables, the
difference is quite evident. For each election the proportion of the
total variance in Conservative voting explained by New Conservative
cleavage variables exceeds that of the New Deal cleavages. A good
deal of variance remains unexplained in Table 5, and the values

Table 6. PREDICTIVE CAPABILITY OF NEW DEAL CLEAVAGE VARIABLES VERSUS
NEW CONSERVATIVE CLEAVAGE VARIABLES FOR CONSERVATIVE
CANDIDATES FOR GOVERNOR AND SENATE, 1962-1970

Conservative	New Deal Cleavage Variables	New Conservative Cleavage Variables	Difference
Governor, 1962	.104	.151	.047
U.S. Senate, 1962	.238	.405	.167
U.S. Senate, 1964	.540	.802	.262
Governor, 1966	.315	.548	.233
U.S. Senate, 1968	.389	.573	.184
Governor, 1970	.145	.347	.202
U.S. Senate, 1970	.223	.447	.224

indicate some interelection differential in the explanatory power of
the New Conservative cleavage variables. Nevertheless, the data do
indicate that the Conservative Party is gaining its support from new,
rather than old, cleavage bases in New York politics.

V. VARIATIONS ON THE GENERAL THEME

The simple correlations in Table 4 and the multiple correlations in
Table 6 do provide an outline of the ecology of Conservative Party
support across New York State. The outline is, however, less than
complete. None of the simple correlations are particularly strong;
and, aside from the case of the 1964 Senate, in none of the elections
was as much as 60% of the total variance explained. Moreover, the
lack of any significant relationship between Conservative voting and
such variables as ethnicity is at odds with the observations of
commentators on New York politics.[17]

As summary measures, correlations mask certain relevant factors.
The consistent correlation between rate of population change and
Conservative voting is, for example, much in line with the findings of
studies on protest movements of the right. But in New York State
patterns of population change tend to take on a regional cast; to
refer to population change is to refer, to a significant extent, to the
New York City metropolitan region. While Conservative support has
been strong in the counties surrounding New York City, it has not
been limited to that region. In fact, if the counties ranking in the
highest quartile of Conservative percentage of the vote in at least
three of four elections (1966 Governor, 1968 Senate, 1970 Governor, and 1970 Senate) are mapped, two rather distinct regions are
evident. This is shown in Figure 1.

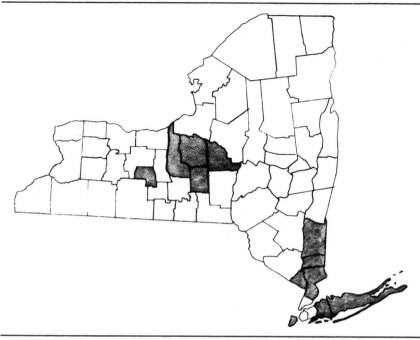

Figure 1: NEW YORK COUNTIES RANKING IN TOP QUARTILE OF CONSERVATIVE
VOTE IN AT LEAST THREE OF FOUR STATEWIDE ELECTIONS, 1966-1972

Twelve of New York's 62 counties are designated as most
Conservative on the map in Figure 1. Seven define a region around
New York City. The other five form a political region bordering on
and including Syracuse (Onondoga County) in the central part of the
state.

The fact of regional imbalances within a political system poses
challenges of interpretation. Concentrations of party strength in
different areas may obviously be a function of underlying similarities
between the areas. Alternatively, the party strength may result from
the interplay of different variables in different areas, two or more
regions may exhibit similar behavior, but not for the same reasons.
Explanations for the pro-Conservative tendencies of the Syracuse
region appear to be unrelated to similarities in the socioeconomic
characteristics of the county units making up the region. Within-
region variations are greater than the within-region similarities. And
excepting the central city of Syracuse and its immediate suburbs, the
region does not mirror even the most gross characteristics—rate of
population growth, density, ethnicity, family income, and so on—of
the New York metropolitan area.[18]

The Conservative tendencies of the Syracuse region are perhaps better explained by the impact of organizational work and regional structures than by underlying socioeconomic factors. From 1962 onward, Syracuse has been a center of upstate Conservative Party activity. The party's first gubernatorial candidate was a Syracuse businessman. During the 1960s the Syracuse mass media were particularly vocal in their opposition to the taxing and spending policies of the Rockefeller administration. Among the most prominent opponents of increased state taxing and spending has been a block of state legislators from Syracuse and Onondoga County. One reason frequently cited for their opposition to the Rockefeller fiscal programs has been their fear of the local press. While the nature of the causal linkage is not a simple one, as to whether the legislators behave as they do out of fear of retaliation from the mass media, or whether they use the threat of retaliation as a rationalization for their behavior thereby enhancing their power in the legislature, the power of the Syracuse media is defined as real within the state and region.[19]

Lacking micro-level data to substantiate the saliency of the mass media as a determinant of Conservative voting considerably weakens our argument. Yet one is hard pressed to offer alternative explanations for the Conservative propensities of the Syracuse area.[20] A number of studies have demonstrated the lack of information, or the nonsalience of issues to voters. Alternatively, it has been recognized that one critical function of the media is that of "agenda setting," defining what politics will be about within a community, stressing which cleavages will be debated. The mass media of the Syracuse area appears to have performed this agenda-setting function. By stressing opposition to the liberal programs of the Rockefeller administration and by endorsing conservative candidates in several elections, the media have helped to create a community context supportive of the Conservative cause.

It is the New York City metropolitan area that has been the most important source of Conservative votes. This is obviously due to the sheer magnitude of the area's population, but it is also the result of the distinct appeal of Conservative candidates to segments of the region's electorate. The extent of Conservative overrepresentation in the region is indicated in Table 7. Categories of the table include all cities and towns in New York State grouped by the criteria of geographic location, population density, and assessed property valuation. The index of overrepresentation is a ratio of category

Table 7. CONSERVATIVE INDEXES OF OVERREPRESENTATION IN
GUBERNATORIAL ELECTIONS, 1962-1970

	1962	1966	1970
New York City	.85	1.13	.63
New York City satellite cities	.93	.84	.88
Upstate central cities	.82	.47	.88
Upstate satellite cities	.34	.29	.71
Upstate independent cities	.74	.51	.86
New York City suburban towns	1.44	1.43	1.33
Upstate central city suburban towns	1.39	.91	1.36
Remainder of upstate	.97	.74	1.38

contribution to the total Conservative gubernatorial vote to category contribution to total gubernatorial vote; as values exceed 1.0, the Conservative vote is overrepresented.[21]

As the data indicate, the region is not of a single piece politically, New York City was overrepresented in its contribution to the Conservative gubernatorial vote only in 1966. The satellite cities, older and established well before the suburbanization of the region, contributed to Conservative party voting in a smaller proportion than they contributed to the total gubernatorial vote. It is in the suburban towns of the counties surrounding New York City that the Conservative Party has found fertile ground. If one is to search out the representative Conservative voter it is in these towns he must look. There, most probably, he will find the middle to upper income white-collar resident troubled by rising property taxes and bothered by the apparent inability of Republicans or Democrats in state government to deal with his most pressing problems.

That Conservative voting was overrepresented in New York City, the national symbol of Eastern liberalism, only in 1966 is not to say that the party is without support in the city. Mayoral candidates in 1965, 1969, and 1973, running as Conservatives or with Conservative endorsement, have received fairly sizable votes. And it is within the city that one does find the most suggestive evidence of a relationship between Conservative voting and the "Social Issue" publics.

When the state legislative districts in New York City are ranked by support for Conservative candidates in the gubernatorial, senatorial, and mayoral elections between 1966 and 1970, 13 of 68 districts consistently fall within the upper quartile. These most consistently conservative assembly districts in the city share a number of common characteristics. Nine of the 13 are located in the traditionally most Republican, least urbanized boroughs of the city (Queens and Staten Island), though all but one of the Queens districts are clustered in the oldest, most densely settled area of the borough. For the most part, none of the 13 displays extremes of wealth or poverty. They are overwhelmingly white and tend to be somewhat more ethnic (primarily Italian but also Irish and German) and less Jewish (as measured by the size of the Russian population) than the city as a whole.

The ethnic-religious characteristics of the districts are suggested by the backgrounds of the state assemblymen elected from the districts. Thus, at least 10 of the 13 assemblymen list Roman Catholic affiliations in their legislative biographies. (All 13 of the assemblymen from these districts voted against liberalization of the state's abortion law during the 1970 legislative session.) Six of the 13 have identifiable Italian surnames, and 2 of the remaining 7 are Irish. Four are Democrats and 9 Republicans (3 of the 4 Democrats are from Queens).

It seems rather clear that it is within these constituencies that urban frustration has been most evident. Traditionally the ethnic Catholic has controlled the machinery of the Democratic Party in New York City, but the post-World War II years have transformed in very fundamental ways the nature and value of that machinery (Glazer and Moynihan, 1970). The decade of the 1960s produced a series of events which led these discontented Catholic ethnics away from the Democrats. And by and large the Conservative Party has benefited.

VI. CONCLUSIONS

There has been a general decline in third party movements over the twentieth century (James, 1974: 57-58). Nevertheless, there has been sufficient minor party activity in recent years to suggest that these parties are of more than simply historic interest. Indeed, if elections at several levels become increasingly candidate oriented and if voters find it easier to desert their traditional political loyalties as the nation moves from one alignment period to another, one might expect even more third party activity in the near future. In New York the Conservative Party has achieved an established position within the state political system in a relatively brief period of time. An indication both of the party's established position and its legitimacy was evidenced in the 1972 presidential and 1974 gubernatorial elections when the candidates of the Republican Party actively sought Conservative endorsement.

One essential factor in explaining the success of the Conservatives is the flexibility of a state election law which is not unduly restrictive on the establishment of new parties. Moreover, provisions of the law allowing minor parties to endorse major party candidates enhance the former's bargaining strength. As James (1974: 58) notes:

> This possibility reduces the critical weakness of a third party, that support for it will result in "vote wasting." In all other states the votes cast on separate ballot lines cannot be added together. Therefore, nomination by more than one party divides and reduces a candidate's support, rather than enhancing it.

While important, formal rules are, at best, a necessary and decidedly not a sufficient condition for minor party success. Obviously there must be a potential constituency with which the party's candidates can successfully interact. The data reported above demonstrate that for the Conservatives there was such a constituency. Interestingly, definition of this aggregate constituency involves a set of variables related to income level, population change, and rate of governmental change. For county units, neither past patterns of voting nor New Deal cleavage variable proved adequate as predictors of the Conservative vote.

As of the mid-1970s the Conservative Party had accomplished much. It had provided a margin of victory or defeat for numerous candidates in local and state legislative electiosn through its endorsement policies. The party had achieved a measure of national prominence by electing a U.S. Senator in 1970. And perhaps most important from the perspective of the party's founders, it had moved the state's Republican leadership to a more conservative stance. This was most evident in the 1970 election when numerous surveys indicated the unpopularity of the candidacy of incumbent Senator Charles Goodell as well as support for Conservative issue positions.

While Governor Rockefeller never publicly repudiated Goodell nor expressed support for Buckley, opinion polls indicated that Rockefeller and Buckley constituted an "unofficial Republican ticket." By late October, 48% of respondents who planned to vote for Rockefeller were also supporting Buckley while 65% of those voting for Buckley declared support for Rockefeller. That Rockefeller and Buckley did, in fact, draw support from the same aggregates within the population is indicated in the autocorrelations of the 1966, 1968, and 1970 elections, at several levels of analysis (see Table 8).

Table 8. REPUBLICAN GOVERNOR (ROCKEFELLER)–CONSERVATIVE SENATOR (BUCKLEY) INTERCORRELATIONS, 1966, 1968, AND 1970

		All Counties (N=62)	New York City A.D.s. (N=68)	Syracuse Wards (N=19)	Buffalo Wards (N=27)
Rockefeller v. Buckley	1966 1968	−.59	.27	.11	.42
Rockefeller v. Buckley	1966 1970	.03	.25	.09	.79
Rockefeller v. Buckley	1970 1968	−.58	.90	.73	.43
Rockefeller v. Buckley	1970 1970	.42	.92	.75	.93

The correlations between Rockefeller's 1966 votes and those of Buckley in 1968 are, with the exception of Buffalo wards, modestly positive or negative. Correlations for the 1970 votes are consistently positive and, within cities, quite strong. That Rockefeller moved to the right because of the Conservative Party cannot be demonstrated. The essential point is that the existence of the minor party provides the electorate with a vehicle for protesting against those candidates of the major parties who fail to hear their grievances. This historic function of minor parties continues to be performed in New York.

NOTES

1. In those cases where both the appropriate individual and aggregate level statistics exist, even more sophisticated types of analyses can be undertaken. Using both types of data it is possible, for example, to determine the contribution of individual and structural independent variables to explaining variance in a particular dependent variable (Valkonen, 1969).

2. This literature stressed the importance of the political party leadership's moving to moderate or slightly conservative issue positions given the alleged "mood" of the late 1960's electorate. Most representative of it is Phillips (1969), Scammon and Wattenburg (1970), and Lubell (1970).

3. Relatively little has been done on New York politics in recent years. The last work to attempt to consider New York politics in any total sense was Straetz and Munger (1960); some updated material is available in Pierce (1972). Much new material on the state government, but relatively little on political parties or elections, can be found in Connery and Benjamin (1974). For any student of New York politics, the *New York Times* is, of course, the major data source. In recent years the weekly *New York* has furnished useful comments on New York City politics.

4. During the 1940s the American Labor Party divided internally on the issue of Communist influence in, and control of, the party. A group opposed to the Communist influence split with the ALP and formed the Liberal Party. By 1952 the American Labor

Party received insufficient votes to continue to be automatically placed on the ballot. Other minor parties such as the Socialist Labor and Socialist Worker continue to appear on the statewide ballot by petitions. The vote of these splinter groups has been so miniscule, however, that we have ignored them in this analysis.

5. An account of the growth and development of the Conservative Party in its early years can be found in Mahoney (1968).

6. This opposition has taken several forms, the most obvious being periodic public statements by former Governor Rockefeller and other Republicans against the Conservatives. Bills have been introduced in the state legislature but have not been passed to disallow endorsement of major party candidates by minor parties. At the local level similar efforts have been made to dilute minor party strength; in Nassau County, a suburb of New York City, for example, both Republican and Democratic leaders have actively worked, until very recently, to prevent their party candidates from accepting minor party endorsements.

7. By 1970, only eight years after its founding, the Conservative Party had at least a county chairman in 54 of the state's 62 counties; the Liberal Party, in existence since 1944, had only 27 county chairmen in the same year.

8. Endorsement by a minor party provides the candidate with an extra ballot line; New York political folklore holds that this enhances the candidate's chances of receiving support from voters who are attracted to him personally but are reluctant to vote his major party label. Conservative Party leadership worked to support Barry Goldwater in 1964 and Richard Nixon in 1968 by endorsing their Republican presidential electors. Their efforts failed, however, due to opposition from Nelson Rockefeller. In 1972, reportedly as a result of a White House request, the Conservatives were permitted to endorse the Republican electors. Rockefeller's successor as governor, Malcolm Wilson, had strong ties to the Conservative wing of the Republican Party and to the Conservative Party. According to news accounts, a quid pro quo of Wilson's endorsement was the withdrawal of Republican opposition to Conservative endorsement of Republican candidates in local elections.

9. In the 1970 election, for example, the Buckley campaign was managed by the consultant F. Clifton White, drew large contributions, and maintained a campaign organization separate from the remainder of the Conservative Party ticket. See, as one illustration, reporter Frank Lynn's account "Adams Cast as Buckley's Poor Cousin" in the September 5, 1970, *New York Times.*

10. Needless to say these were atypical elections in that the Republican candidate (Javits in 1968 and Goodell in 1970) rather than Democratic candidates received Liberal Party endorsement. Also as one moves toward the lower right corner of the table, correlations between the votes for candidates in the same election are being read.

11. This is only a slight exaggeration. For those accustomed to autocorrelations approaching .9 in the comparison of pairs of elections, the autocorrelations of Conservative candidates are revealing:

Office	Election Pairs	r
Governor	1962 v. 1966	.51
	1966 v. 1970	.53
U.S. Senate	1962 v. 1964	.66
	1964 v. 1968	.83
	1968 v. 1970	.77

12. All of correlations and regressions included in this study are based upon census data and election returns that are temporally closest. That is, the 1962 and 1964 elections are related to the 1960 census and the 1966, 1968, and 1970 elections to the 1970 census. It makes little conceptual sense and violates the assumptions of causality to correlate static 1970 census data with earlier elections. Further, when both 1960 and 1970 census variables are correlated with each election, the differences in the size of the resulting correlations are modest.

13. It is not clear as to whether the decline in explanatory power is a function of the office or of Nelson Rockefeller's impact on that office, or both. One might suspect that it is a Rockefeller (or incumbent) phenomenon. The R^2s for the Republican vote in presidential elections have exhibited reasonable stability over the time period: 1956, .57; 1960, .77; 1964, .32; 1968, .77; and 1972, .81.

14. It goes without saying that the lack of a consistently strong and positive correlation here, or with any of the other variables, is not proof of anything. The crudity of the indicators of lower middle class status and Catholocism undoubtedly inhibit the discovery of any real world relationship.

15. In terms of causal inference making it is suggestive that a time lag of sorts exists between tax increases and electoral response. Voters seem to have reacted more to the property tax increases of the prior period (1962-1967) than to those of the immediate period (1967-1972).

16. Six independent variables are included in the multiple correlation: (1) percent increase in population, (2) percent population ethnic, (3) median family income, (4) percent work force employed outside county of residence, (5) percent work force white collar, and (6) percent increase in total property taxes, 1962-1967.

17. Commenting upon the impact of Liberal and Conservative decisions to run independent candidates or to endorse Republicans or Democrats, Richard Reeves wrote in the April 12, 1970, *New York Times:*

> The Liberal vote is won at Democratic expense, but there is some uncertainty about whether the Conservatives have the same impact on the Republicans. Many politicians believe that the majority of votes on the Conservative line are cast by Irish and Italian voters who are registered Democrats.

18.

	Onondoga	Cayuga	Cortland	Madison	Yates
Density per square mile, 1960	534	106	82	83	54
Percent population change, 1950-1960	23.8	5.4	10.6	18.7	5.7
Percent ethnic stock, 1960	27.4	24.4	15.1	15.6	13.0
Median family income, 1960	$6,691	$5,384	$5,505	$5,451	$4,799
Percent work force white collar, 1960	48.6	35.3	34.1	37.5	32.8

19. This was dramatically illustrated during the 1971 legislative session when Governor Rockefeller was confronted with a "rebellion" against proposed tax increases from both Democrats and a bloc of Republicans, including several from the Syracuse area. Frank Lynn in the *New York Times* of March 28, 1971, noted:

> The concern over this apparent rebellion was evident when Governor Rockefeller sent his personal plane to Syracuse yesterday to bring the publisher of the *Syracuse Herald-Journal,* Steve Rogers, here for a luncheon at the executive mansion.
>
> The newspaper and the affiliated *Syracuse Post-Standard* have repeatedly editorialized against state spending and tax increases.
>
> Some of the Syracuse legislators have privately conceded that they are fearful of the impact of the stand of the newspapers, which are credited by some politicians with playing a major role in the defeat of former Assembly Majority Leader Charles Schoeneck, who had voted against the sales tax several years ago.

In another *Times* story (March 30, 1971), Lynn reported:

> Senator Hughes (the senior member of the Syracuse delegation), . . . denied that the legislators were overly influenced by the [Syracuse newspaper] editorials, although he hastened to add that, "I don't mean that they don't have any *effect.*" He said the newspapers tended to stir up people beyond what might happen in another *community.*

20. In any given metropolitan area the probability of a suburban area being more supportive of a Conservative candidate than the central city is very high. But the central city of Syracuse has been consistently more Conservative than other upstate central cities *or* their suburbs. When the 1968 and 1970 Senate vote for individual central cities and the average of the vote cast by their neighboring suburban towns, the following is obtained:

City and Suburb	Percent Conservative Senate, 1968	Percent Conservative Senate, 1970
Albany City	6.1	19.3
Suburban towns	9.6	30.6
Binghamton City	7.5	29.5
Suburban towns	7.8	31.2
Buffalo City	5.6	20.9
Suburban towns	8.3	33.2
Niagara Falls City	7.7	24.8
Suburban towns	9.6	35.8
Rochester City	7.7	30.6
Suburban towns	12.4	44.6
Utica-Rome City	13.4	39.3
Suburban towns	16.7	47.6
Schenectady City	10.6	28.7
Suburban towns	15.4	37.1
Syracuse City	22.8	42.8
Suburban towns	30.1	53.5

For the two elections, the Conservative leanings of Syracuse and its suburbs are evident. In 1968 Syracuse was more Conservative than any other central city and all suburbs excepting its own. In 1970 only the suburbs of Rochester, Utica-Rome, and Syracuse gave Buckley a higher percentage of the vote than Syracuse central city.

21. This index of overrepresentation is drawn from Alker (1965). The only vote returns published by the New York State secretary of state in sufficient detail to permit the type of reporting in Table 6 are those for governor. However, even with a less detailed breakdown of the Buckley Senate vote in 1968 and 1970, the point of Conservative overrepresentation in the New York City suburbs is made:

	1 Category % of Total Buckley Vote, 1968	2 Category % of Total Senate Vote, 1968	3 Ratio 1/2, 1968	4 Category % of Total Buckley Vote, 1970	5 Category % of Total Senate Vote, 1970	6 Ratio 4/5, 1970
New York City	41.8	38.0	1.10	34.8	37.6	.93
New York City suburban counties	30.9	22.5	1.37	27.4	22.5	1.22
Upstate central city counties	14.8	22.2	.67	20.0	22.4	.89
Remainder of upstate	12.6	17.3	.73	17.8	17.5	1.02

REFERENCES

ALKER, H. (1965) Mathematics and Politics. New York: Macmillan.
BELL, D. [ed.] (1963) The Radical Right. New York: Doubleday.
BURNHAM, W. (1970) Critical Elections and the Mainsprings of American Politics. New York: Norton.
——— (1969) "The end of American party politics." Trans-Action 7 (December): 12-22.
——— and J. SPRAGUE (1970) "Additive and multiplicative models of the voting universe: the case of Pennsylvania, 1960-1968." American Political Science Review (June): 471-490.
CAMPBELL, A. et al. (1960) The American Voter. New York: Wiley.
CONNERY, R. and G. BENJAMIN [eds.] (1974) Governing New York State: The Rockefeller Years. New York: The Academy of Political Science.
CONVERSE, P. (1966) "The concept of the normal vote," in A. Campbell et al., Elections and the Political Order. New York: Wiley.
——— (1964) "The nature of belief systems in mass publics," in D. Apter (ed.) Ideology and Discontent. New York: Free Press.
——— et al. (1969) "Continuity and change in American political parties and issues in the 1968 election." American Political Science Review (December): 1083-1105.
DAWSON, R. (1973) Public Opinion and Contemporary Disarray. New York: Harper.
DeVRIES, W. and L. TARRANCE (1972) The Ticket-Splitter. Grand Rapids, Mich.: Eerdmans.
DOWNS, A. (1957) An Economic Theory of Democracy. New York: Harper.
FEIGERT, F. (1973) "Conservatism, populism, and social change." American Behavioral Scientist (November/December): 272-278.
GLAZER, N. and D. MOYNIHAN (1970) Beyond the Melting Pot. Cambridge: M.I.T. Press.
JAMES, J. (1974) American Political Parties in Transition. New York: Harper.
KEY, V. O. (1958) Politics, Parties, and Pressure Groups. New York: Crowell.
LADD, E. (1970) American Political Parties: Social Change and Political Response. New York: Norton.
LIPSET, S. (1963) "Three decades of the radical right: Coughlinites, McCarthyites, and Birchers–1962," in D. Bell (ed.) The Radical Right. New York: Doubleday.
——— and E. RAAB (1970) The Politics of Unreason. New York: Harper.
——— (1969) "The Wallace backlash." Trans-Action (December): 23-35.
LUBELL, S. (1970) The Hidden Crisis in American Politics. New York: Norton.
MAHONEY, J. (1968) Actions Speak Louder. New Rochelle, N.Y.: Arlington House.
McNALL, S. (1969) "Social disorganization and availability: accounting for radical rightism," in R. Schoenberger (ed.) The American Right Wing. New York: Holt, Rinehart and Winston.
MacRAE, D. and J. MELDRUM (1960) "Critical elections in Illinois: 1888-1958." American Political Science Review (September): 669-683.
PHILLIPS, K. (1969) The Emerging Republican Majority. Garden City, N.Y.: Doubleday.
PIERCE, N. (1972) The Megastates of America. New York: Norton.
PRICE, H. (1970) "Rise and decline of one-party systems in Anglo-American experience," in S. Huntington and C. Moore (eds.) Authoritarian Politics in Modern Society. New York: Basic Books.
ROHTER, I. (1969) "Social and psychological determinants of radical rightism," in R. Schoenberger (ed.) The American Right Wing. New York: Holt, Rinehart and Winston.
SCAMMON, R. and B. WATTENBERG (1970) The Real Majority. New York: Coward-McCann.

SCHOENBERGER, R. (1969) "The Conservative movement: a view from the East," in R. Schoenberger (ed.) The American Right Wing. New York: Holt, Rinehart and Winston.

SOARES, G. and R. HAMBLIN (1967) "Socio-economic variables and voting for the radical left: Chile, 1952." American Political Science Review (March): 1053-1065.

STRAETZ, R. and F. MUNGER (1960) New York Politics. New York: New York University Press.

SUNDQUIST, J. (1973) Dynamics of the Party System. Washington, D.C.: Brookings.

WOLFINGER, R. and F. GREENSTEIN (1969) "Comparing political regions: the case of California." American Political Science Review (March): 74-85.

VALKONEN, T. (1969) "Individual and structural effects in ecological research," in M. Dogan and S. Rokkan (eds.) Quantitative Ecological Analysis in the Social Sciences. Cambridge: M.I.T. Press.

Chapter 6

PARTY REFORM AND POLITICAL PARTICIPATION: THE DEMOCRATS IN MAINE

L O U I S   M A I S E L

In 1972 the business of the Democratic Party was for the first time conducted under the guidelines established by the Commission on Party Structure and Delegate Selection (the McGovern-Fraser Commission). That commission, appointed in 1969 by National Chairman Fred Harris at the direction of the 1968 National Convention, operated under a mandate to reform party procedures in order to afford "all Democratic voters . . . a full, meaningful, and timely opportunity to participate"[1] in the party's decision-making processes. What was the effect of the reforms on participation within the Democratic Party in Maine?

The foundations of the Democratic Party, nationally and in many of the states, were shaken by the 1968 presidential nomination. First Senator Eugene McCarthy and later Senator Robert Kennedy asked hundreds of thousands of Americans—many of them young and

AUTHOR'S NOTE: This paper was made possible in part by a grant from the Research, Travel and Sabbatical Committee of Colby College. The author would like to thank Patricia Rachal for her assistance in collecting the information upon which this study is based. He would also like to thank Thomas Morrione for his help in questionnaire design, Ward Shaw for his help in computer programming, the staff of Maine's Democratic State Committee for their cooperation throughout the time spent on the project, and John Donovan, George Mitchell, and Frederick Sontag, each of whom commented on earlier drafts of this paper. None of them is in any way responsible for any errors of fact or interpretation which may appear in this paper, but the study would not have been possible without the help of them all.

idealistic, most of them disenchanted with the Vietnam War—to seek to alter governmental policies by working within the Democratic Party, not by "voting with their feet." The party system was put to a severe test and was found wanting. The national convention in Chicago ended with violence in the streets and with the party terribly divided.

The McGovern Commission's task was to analyze why the system was so unresponsive to the expressed will of the rank and file; its mandate was to institute procedural changes to compensate for this failure. Party leaders—those who won in Chicago as well as those who lost—felt that the very existence of the Democratic Party and even of the two-party system was threatened if voters were not made to feel that their participation could produce the desired effects.[2]

In Maine the impetus to reform was felt before the national convention met in Chicago. Meeting in May 1968, the Democratic State Convention established a special committee to review the structure of the party in the state. That committee, chaired by National Committeeman George J. Mitchell, undertook the task assigned by the McGovern Commission as well as the broader task of examining the openness, relevance, and functioning of the party organizations within the state.

The reforms eventually instituted guaranteed a system in which no step in the delegate selection process was to begin before the calendar year of a presidential election. All meetings were to be well publicized and opened to the public. Most important, the state parties were to take steps to see that those groups which had been traditionally underrepresented—women, youth, and minorities—were represented in approximate proportion to their numbers. The same theme pervaded all the guidelines: make the party organization more meaningful to more people.

Political science literature tells us a great deal about the functions of party organization (Key, 1964; Key, 1967: ch. 1; Eldersveld, 1964: parts 3, 4; Sorauf, 1972: parts 2, 3, 4; Caraley, 1966: part 2; Abbott and Rogowsky, 1971: parts 1, 2, 3). The importance of the various reforms implemented by the Democratic Party rests on two assumptions. First, if the party did not reform, a significant portion of the politically relevant population would turn elsewhere to accomplish what parties have traditionally done, that is, provide meaningful choices between those in power and those out (Key, 1967: 11-14); such a reaction would profoundly alter American politics as we know it. Second, party reform could lead to increased participation as a matter of course; subsequently party organizations could be performing significantly different functions in our system, for example, they could become more issue-oriented.

This paper represents but a first step. It describes the effects of the reforms on participation at several levels of party organization in Maine in 1972. The implications of these changes for the American party system are raised in the concluding section.

I. THE SETTING

Although Maine is a predominantly rural state, her political geography marks her as an interesting object of study. The state's sixteen counties range from largely urban to totally rural; some are experiencing rapid growth as new citizens seek the peaceful tranquility which contrasts so pointedly with the environments of nearby metropolitan centers, while others show population declines typical of many aging rural communities. The counties span the spectrum from heavily Democratic to heavily Republican; but these partisan leanings do not necessarily coincide with urban-rural differences. Consequently variations among the experiences in different types of counties can be observed. The Democratic organization in some counties is almost dormant; in others it is quite active and many citizens are involved in all party decisions; in one, Androscoggin, a classic political machine controls the political process in a way that Mayor Daley would recognize favorably.

Duane Lockard (1959: ch. 4) described Maine as a strong one-party Republican state whose politics was dominated by one overwhelming interest, lumber. Thanks to a Democratic rejuvenation sparked by Edmund S. Muskie as he won first the governorship and later a seat in the U.S. Senate, after the 1970 election Austin Ranney (1971: 87) classified Maine near the Democratic end of his two-party state category.[3]

Viewed in 1974, Maine has moved even closer to the classic two-party pattern. The secretary of state's records show that the Democratic enrollment has grown by approximately 40,000 since 1968, while the Republicans have shown no sizable increase. Enrollments as of the 1974 primary were 237,828 (39.4%) Republicans and 212,175 (35.2%) Democrats; 153,224 (25.4%) registered voters did not enroll in one of the major parties. While the Republicans retained control of the state senate in recent elections, the Democratic sweep in house races not only captured control of that body but also provided a sufficient number of votes so that the Democrats could control the legislative caucus which selects the attorney general, secretary of state, and state treasurer. One incumbent congressman, William Cohen (R), won reelection easily, but Democrat Peter Kyros, who had held the First District seat for his party since 1966, was apparently upset by David Emery.[4] The surprising victory of Independent James Longley in the gubernatorial race strays from any conception of a two-party model, but the fact that the Republican candidate finished a poor third demonstrates how far Maine has come from when she was a one-party bastion.

When viewed from afar, Maine appears quite homogeneous, but a closer look at the Democratic organizations within the state reveals that they vary considerably. The two parties are quite competitive statewide and in many areas of the state; however, pockets of one-party dominance, favoring either party, are also in evidence. The Democratic Party was rejuvenated approximately fifteen years ago and has continued to edge into Republican strongholds. With 18 year olds obtaining the vote and with the Democrats seeking to gain majority status, Maine serves as an excellent arena in which to view the effects of party reform on political participation.[5]

II. METHODOLOGY

Three prime data sources provided the information for this study. First we examined caucus papers for every town that caucused in 1968, 1970, and/or 1972.[6] From these records we gathered information on participation by women, specifically town offices held and participation at state conventions. However, caucus papers do not reveal the ages of participants,[7] nor do they record the number of participants.

In January 1973, we mailed a questionnaire to each of the 354 town and ward chairpersons listed by Democratic state headquarters.[8] After a follow-up mailing, our response rate was over 60%.[9] Our return rate was probably higher than that, as most close observers of the Democrats in Maine feel that many of the smaller towns have party officers on paper only—that is, officers' names have been submitted after the town caucus, but those named have no intention of serving in the post. After careful analysis and after noting that more heavily populated areas are slightly overrepresented in our sample, we decided that the responses to our questionnaire were from a sufficiently broad sample to be included in our analysis.[10] From questionnaire responses we drew information on general levels of participation, participation by youth, efforts to stimulate participation, orientation of those involved in the party, and like matters.

Finally, we interviewed many of the most active participants. Every county chairperson and most of the large city chairmen were interviewed during the first two months of 1973. The availability of these persons for interviews points to another advantage of studying a state such as Maine (compare Bowman and Boynton, 1966: 7; Hirschfield et al., 1962: 490; Eldersveld, 1964: 103-104). In addition, we sought the views of a large number of candidates, party officeholders, and party staff members. These interviews were all structured to include a set of open-ended questions and to permit those interviewed to add other information they deemed relevant. As the interview data are less easily systematized, they have been used to augment information gained from the questionnaires and analysis of caucus records.

III. GENERAL LEVEL OF PARTICIPATION

Democratic party leaders across the nation were concerned that citizens would turn away from their party. The objectives of the reform movement included increasing participation by altering procedures so that citizens would see political activity as meaningful and by stressing the openness of the party so that those who had not participated in the past felt welcomed into the party.

A number of indices measure levels of participation in party organizations. First, one can determine the number of governmental units which have been organized politically. Most urban areas have some type of political organization; in a rural state like Maine, however, politics has not always reached to some of the smaller, more remote areas. The Democratic State Committee made a determined effort to organize many small towns which never before had taken part in Democratic politics. In 1972, 68 towns caucused for the first time; the total number of towns and cities caucusing was 346 as compared to 278 in 1970 and 275 in 1968.[11]

Although the increase in the number of towns organizing is important, one must realize that most of the new towns are quite small, having fewer than 500 residents; therefore, it is perhaps more significant to examine the attendance at the 1972 caucuses as compared with that in earlier years.

Table 1 reveals that most respondents to our questionnaire felt that attendance at their caucus in 1972 was greater than it had been in previous years.[12] That is, the percentage of towns with smaller caucuses was declining while more towns had larger caucuses. Caucus data are of necessity imprecise as attendance records are not maintained; however, a pattern seems clear: 39.4% of the respondents felt that their town's caucus in 1972 was larger than it had been in past years while only 12.7% felt that the 1972 meeting was smaller. Nearly half of those reporting (47.9%) did not estimate the difference to be substantial enough for them to change response category.

Attendance at caucus is a one-time affair; it is significant in that it might demonstrate a desire to participate in the selection of the presidential nominee, the minimal level of commitment sought by the McGovern Commission. Many of those interviewed attributed the increased attendance to commitment either to Senator Muskie, demonstrating that Maine still supported the faltering frontrunner, or to Senator McGovern or Congresswoman Chisholm, the only other candidates with workers active in the state. As one urban chairperson described the situation, "Our caucus was actually taken over by new McGovern and Chisholm people. The caucus was literally utter chaos at first. . . . We weren't prepared for such a crowd. Attendance was twice what we had ever had before."

Caucus attendance does indicate a certain level of awareness of town activities. In another of the urban centers, the chairperson felt that caucus attendance was swelled by a potential fight over his job. This concern for local party politics, apparent in a number of areas in which caucus attendance was unusually high, might be considered an

Table 1. ATTENDANCE AT MUNICIPAL CAUCUSES (in percentages)

	Average, 1964-70	1972
No caucus	8.5	1.9
Fewer than 10 people	35.8	31.6
10-20 people	30.7	35.8
21-30 people	9.4	12.3
31-50 people	4.7	9.5
More than 50 people	4.2	7.5
Don't know	6.7	1.0
n = 212		

unanticipated by-product of the McGovern reforms in that more people felt their participation was desired and thus became involved at even the most local level. Maine's Mitchell Commission, moreover, set this type of participation as one of its primary objectives. In the introduction to its report to the 1970 Maine State Democratic Convention, the Commission specified that its "goal . . . extends beyond the Presidential selection process" (Mitchell Commission, 1970: 1) to building a strong, involved, participatory party at all levels.

Membership on municipal party committees in Maine demonstrates a continuing interest in the party (Mitchell Commission, 1970: 8). Thus, an examination of the size and composition of the town and ward committees will indicate whether the trend observed in viewing caucus attendance was carried over into longer-lasting commitments.

Table 2 reveals that membership on municipal party committees increased significantly. Many more towns and wards reported larger committees while the number reporting committees of 5 to 10 members declined. The slight increase in the very small committees follows from a combination of two factors: (1) many towns caucusing for the first time and having very small committees which is partially offset by (2) some of the towns previously reporting very small committees having larger ones in 1972.[13]

Anyone who has served on a party committee at the town or ward level will attest that membership on such a committee involves limited or no participation at all except at registration and election times. This is particularly so in a state like Maine wherein an expression of a desire to serve is tantamount to election to these committees. Officers of these committees, however, invest a good deal more of their time (and money) and are involved in making decisions on party matters throughout the year. They assume responsibility for maintaining committee records and stimulating whatever organizational activity goes on between elections, as well as

Table 2. MEMBERSHIP ON MUNICIPAL DEMOCRATIC COMMITTEES (in percentages)

	1970	1972
Fewer than 5 members	16.5	18.6
5-10 members	24.6	17.1
11-20 members	19.6	20.3
More than 20 members	14.1	24.2
No answer	25.0	19.8
n = 212		

directing campaign efforts (cf. Eldersveld, 1964: chs. 13-16). Additionally the officers are the contact points for county committees and the state committee and as such are kept continuously aware of party activity. Thus, it is important to see how many new people assumed municipal office in 1972.

Table 3 lists the percentage of towns with each possible number of new officers in 1970 and 1972. Four hundred and sixty-five individuals who had not been serving prior to 1970 served as town committee officers from that year until 1972; 617 Democrats who had not previously held municipal offices were elected in 1972. This rise is attributable both to towns caucusing for the first time and to new people serving in towns which had previously caucused.[14] The two largest shifts occurred in the percentage of towns having no new officers and in those having four new officers. In each case the shift was in the direction reflecting more new participants in 1972.

While the argument to this point shows more party organization participation in 1972 than before, one could argue persuasively that this stepped-up activity was artificially stimulated by Senator Muskie's candidacy and thus cannot be attributed to the party reforms. To counter this latter view, it is necessary to look at activity after Muskie was no longer a factor.

The municipal leaders were asked whether more new people had participated in the 1972 election campaign than previously. Of the 213 respondents, 61% (130) felt that more new people participated while only 33% (70) felt that there had been the same number or fewer new participants. Those responding affirmatively to the question "Were there more new participants in this campaign than has normally been the case?" were asked to choose the most appropriate statement from those listed in Table 4.

Thus, municipal party leaders did perceive a meaningful impact by new people working in the fall campaign. Generally these newcomers did not replace those who have always worked; rather, they worked alongside them or engaged in new types of activities.

Table 3. NEW OFFICERS ON MUNICIPAL COMMITTEES

	1970	1972
Percentage of towns with		
no new officers	19.2	13.3
1 new officer	26.8	26.0
2 new officers	27.1	24.0
3 new officers	19.7	18.4
4 new officers	9.2	18.4
n =	286	354

Table 4. ACTIVITIES IN TOWNS REPORTING MORE NEW PARTICIPANTS

Statement	Percentage
Most of the campaign work was done by the same people who have worked in the past, but there were new workers who had significant impact.	46.7
New participants took over a large portion of the campaign activity while those who worked in the past did less.	18.2
New participants took over a large portion of the campaign activities while those who worked in the past continued on as before and/or increased their activity.	25.6
Almost all of the work was done by new participants.	9.5
Almost all of the work was done by old participants.	0.7
n = 138	

Interview data reveal that county leaders were cognizant of these new activities. They commented that new participants (who were invariably referred to as "they" or "the McGovern people" by the older party leaders and "we" by the new ones) did a good deal of door-to-door canvassing which rarely had been tried in the past.

Apparently the level of activity by new people varied considerably from county to county. Two county leaders felt that new participants hurt the party's cause. One commented:

Almost all of the new people were for McGovern, but a lot of them went to the convention and then disappeared. The new people worked only for McGovern while the old Democrats helped more on the county campaign. . . . This resulted in some real battles and some hard feelings.

However, a more common and more optimistic view was that expressed by one of the city chairmen:

Some were just in for one shot, but some came in as McGovern people and were really taken with politics. These "issue-oriented" people need an organization to direct them, otherwise they can antagonize voters because of duplication and everything. But things worked out okay.

In at least one and possibly two heavily Republican areas, new Democrats have completely replaced the old organization. In these areas the Democratic organization had been nearly dormant; the regulars functioned mainly as delegates to conventions, state committee members, and the like. They could not adjust to an active role in a campaign. One of the new county leaders described the situation:

A: Exactly. We did [take over the party]. And we put on quite a campaign. We had lots of participation and raised lots of money. We've tried to keep the party regulars back in, but we've had lots of trouble. . . . ——— [a regular] said they [the new people] would all back out and leave me high and dry. Well, at our first meeting there were 19 people and 17 of them were McGovern people. That's good attendance for us.

Q: Do you think the Old Guard will return?

A: Oh no. I'm confident they will back out. They never manned a headquarters, did any of the door-to-door campaigning, really divorced themselves from the whole thing. Of course, they had never done any of it before either.

The caucus activity could have been stimulated by Senator Muskie's candidacy; the fall campaign could have resulted from the intense commitment that McGovern supporters felt. However, the fragments of evidence since the 1972 campaign indicate a continued high level of participation. In November 1973, for example, Waterville Democrats caucused to nominate a mayoral candidate. Caucus attendance of over 1,250 surpassed the previous record high turnout by nearly 40% and represented approximately 30% of all registered Democrats. The caucuses in February 1974 to select delegates to the state convention appeared to continue the trend toward increased involvement, though no hard data are yet available. Finally, more Democrats are seeking office than ever before. Six men entered the gubernatorial primary, and each of the congressional nominations was contested. Democrats filed for all but 4 of the 154 seats in the state house of representatives and all but 2 of the 33 senate seats, totals never before attained. In many districts, fierce primaries were fought. As an example, in Portland, 19 Democrats sought the 10 nominations available in the one multimember district.

This evidence all points to the finding that the reform movement was successful in achieving its goal of increased awareness of and participation in Democratic Party activities. We must go further, however, to determine if this increase was reflected in the activities of the specific groups singled out by the McGovern Commission.

IV. PARTICIPATION BY WOMEN

In summarizing its guidelines to state parties for selecting delegates to the 1972 National Convention, the McGovern Commission mandated that the state parties "overcome the effects of past discrimination by affirmative steps to encourage representation on the National Convention delegation of minority groups, young people, and women in reasonable relationship to their presence in the population of the State." Interestingly, the Mitchell Commission's recommendations on citizen participation specify youth participation and emphasis on issues; the commission did not feel it necessary to spell out recommendations regarding women (Mitchell Commission, 1970: 3).

Although many of the county leaders did take particular steps to encourage women, a majority agreed with the implicit assumption of the Mitchell Commission that women's participation was not a problem in Maine.

Women have always been active. . . . Our women do all the work, the absentee work, the telephoning, everything.

The women are more active than the men. There is a ——— County Democratic Women's Club which is much more active than the men. They meet monthly and get far better turnouts than the County Committee does. All our Election Day workers are women.

However, the important question becomes whether women are workers in the party without sharing in the rewards and without equal status in the decision-making processes. One county chair*man* hinted at this when he said, "Well, the County Committee has always been dominated by women. Of course, there's never been a woman Chairman that I know of." Thus, although the Mitchell Commission did not make recommendations about women, it is important to examine their level of participation and how significant it was in 1972.

Table 5 summarizes the situation regarding women at 1972 municipal caucuses. It reveals that while most towns reported approximately the same number of women participants as in the past, a large percentage of towns showed substantial increases.

In response to the question "Did you or your town or ward committee take any specific action aimed at interesting women in coming to your caucus?" only 36.3% (77) of the respondents answered affirmatively while 56.1% (119) answered negatively. Table 6 shows the relationship between this information and that on women's caucus attendance. These data clearly reveal that those municipal committees which made an effort to attract women

Table 5. PARTICIPATION BY WOMEN IN 1972 MUNICIPAL CAUCUSES

Statement	Percent Agreeing
Many more women attended this year's caucus than have attended in the past	15.1
A few more women attended this year's caucus than have attended in the past	20.3
About the same number of women attended this year's caucus as have attended in the past	52.4
Fewer women attended this year's caucus than have attended in the past	0.9
Have not caucused in the past	4.2
Cannot estimate the attendance by women	7.0
n = 211	

—through speeches before women's groups, personal recruitment, use of media—were significantly more successful in attracting women to party caucuses than were the committees that did not partake in such activities. This suggests that the feeling that women always have participated enough is something of a self-fulfilling prophecy; that is, if one believes this and takes no affirmative steps, only the same women will participate, whether this is an adequate number or not.

Comparing participation by women county by county does not show any substantial differences, though these data are somewhat difficult to work with because the number of respondents from each county was quite small. Similarly, no statistically significant correlation was found when controlling for size of community. Apparently largely urban Cumberland County (Portland) had a larger increase in participation by women than did other counties, but again the number of respondents was too small to state this with any degree of certainty.

Table 6. RELATIONSHIP BETWEEN MUNICIPAL COMMITTEES' EFFORTS AND CAUCUS PARTICIPATION BY WOMEN IN 1972

	Percent Making an Effort	Percent Making no Effort
Many more women attended	26.0	7.6
A few more women attended	27.3	18.5
About the same number of women attended	35.1	62.2
Fewer women attended	0.0	0.8
Have not caucused in past; cannot estimate	11.6	11.0
n =	77	119
	$X^2 = 20.16$	$p = .01$[a]

a. Chi squares have been provided for the information of the reader only when tables have been used to show statistical relationships.

Table 7. RELATIONSHIP BETWEEN PARTISAN COMPLEXION OF MUNICIPALITY
AND CAUCUS PARTICIPATION BY WOMEN IN 1972

	% Highly Demo-cratic	% Slightly Demo-cratic	% Com-petitive	% Slightly Repub-lican	% Heavily Repub-lican
Many more women attended	20.8	10.5	15.4	15	13.4
A few more women attended	12.5	13.2	17.9	25	28.3
About the same number of women attended	56.3	60.5	51.3	45	50
Fewer women attended	0.0	2.6	0.0	0	1.2
Have not caucused in past; cannot estimate	18.8	13.0	15.4	15	7.4
n =	24	38	39	20	82

However, Table 7 does reveal that many more women participated in more highly Republican areas, as identified by respondents to the questionnaire. This suggests that the Democratic organizations in these areas were dormant, and women saw an opportunity to participate in a meaningful way. In fact, the Democratic organization in one highly Republican county—and those in many of its towns—was completely taken over by a group of new Democrats who then chose a woman to head the county committee.

The corollary of this finding, of course, is that it is harder for new women to participate where strong organizations already exist. That is, party leaders in office, where that office has some potential influence, appear to be less anxious to encourage new participants to try to enter the system.[15]

The figures on attendance by women at caucus run parallel, as one would imagine, to the number of women on town committees. Many more women were on 36.3% (77) of the respondents' municipal committees in 1972 than in 1970. On 47.4% (101) the same number of women served, and on 16.4% (35) there were fewer women.

Again, it is important to look at influence as well as at participation. For that purpose, the figures on municipal officers are relevant. Table 8 shows that more municipal committees had more women serving as officers in 1972 than in either 1968 or 1970. In 1968, 32.1% of the municipal committees had less than equal representation by sex on their officer slates; in 1970, this figure rose slightly, to 33.4%, but in 1972 in dropped to 27.1%. In terms of actual numbers, 492 women served in local party offices in 1968, 503 in 1970, and 667 in 1972.[16] Obviously some of this large

Table 8. WOMEN OFFICERS ON MUNICIPAL COMMITTEES

	1968	1970	1972
Percentage of towns with			
no women officers	12.7	12.9	7.9
1 woman officer	20.1	20.4	19.2
2 women officers	50.5	47.6	52.8
3 women officers	13.8	15.4	16.7
4 women officers	2.8	3.5	3.4
n =	283	286	354

increase was due to the increased number of municipalities which caucused and elected officers. However, the 68 towns that did caucus in 1972, not having done so in 1970, elected only 272 new officers, so women did not just keep an equal position; their position improved. Of the total number of local party officers elected in 1968, 43.5% were women; in 1970, 44.0%; in 1972, the figure rose to 47.1%.

While the number of officers on municipal committees is of some significance, these data are susceptible to misinterpretation. Although service as a town or ward officer does show an increased level of commitment, those who have served on these committees will attest that the secretary and the treasurer do much of the work, but the chairperson makes most of the decisions. The position of secretary has traditionally been viewed as "women's work," and the data on Maine's local party committees bear this out. Although more Maine women chaired Democratic Party committees after the 1972 caucuses than ever before, four times as many were still taking notes. Women appeared to be ready to participate, but not to take the larger step into decision-making power. This is further demonstrated by the fact that, while there were contested elections for chairperson in 68% of the municipalities whose officers responded to the questionnaire, only 10.9% of the losers were women. Thus, where women ran, a large majority of them won, but few ran. In this instance, men were not keeping women "in their place," but rather women were unwilling to compete for their share of the power, and existing organizations were not encouraging them to do so.

This situation for town and ward chairperson was paralleled at the county level. In 1972, only three Democratic county committees were chaired by women. One of these was serving her third term, while the others were newly elected. All of those interviewed agreed that few women have served as county leaders in the past, though many have held county office. The reaction of one male county leader to the status of women in this area is typical.

Table 9. MUNICIPAL COMMITTEES WITH FEMALE CHAIRPERSONS
AND/OR SECRETARIES

	1968	1970	1972
Female chairperson, %	12.7	15.7	19.5
Female secretary, %	76.9	77.3	79.4
n =	283	286	354

There was no real need to emphasize women here. . . . We have a good cross-section. We have a lot of couples interested—like ——— [his wife] she knows at least as much about the party as I do.[17]

Yet, he had no answer when asked why he had been county chairman for many years and she had never served.

Finally, because the McGovern reforms were specifically related to selection of the presidential nominee and because Maine chooses national convention delegates at its state convention, it is important to look at the composition of delegations to the state conventions.

It is impossible to compare the 1972 delegations ward-by-ward and town-by-town with previous conventions because the total number of delegates and alternates was decreased by over 10% as a result of changes made after the 1970 State Convention. We can say with certainty that many women have always attended state conventions, although the methods by which they were selected were considerably less than democratic. One city leader discussed the selection process in his area:

Because of the reforms the entire delegate selection process was more wide-open. In the past this was done solely by the City Committee. We would get together and make a list of us and our friends and would choose whoever wanted to be delegates. Usually most of the women were wives. Like a husband would be the delegate and his wife the alternate. It made a nice weekend trip to wherever the Convention was held.

In 1972, 33.3% of the delegates eligible to attend the state convention and 49.3% of the alternates were women. Although in raw figures the number of women may have decreased, because the size of the entire convention decreased, it is clear that the process by which the women were selected and probably the percentage of women in attendance improved.[18]

The McGovern Commission concerned itself with the manner in which those delegates who nominated the party's presidential candidate were chosen. The members of Maine's State Convention do this in caucuses of the members from specially designed delegate selection districts. For the Miami National Convention, the delegation was comprised of 15 males and 5 females.[19] This delegation was challenged as not conforming with the guidelines set down by the McGovern Commission. After an extensive hearing and review of the relevant caucus and state convention data, the hearing examiner for the Credentials Committee ruled that Maine had taken significant affirmative action toward encouraging women to participate and in fact had made substantial progress from the situation in Chicago in 1968 when only 13% of the delegates (4 of 30) were female. The findings of the hearing examiner were accepted by the Credentials Committee, and the delegation as elected by the state convention delegates was allowed to sit. Again, the conclusion follows that women showed a desire to participate, an awareness of the new rules (including those for challenges), and made some progress toward equality, though falling far short of that point.

One of the major goals of the 1972 reforms of the Democratic Party was to encourage women to become more active in all aspects of party work and decision making. Maine, perhaps because of its rural nature or perhaps for other reasons, is apparently unusual in that women have traditionally played an active role, so much so that the state's reform commission did not find it necessary to specify actions to encourage women.

As a result of the reforms, many more Democrats participated in party affairs in 1972 than had in the past. This general increase was more than paralleled by increased activity by women. However, the evidence seems to indicate that women in Maine in 1972—as in the past—have been typecast into particular political roles. They are workers on committees in far greater percentages than they are officers; when they do hold office, they serve as secretary far more often than as chairperson. At conventions, more women are alternates than delegates. The reforms made Maine Democrats more aware that this was a problem; although some progress was made, much more needs to be done to change the situation significantly.

V. PARTICIPATION BY YOUTH

Some of the same dissatisfaction which provided the impetus for the reform movement within the Democratic Party also increased activity on behalf of granting 18 year olds the right to vote. The final success of this effort to extend the franchise led to a substantial increase in the size of the potential electorate in 1972.

Within the Democratic Party, two forces were at work to increase the influence of young people. First, because of the change of law, the new group of 18 to 20 year olds was eligible to participate for the first time; in addition, the large number of individuals who had turned 21 since the last election further increased the potential size of the youth bloc. Second, and augmenting the impact of the sheer size of the youth bloc, the party reforms pointedly sought to stimulate meaningful participation by younger Democrats.

Maine's Mitchell Commission Report included three specific recommendations on younger voters (1970: 7). First, it called for action to lower the voting age and interim steps to let 18 to 20 year olds participate in party matters even before they were enfranchised. Furthermore, two additional recommendations emphasizing issue orientation were designed to make the party more relevant, particularly to some young voters who had not participated in the past in proportion to their numbers. Finally, the Maine Young Democrats were specifically given two voting positions on the state committee.[20]

The McGovern Commission guidelines called for specific action by state parties to increase participation by younger Democrats. In Maine nearly every county chairman responded that an effort had been made to appeal to younger voters.[21] Of the 212 respondents to the questionnaire on this issue, 57.1% claimed that they or their committee had taken "specific action aimed at interesting voters under 30—either new voters or those who had not been eligible before—in coming to [their] caucus." The actions most frequently specified were personal recruitment, speaking at high schools, or appearing on local radio and television shows.

Table 10 shows that a majority of those who answered the questionnaire felt that more younger Democrats did participate in municipal caucuses in 1972 than had in the past. A majority of those interviewed felt that youth participation contributed a substantial share to the total increase in participation noted earlier.

Once again the level of youth participation differed considerably in those towns where local committees made an effort to influence youth from those in which no effort was made. This finding, coupled with that on women in Table 5, points directly to the impact of the reforms. The much-maligned "quota system" for delegates to the national convention was not really the goal of the reform guidelines;

Table 10. PARTICIPATION IN CAUCUSES BY DEMOCRATS UNDER 30

Statement	Percentage
Many more voters under 30 attended this year's caucus than have attended in the past	19.3
A few more voters under 30 attended this year's caucus than have attended in the past	33.0
About the same number of voters under 30 attended this year's caucus as have in the past	27.8
Fewer voters under 30 attended this year's caucus than have attended in the past	3.8
Did not caucus in the past, no estimate, etc.	16.1
n = 212	

rather the number of delegates to the convention served as an index to measure the success of state parties in attracting women and younger voters (and minorities) into the workings of the party. The goal of the guidelines was to eliminate discrimination—overt or covert—in party circles. The means was to take specific affirmative actions to convince those who had been the victims of past discrimination that their participation was earnestly desired and could have a meaningful impact. The data from the state of Maine indicate that the assumption upon which the McGovern Commission based its reforms was accurate. In those communities where specific action was taken to bring new participants into the process, women and youth (as shown in Table 11) participated in greater numbers than they had in the past and in significantly greater numbers than did women and youth in areas wherein local committees took no action.

As was the case with the data on women, no clear differences existed among Maine's counties nor among communities of different sizes. However, again in this case, largely urban Cumberland County

Table 11. RELATIONSHIP BETWEEN MUNICIPAL COMMITTEES' EFFORTS AND CAUCUS PARTICIPATION BY YOUTH IN 1972

	Percent Making an Effort	Percent Making no Effort
Many more under 30 attended	24.0	13.3
A few more under 30 attended	37.2	29.3
About the same number under 30 attended	21.5	37.3
Fewer under 30 attended	5.0	1.3
Have not caucused in past; cannot estimate	13.4	18.7
n =	121	25
	$X^2 = 10.67$	$p = .05$

Table 12. RELATIONSHIP BETWEEN PARTISAN COMPLEXION OF MUNICIPALITY
AND CAUCUS PARTICIPATION BY YOUTH IN 1972

	% Highly Democratic	% Slightly Democratic	% Competitive	% Slightly Republican	% Heavily Republican
Many more under 30 attended	20.8	10.5	20.5	20	20.8
A few more under 30 attended	25.0	28.9	25.6	35	42.7
About the same number under 30 attended	37.5	42.1	30.8	25	19.5
Fewer under 30 attended	0.0	5.3	0.0	5	3.7
Have not caucused in past; no estimate	16.7	13.2	23.1	25	13.4
n =	24	38	39	20	82

had a more marked increase in youth participation than did the others. Also, as was observed from the data on women, there was an obvious difference when one divided the towns and wards according to political complexion. As Table 12 demonstrates, many more of the highly Republican towns—as so classified by local party leaders—had increased participation by youth than did those in any other category. Party leaders concurred that many young McGovern supporters went to the caucuses in towns which previously had had minimal participation. In a number of towns they controlled the caucuses. In many more they at least elected delegates to the state convention.

Once more one must question whether this caucus participation was a one-shot affair. In some towns the young participants seemed to disappear right after the caucus or the convention. In others they continued to work but never joined in with the regular organization, as indicated by the following response:

> Mainly the new groups—the McGovern backers—created a schism between themselves and the regulars. The resentment was shown by each group going out on its own.

One should remember that much of this split was caused because the new young participants tended to back Senator McGovern whereas the regular Democrats favored Senator Muskie for the nomination. The resentment, therefore, was not so much one of new versus established, or young versus old, as it was of McGovern versus Muskie. This resentment was intensified because of the personal commitment of many Maine Democrats to Muskie but was not a phenomenon unique to this state or these candidates.

Despite this potential cleavage, in some counties the new young participants blended with the regulars and performed important campaign functions. One county leader summarized his experience:

> The McGovern people were new, more younger people. . . . And they got votes out we had never seen before. I've been a Ballot Clerk for seven years and there were people voting I didn't even know lived in this town.

The participation by younger Democrats was reflected in membership on town committees. Responding to the questionnaire, municipal party leaders felt that, in 45.1% of their communities, local party committees had more members under 30 than they had before the 1970 caucuses, whereas 40.1% had the same number and only 14.1% had fewer.

As mentioned above, however, it is important to examine influence in decision making in addition to participation in campaigns. Table 13 compares the percentage of municipal committees with each possible number of officers under 30 in 1970 with that in 1972. The high "don't know" figure reflects the difficulty in estimating ages, as well as the fact that some of the towns did not elect officers in 1970.

While 56.8% of those responding had the same number of officers under 30 in 1972 as they had in 1970—mostly none—30.5% had more in 1972 and only 12.7% had fewer. Again, as was true of women, most of those under 30 who ran for office won. While there was competition for town and ward office in 68% of the communities whose officers responded, in only 8.5% were any of the losers under 30. Finally, while there was some resentment that new participants were trying to take over, 16% of the towns and two of

Table 13. OFFICERS UNDER 30 ON MUNICIPAL COMMITTEES

	1970	1972
Percentage of towns with		
no officers under 30	64.1	46.7
1 officer under 30	17.0	25.0
2 officers under 30	6.6	15.1
3 officers under 30	2.8	7.5
4 officers under 30	0.0	2.8
don't know, no 1970 caucus	9.4	2.8
n = 212		

the sixteen counties elected party leaders who were under 30 years old.

It is evident, therefore, that young voters did become more active in Maine's Democratic Party, that they participated in the political process, that they competed in party elections, and that, while they did not always blend in with the more established Democrats, they did take a share of the party power. These findings are confirmed when one looks at participation in the 1972 State and National Conventions.

Although records of delegates' ages have not been maintained, our sample yields interesting data. In 29.1% of the municipalities responding, party leaders said that there were more delegates under 30 in 1972 than there had been in 1970. Only 13.1% felt that there had been fewer in 1972. The majority of the sample (57.7%) felt that the number was the same, again usually zero. The estimates concerning alternates were essentially the same. The number of communities reporting more delegates under 30 is especially important when one recalls that the size of most town and ward delegations was decreased.

In 1968, only one of Maine's 30 delegates to the Chicago Convention was under 30 years old. In Miami in 1972, three of the twenty delegates were under 30 and a fourth was exactly 30; three of the twenty alternates were also under 30, including two of the three alternates pledged to Senator McGovern.[22] Thus, the index used by the McGovern Commission indicated that the affirmative steps taken in Maine had indeed produced the desired result.

The percentage of young voters participating in the political process has always been surprisingly low. In 1972, the number of young Democrats eligible to participate increased dramatically. More important for our purposes, because of the appeal of Senator McGovern—and because of the positive steps taken by Maine Democratic Party leaders—an increased percentage of Maine's younger voters became active in party matters and contributed in a meaningful way to the party decision-making processes at all levels.

VI. CONCLUSIONS

Obviously the importance of these findings does not follow directly from the specific data generated by this research. Rather, it is a function of what these findings might mean for the future of the party system in America as we know it.

Political scientists and political journalists have been debating the future of parties for some time. Some, such as Kevin Phillips (1970) or Richard Scammon and Ben Wattenberg (1970), have concerned themselves with partisan alignments in the future, seemingly assuming that parties will continue to function as they have in recent years. Others, such as Frank Sorauf (1972) or Walter Dean Burnham (1970), feel that parties have begun to lose their primary position on the American political scene. Still others, like David Broder (1971) or John Saloma and Frederick Sontag (1973) or perhaps Burnham as well, see this decline of party's functions but regret the fact and plead for a reversal of the trend.

This paper has demonstrated that in one party in one state during one election year, the trend toward a decline in participation in party affairs was reversed. More Maine Democrats participated in every aspect of the political process, from caucus through active campaigning. Specifically these groups who had participated least in the past, women and younger voters, participated in greater numbers, particularly in those areas wherein a concerted effort was made to encourage them to do so. While all of the past was not reversed, while sex typecasting still existed, while animosity between younger and older activists was often as much in evidence as were harmonious arrangements, movement was clearly in a participatory direction as called for by the national and state party reform commissions. All of this was in spite of the fact that the national standard bearer was even more unpopular in Maine than he was nationally, having wrested his nomination from the state's favorite political son.

One must remember, however, that although these findings indicate a movement in the direction of increased participation, no one can claim that this movement was massive. More people were active in 1972 than had been in the past—and the reforms guaranteed that those who were active covered a broader spectrum of society— but many more people chose to remain inactive in 1972, just as they had in prior years.

The 1972 Democratic National Convention called for the establishment of a National Charter Commission and a National Delegate Selection Commission. The work of each of these will be important in determining the future direction of political parties. The mere fact that the Democratic Party had never before had a charter is significant. The Charter Commission, chaired by Duke University President Terry Sanford, the former governor of North Carolina who was, for a short time, a candidate for the party's presidential nomination in 1972, has wrestled with very difficult, basic problems. The question of the role of a political party involves answering preliminary questions. How many people can one actually expect to interest in political affairs? What type of party will interest most? What should be the nature of the relationship between party workers and rank and file? Party leaders and party workers? Party leaders and elected officials? What happens to parties between elections? Can one counter the debilitating effects of the Watergate scandal or will all progress be reversed as people "turn off" to politics and dismiss all politicians as corrupt and to be avoided?

In Maine 50% of the respondents to our questionnaire (n = 212) defined the role of the Democratic Party in their area as a "skeleton organization year round; most activity center[ing] around campaigns." An additional 22.2% responded "campaign activity only." Toward the more activist end of the scale, only 1.4% said that the party served as a "forum for discussion of governmental issues" and 9.0% defined the role of the party as a "year round organization providing services and/or assistance to party members."

However, when these same local party officials were asked what role the party should play in their area, they responded as noted in Table 14.

This demonstrates that local party leaders want to move the party in a more activist direction. My findings also indicate that increased effort can be successful in involving more people. But one must be cautious. I agree with those who feel that this is a desirable goal, that parties perform a meaningful role in our system of government, that they can be a mechanism for citizen participation and issue awareness, and that large numbers of citizens can be encouraged to

Table 14. PARTY LEADER PREFERENCES

Role of Party	Percentage
Forum for discussion of governmental issues	7.5
Year round organization providing services and/or assistance to party members	34.4
Skeleton organization year round; most activity centers around campaigns	20.3
Campaign activity only	3.8
Combination—forum for discussion of governmental issues and service organization	15.6
Other combinations—scattered	8.0
No answer	10.9
n = 213	

work for policy change through the political process, this last conclusion being the one sure lesson of the Eugene McCarthy movement and the early McGovern primary victories.

At the same time, however, this revitalization can only be a slow process. Citizens will have to be convinced that party politics merit their attention, and in light of Watergate this convincing will not come easily. Fewer than 70 people attended the Charter Commission's open hearing in Maine; that this small turnout was not unusual leads one to question the level of commitment on the part of party activists to party reform. Even activists are not interested in party per se; they are interested in what the party can do for them. It is clear that parties must demonstrate that commitment to them will lead to substantive results if they are to thrive.

Some have come to question whether the Democrats will continue to reform. Party regulars have attempted to make the reforms in the delegate selection process the scapegoat for the McGovern electoral debacle in 1972 and thus the current Delegate Selection Commission has done away with "quotas." However, the commitment to affirmative action has remained intact; the work and progress of the McGovern Commission have not been undone.

That the reforms have survived is not the same as saying that the two-party system is totally healthy. One grave danger that stems from the picture of American politics emerging from Watergate is that more citizens will turn away from political participation, no longer viewing it as a means to achieve the government they desire. If citizens view the system as corrupt and all politicians as self-serving, apathy, a danger endemic to our system, will stand as an even greater threat.

If political parties are to overcome apathy and counter Watergate, they must pursue a definite strategy. First, the commitment to a participatory system must be reaffirmed; citizens must feel that the smoke-filled room is a relic of another era, that small groups of men will not again usurp the political process, that their efforts can shape the direction the party is taking. Second, the parties must continue to expand their bases; women, youth, and minorities, extremists as well as centrists, must find that they have a place in the two-party system, that the issues which concern them will be aired and debated. Barring this, these people will turn to other means for expressing their legitimate concerns, and the two-party system will suffer. Most important, however, the spirit that led to the procedural reforms must be linked to substantive changes in policy. The system must demonstrate that it can respond to citizen pressure, not just to the pressure of big money. Parties and politicians must confront the issues that affect the people in a forthright manner and propose constructive solutions.

This paper has demonstrated that the procedural reforms mandated by the McGovern and Mitchell Commissions did lead to increased participation by Maine Democrats, especially by women and youth where their participation was actually sought. But the real evidence of the health of party politics in Maine was demonstrated by the 1974 primaries, fought as the Watergate crisis was reaching its lowest depths.

Rather than looking to Washington, Maine Democrats debated the key issues facing the state, stressing differing philosophies and programs, seeking volunteer and voter response on the basis of substantive differences. Six Democrats sought the party's gubernatorial nomination.[23] The candidates all drew heavily on young people and women to run their campaigns. The policy differences that separated the candidates were apparent in the attitudes of the volunteers attracted to the campaigns.

In addition, a woman, Jadine O'Brien, challenged incumbent Congressman Peter Kyros for the Democrats' First District nomination. Her campaign, based on strong personality and issue differences, brought into politics a corps of volunteers who had never before been active. They fought to have their views carry the day; while they lost this battle, there is little question that they gained valuable insights and will return to fight another day.

The future of the Democratic Party in Maine appears to be bright. The party has drawn new activists who are committed to working for substantive change through the system. Not fearing to air controversial differences, as they did with convention floor fights over platform planks on amnesty and Gay Liberation, the Democrats have shown doubters that the spirit of reform will encompass substantive debate as well as procedural issues. The Republicans will have to respond to this spirit or lose the new generation of active politicians.

Doubters chide, "To change is not necessarily to reform." However, if change is meaningful, if it reaches the problems that are afflicting the system, then it is reform in its most positive sense. Party politics have been afflicted by disillusionment and apathy caused largely by closed decision-making processes and unresponsiveness. The reforms in the Democratic Party, nationally and in Maine, have made inroads on these problems. The parties must continue to make citizen participation easier and more meaningful. They must echo Macaulay's famous dictum: "We reform that we may preserve."

NOTES

1. This language, adopted by the McGovern Commission, is a composite of two varied, but not inconsistent, phrases accepted by the 1968 Convention. The convention approved both the majority report of the Credentials Committee, calling for a "meaningful and timely opportunity," and the minority report of the Rules Committee, seeking a "full and timely opportunity" for participation.

2. This sense of urgency is expressed in the concluding section of *Mandate for Change,* the Report of the McGovern Commission:

> If we are not an open party; if we do not represent the demands for change, then the danger is not that people will go to the Republican Party; it is that there will no longer be a way for people committed to orderly change to fulfill their needs and desires within our traditional political system. It is that they will turn to third or fourth party politics or to the anti-politics of the street. (Punctuation as in the original)

The entire report is available from the Democratic National Committee; it was reprinted in the *Congressional Record* on September 22, 1971.

3. Ranney's classifications are based on popular vote for governor, percentage of seats held in the state senate, percentage of seats held in the state house of representatives, and the percentage of all terms for governor, senate, and house held by each party over a period of fourteen years ending in 1970 (Ranney, 1971: 84-91).

4. The outcome of the race in the First Congressional District remains in doubt as Congressman Kyros has requested both an inspection of the ballots and a recount.

5. The unsuccessful presidential campaign of Senator Edmund Muskie presents some difficulties. One could argue that participation was artificially stimulated because the state's senior senator was so deeply involved in national politics and many people wanted to be associated, however remotely, with his campaign. On the other hand, one could argue that the Muskie balloon had burst by the time Mainers were organizing in 1972; Maine's uniform caucus period is in the third week in March, which in 1972 was after the handwriting was on the wall for Muskie. While I was aware of this factor, I could not accurately gauge its effect. However, I did keep it in mind throughout my analysis and will refer to it when appropriate.

It should also be noted that this research was completed before the effects of the Watergate scandal had begun to be felt. While I do not feel that my research is "inoperative," my conclusions concerning political participation have had to take into account events happening after my data were gathered.

6. Records prior to 1968 are incomplete; thus we could go back no further for comparison.

7. The McGovern Commission was concerned with discrimination—either overt or unintentional—against women, youth, and minority groups. Maine has no prominent racial minority; American Indians comprise 3% of the population and are the largest such group. Americans of French descent are the largest ethnic minority; a preliminary surname check in areas with large Franco-American populations revealed that they were represented in numbers at least proportional to their percentage of the total population. Thus, this study concentrates on the general level of participation and the participation by youth (defined, with the McGovern Commission, as those under 30) and by women.

8. Most of the cities in Maine are divided into wards; however, prior to 1972, the cities did not tend to break down to the ward level for caucuses and did not elect ward officers. In 1972, as stipulated in the Mitchell Commission guidelines, most cities did caucus by ward. However, ward organizations, except in the largest cities, are still sketchy and lists of ward officers are often unavailable. Consequently, the 354 questionnaires were sent to town chairpersons, city chairpersons, and the ward chairpersons listed at state headquarters.

9. Others who have studied local party officials have also noted problems in achieving high response rates (see Bowman and Boynton, 1966: 669).

10. The questionnaires, while anonymous, were coded according to county and included certain questions relating to size and political characteristics of the town. Comparison of these figures with those for the entire population revealed that some of the smaller counties were slightly underrepresented in our sample; the larger cities were the most overrepresented. However, none of this variation was of significant magnitude and a sufficient number of responses was recieved from all types of communities. Consequently, we felt that reliance on the questionnaire data was warranted.

11. A few towns have caucused inconsistently, for example, in 1968, but not in 1970. As Maine's governor is elected in "off" presidential years, however, sufficient incentives exist to maintain organizations.

12. See note 5 for possible causes of this increase unrelated to party reforms.

13. Twenty percent of the towns with committees of four or fewer members in 1970 reported more than four in 1972. Because adequate records have not been maintained, it is not possible to ascertain if a cyclical pattern exists, showing an increase of activity (as reflected in committee membership) in presidential years and a decrease in "off" (i.e., gubernatorial) years. Those interviewed were of the impression that changes in 1972 were of a different magnitude than anything experienced before.

14. Determining the number of new officers per town was not so easy as would be imagined. First, because our interest was in new participants, we wanted to eliminate consideration of in-and-outers, that is, those who served one year, did not serve for a while, and then served again. This could not be done systematically because of the lack of old caucus papers. Judging from the records which were available, however, we felt that this was not a common pattern. Second, we had to consider that individuals might switch offices. While recognizing that a chairperson obviously spends much more time than does a treasurer, for example, we only counted those who held no office whatsoever in the previous biennium.

It is interesting to note that the turnover rate for town and ward officers is generally quite high. This is not inconsistent with what others have found elsewhere (Bowman and Boynton, 1966); this reflects the fact that service as an officer of a local party committee tends to be a duty rather than a privilege and is accompanied by few gratifications.

15. This reasoning has led some reformers, such as Frederick Sontag, to conclude that sex-rotation of party officers is essential if women are ever to achieve a position of true parity.

16. Additionally, in 1972, 16.9% of the towns reported that some women had run for office and lost. This figure cannot be accurately converted into raw numbers because it is based on the questionnaire sample and not caucus papers. Comparable figures are not available for earlier years, but this does show that women were willing to enter the political fray even if losing was a possibility.

17. It should be noted here that early in 1973 State Chairman Severin Beliveau resigned. Violet Pease, elected his successor by the state committee in a hard-fought, three-way contest against two males, became the first woman elected to head a state committee.

18. Prior to 1972, the state headquarters never broke delegations down by sex. Consequently no accurate figures for previous conventions exist.

19. Of the 15 alternates attending the convention, 4 were female. Five additional male alternates were elected but did not travel to Miami.

20. Women were already guaranteed representation on the state committee. Minimum county representation on the state committee is two, one person each of each sex. County representation above the minimum varies with the population of the county and Democratic voters in the county, with no stipulation regarding the sex of the representatives.

21. Only one felt that no effort was made in his county. Most of those interviewed emphasized the newly eligible voters, not the group of 21 to 30 year olds also included in the McGovern Commission's definition of youth.

22. All of the delegates and the rest of the alternates went to Miami pledged to Senator Muskie, although a number of them had specified at caucuses that they would vote for Senator McGovern were Muskie no longer a candidate.

23. While this article deals only with the Democrats in Maine, it should be noted here that four Republicans sought their party's nod; these men also differed markedly on the issues and debated these points throughout the state. Furthermore, three Independents filed petitions to be placed on the November ballot. One of these, James Longley, has attempted to build a volunteer organization comprising those most concerned with efficiency and economy in government.

REFERENCES

ABBOTT, D. W. and E. T. ROGOWSKY [eds.] (1971) Political Parties: Leadership, Organization, Linkage. Chicago: Rand McNally.

BOWMAN, L. and G. R. BOYNTON (1966) "Recruitment patterns among local party officials: a model and some preliminary findings in selected locales." American Political Science Review (June): 667-676.

BRODER, D. S. (1971) The Party's Over. New York: Harper and Row.

BURNHAM, W. D. (1970) Critical Elections and the Mainsprings of American Politics. New York: Norton.

CARALEY, D. [ed.] (1966) Party Politics and National Elections. Boston: Little, Brown.

ELDERSVELD, S. (1964) Political Parties: A Behavioral Analysis. Chicago: Rand McNally.

HIRSCHFIELD, R. S., B. E. SWANSON, and B. D. BLANK (1962) "A profile of political activists in Manhattan." Western Political Quarterly: 489-506.

KEY, V. O. (1967) American State Politics: An Introduction. New York: Knopf.

––– (1964) Politics, Parties, and Pressure Groups. New York: Crowell.

LOCKARD, D. (1959) New England State Politics. Princeton: Princeton University Press.

McGovern Commission (1971) Mandate for Change. Washington, D.C.: Democratic National Committee.

Mitchell Commission (1970) Report of the Maine Democratic Commission on Party Structure and Delegate Selection. Augusta: Maine State Democratic Committee.

PHILLIPS, K. P. (1970) The Emerging Republican Majority. Garden City, N.Y.: Anchor Books.

RANNEY, A. (1971) "Parties in state politics," in H. Jacob and K. N. Vines (eds.) Politics in the American States. Boston: Little, Brown.

SALOMA, J. S. and F. H. SONTAG (1973) Parties. New York: Vintage Books.

SCAMMON, R. M. and B. J. WATTENBERG (1970) The Real Majority. New York: Berkley.

SORAUF, F. J. (1972) Party Politics in America. Boston: Little, Brown.

Chapter 7

CLIENTELE MARKETS, ORGANIZATIONAL DYNAMICS, AND LEADERSHIP CHANGE: A LONGITUDINAL COMPARISON OF THE NORWEGIAN AND BRITISH LABOR PARTIES

E. SPENCER WELLHOFER
VICTOR J. HANBY
TIMOTHY M. HENNESSEY

I. INTRODUCTION

The future of political parties is a topic that has received considerable attention in the post-World War II period. Opinions on the subject are highly divergent and largely normatively informed. Yet one issue of persistent concern is the appropriate organizational configuration of parties to facilitate party democracy and responsibility.

An understanding of the institutional forces that create the conditions for leadership accountability and responsiveness is a prime requisite for any understanding of the democratic process. In modern industrial societies, large organizational structures have come to dominate political, social, and economic life. In the realm of politics, professional organizational men have replaced the dilettante. Yet despite such organizational dynamics and the importance attributed to political parties in democracy, little rigorous analysis of the structural characteristics of political party development exists.

AUTHORS' NOTE: An earlier draft of this paper was presented at the Annual Convention of the American Political Science Association, August 29-September 2, 1974, Palmer House Hotel, Chicago, Illinois. We wish to thank Professors James Christoph, Penny G. Martin, and James Fay for their comments on an earlier draft. We also wish to thank our respective institutions for financial and clerical support and particularly the Center for International Programs of Michigan State University whose initial financial support made the Political Party Institutionalization Project, of which this paper forms a part, possible.

Traditionally scholars have demonstrated an ambivalence toward organizations. Some, like Michels (1962), saw party leaders as seduced by a fundamental organizational conservatism which led them to abandon their ideological tenets for the security of pragmatic incrementalism. Others, such as Weber (1946), argued for the positive as well as negative attributes of strong party organizations. He suggested that while party organizations did project inherent oligarchical tendencies, they also acted to modify ideological extremism and thus facilitated a realistic party and national leadership, unconstrained by ideological commitments, which could contribute to democracy in the larger society.

Moisei Ostrogorski (1964) was the first modern scholar to point to the inherent organizational pressures on parties operating under conditions of universal suffrage, which ultimately led to oligarchic control, manipulation of the electorate, and the blurring of ideological differences. Ostrogorski's analysis thus constituted the groundwork for a theory of party organization and bureaucracy; and, by emphasizing the role of structural factors, he was able to develop what, by the standard of his contemporaries, was a relatively systematic comparative analysis of party development.

Although the tensions between ideological consistency and organizational incrementalism, between leadership maneuverability and internal party democracy, seem to have been a center of focus and debate in the study of political parties for some time, much of the literature was descriptive by nature and unsystematic in scope. In addition, recent American scholars have tended to idealize the strong party organizations of Europe as models for American parties. Wright's (1971) categorization based on "Rational-Efficient" and "Party Democracy" models is an analysis along these lines. Wright sets forth several dimensions to distinguish two ideal types, with American parties presumably placed near the "Rational-Efficient" and European Socialist parties placed near the "Party Democracy" ideals.

Recent reforms in U.S. party organizations seem designed to move American parties closer to the "Party Democracy" model. These reforms include attempts to reduce the influence of old-line patronage organizations, to introduce greater ideological and policy consistency, to create membership organizations and a full-time administrative apparatus. The introduction of these reforms has produced some unintended consequences (Cavala, 1974; Ranney, 1974).

But whatever position is assumed in the debate, one facet has been given insufficient attention to date: namely, a careful, theoretical and empirical assessment of what the conditions of political party development have been since the inception of the particular party or parties in question. Until this is done, it is unlikely that light will be substituted for heat in the debates. In the paper that follows, we seek to present and analyze a set of data in terms of which to compare the development of two European Socialist parties: the Norwegian Labor Party from 1886 to 1971 and the British Labor Party from 1900 to 1971.

Our fundamental assumption is that the behavior of political parties in a democratic system is in large part determined by a combination of organizational processes, the changing levels of citizen activity and sophistication to which the party is expected to respond through periodic elections, and patterns of leadership change. Proceeding from this assumption, we seek to examine the conditions under which these various elements interact to influence the processes of political party development. In this paper we shall concentrate on three of these: (1) *resources*—party membership and electoral support; (2) *organizational development*—number of party centers; and (3) *leadership change.* In short we seek to understand the relationship, if any, among these three sets of factors.

II. CONCEPTS AND MEASURES

In our previous research, we set forth the stages of organizational development (Wellhofer and Hennessey, 1974b; Wellhofer, 1972; 1974). As organizations, parties must have sufficient resources to carry out their programs. *These resources include the size of the popular vote, the number of dues-paying members, and the size and structural complexity of the affiliated organizations.* We have chosen to call these the "resource markets." The growth of these markets is likely to fluctuate over time as the party experiences a process of trial and error, developing an appeal to its potential clientele base.

POLITICAL PARTIES AS ORGANIZATIONS

Any reading of the vast literature on organizations makes one immediately aware that there is no consensus on a precise definition of "organization." Most writers on the subject, however, generally agree that the necessary, but not sufficient, characteristics of an organization are "1) a set of stable social relationships; 2) deliberately created; 3) with the intention of continuously accomplishing some specific goals or purposes" (Stinchombe, 1965: 142).

Moreover, in the study of organizations, considerable emphasis is placed on the dynamic processes that define the transformation of organizational character (Zald and Denton, 1963; Gusfield, 1955): "Metamorphous models focus on the structural changes which the model builder judges to be dominant and critical" (Starbuck, 1971: 276). In a similar vein, see Starbuck, 1965; Whyte, 1948; Tsouderos, 1955; Messinger, 1955; and Simpson and Gulley, 1962. In general most writers employ two sets of variables of organizational growth and development: the expansion of organizational clientele markets, and the elaboration of administrative structures. As a measure of clientele market development, we suggest that dues-paying membership and votes received in popular elections are appropriate. To measure the administrative elaboration, we employ the growth of administrative subunits: party centers, constituency organizations, affiliated groups such as cooperatives, youth groups, women's groups, and so on.

LEADERSHIP AND LEADERSHIP CHANGE

Ours is a structural analysis of party organization and leadership, and we thus define the leaders by the official positions they hold in the executive organs of the party. For the British Labour Party "leadership" covers the chairman, vice-chairman, treasurer, and other members of the National Executive Committee from 1900 to 1971. For the Norwegian Labor Party we include chairman, vice-chairman, secretary, editor, economic secretary, organization secretary, labor secretary, local government secretary, legal information secretary, women's secretary, and information secretary of the party, the membership of the national and central committees, and the chairman and secretary of the Oslo Federation. The latter are included because of the central role played by the Oslo Federation in the party.

The measure of elite turnover is the circulation index developed by McGregor (1974) and defined as the inverse of the proportion of immobility or the inverse of the percent of officeholders at time, t_1, who occupy the same position in time, t_2. The index employs paired years with the midpoints plotted on Figures 2 and 4. For example, for Norway the plot point of the year 1892 is a comparison of the years 1891 and 1893 with the index showing that 50% of the officeholders in 1891 occupied the same positions in 1893. The index can vary from 0.0 if all individuals occupy the same positions in the two years to 1.0 if no individuals do. By calculating the index in this manner, we control for the expanding size of the elite as new positions are created.

Such an approach to party organization permits us then to examine the relationship between the organizational development and the patterns of leadership change. Here the central question to which we shall address ourselves is: What is the relationship between organizational development and changing leadership patterns?

III. DEVELOPMENTAL PATTERNS OF NORWEGIAN LABOR PARTY

The first stage of the Norwegian Labor Party's development dates from the party's founding in 1887 to 1904 when several major administrative reforms were instituted. During this period the predominant organizational problem was one of defining an appeal to a potential social base. The result was the emergence of a moderate form of socialism which appealed principally to the small handicraft or skilled worker unions and so-called worker societies. During this period the bulk of the party leadership was recruited from the ranks of the skilled workers.

The series of administrative reforms in 1904 established a national committee in addition to the central committee, formalized rules for the meetings of the national party congresses, and attempted to coordinate local party centers into provincial party federations. In addition, a number of factors heightened the need for administrative coordination: suffrage expansion (1898), electoral reform (1904), and dissolution of the Union with Sweden (1905) acted to open the way for more meaningful electoral activity. This, in turn, necessitated a more professional administrative apparatus.

The most turbulent period in the party's history was in the late 1910s and early 1920s. During this period the Norwegian Labor Party was shaken by rapid social change; the resulting dislocations and conflicts produced a major confrontation over party control between the moderates of the skilled trade unions on the one hand, and the syndicalist sector on the other. A Bolshevik youth movement was also active in the conflict. By 1918, the moderates were forced

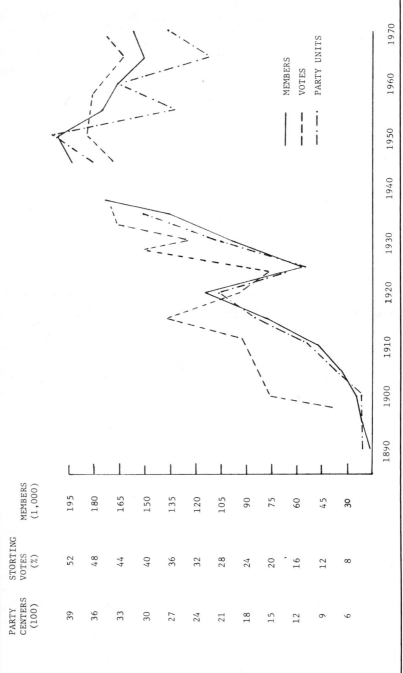

Figure 1: DEVELOPMENT OF THE NORWEGIAN LABOR PARTY

out of control, and the established social base was disrupted by the rapid industrialization of the period. From 1918 to 1921 the moderates remained in the party as active critics of the new order; unable to regain control, they left in 1921 to form the Social Democratic Labor Party (NSA). The new, more radical leadership of the DNA set about to build a new social base more in line with their ideological preferences. In 1923, the Bolshevik elements split to form the Communist Party (NKP). These machinations resulted in a withdrawal of support from all factions by the Federation of Labor in 1925.

Reunification of the party took place in 1927. The struggles between the factions were eventually resolved (1930) and, with the winning of governmental control in 1935, the party shifted its ideology from class struggle and dictatorship of the proletariat to national unity and working within the capitalist system. In 1939 the national congress reaffirmed the new directives. The period from 1930-1950 represents the "takeoff" stage for the party.

The period from 1950 to 1970 was marked by internal party disputes, the most notable of which culminated in the formation of a splinter group which broke away to the left to form the Socialist Peoples Party in 1961. During the period from 1955 to 1970, the electoral success of the party declined and it was forced into coalition (Heidar and Lafferty, 1973).

IV. DATA ANALYSIS: NORWAY

CLIENTELE AND ORGANIZATIONAL VARIABLES

The preceding historical discussion is in large part supported by the data in Figure 1. For all three organizational and clientele variables—party centers, party membership, and Storting votes—the data reveal a positive linear growth until the early 1920s when this pattern is disrupted by a sharp decline beginning in the early 1920s and lasting until the early 1930s. By the middle to the late 1930s, however, party membership and party centers are able to match previous periods of growth and eventually surpass them. Storting votes, by contrast, show a "two-humped" curvilinear pattern, that is, a sharp decline in votes in the 1920s and a large increase in the late 1920s, another decrease and then a recovery in the late 1930s which surpasses all previous percentages of the vote.

As our previous discussion of the Norwegian party development suggested, this disruption in growth patterns and the resulting period of decline undoubtedly can be largely explained by the internal conflicts that shook the party, particularly the dispute between the moderates of the trade unions and the syndicalist sector and later the Bolshevik group which split to form the Communist Party in 1923. In the late 1930s, the party dramatically recovered and exhibited a smooth positive linear growth for all of the variables until the war. Indeed, this growth pattern continued in the years immediately following the war until the mid-1950s, at which time the party centers and membership declined; they have shown only a slight improvement in recent years. Storting votes, however, have not declined, but have remained at their highest levels. The slight decrease in 1965 is a reflection of the foreign policy disputes in the Storting and the creation of the splinter group which called itself the Socialist Peoples' Party.

LEADERSHIP CHANGE

To measure the degree of leadership change, we employ the circulation index. Figure 2 plots the circulation index from 1890 to 1970, interrupted only by the war period. The least circulation or change takes place in 1908, 1932, and 1951, whereas the greatest circulation occurs in 1904, 1912, and 1921.

During the early years of the party, while the circulation index is relatively high, it is also punctuated by a low in 1908. Such a pattern would be typical of a young organization experimenting with different leadership combinations to develop most successfully its clientele base.

Perhaps the most striking feature of the data presented in Figure 2 is the drastic decline in leadership circulation from 1921 to 1932. This phenomenon is a particularly striking one given the fact that organizational and clientele factors are declining and internal disputes in the party are at an all-time high. One would suspect that such conditions would lead to a great deal of leadership change. Yet the level of circulation after 1921 is not positively associated with the disputes of 1921 and 1923, but rather seems to be negatively related; that is, the greater the internal party conflict, the lower the leadership circulation.

One possible interpretation of this finding is that the leaders who took over after significant conflict in 1921 were able to maintain a

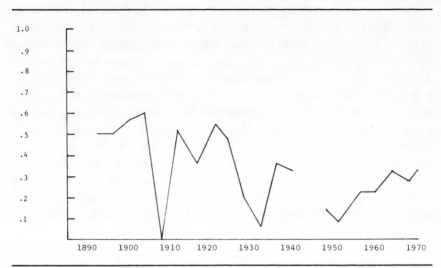

Figure 2: CIRCULATION INDEX FOR THE NORWEGIAN LABOR PARTY

modicum of control until the mid-1930s, and the decline in circulation simply reflects their continued control of the party. This interpretation would be misleading, however, because there are significant changes in leadership, changes that appear insignificant when compared with the high circulation levels of 1921. One must keep in mind that 1921 is the second highest point of circulation. Hence, it is important to note that in 1924 close to 50% of the leadership changed and in 1925 over 40% changed. Indeed, it is not until 1928 and 1932 that the circulation index is startlingly low. However, by 1936 leadership circulation has increased to nearly 40%.

Immediately following World War II, circulation is again very low, approximating the 1932 levels. The index then shows a consistent and regular stepwise increase until 1970, although it never again comes close to pre-1930 levels. The postwar period is also interesting because increases in leadership circulation, as minimal as they are, are accompanied by decreases in membership and administrative elaboration and increases in votes, with the exception of 1965 which undoubtedly reflects the dispute and the establishment of the Norwegian Socialist Peoples' Party.

V. DEVELOPMENT OF BRITISH LABOUR PARTY

As was true in Norway, the British Labour Party began as an alliance of liberal, middle-class intellectuals and trade unionists. The growth of the organization was relatively slow as the leadership structured an appeal to a potential social base. The result was a party broadly committed to the cause of the working class but without a clear ideological program, depending in many circumstances on tacit Liberal support for its candidacies and deriving most of its financial and electoral support from a curious alliance between some older craft and skilled worker unions and the newer, developing unions whose main catchment area was the unskilled component within society's lower occupational strata. A new party constitution in 1918 rendered three significant changes in internal party organization: direct as well as indirect membership extending the social base to individual members, the development of a women's section further expanding the party's appeal, and, finally, a formal policy statement, *Labour and the New Social Order,* explicitly committing the party to socialism, albeit of the moderate, evolutionary kind. The collapse of the Liberals in 1918 (when their vote declined to 26% from 43% in 1910) and the extension of suffrage made many new members and voters available for Labour appeals. In the membership market, because of the difficulties encountered as the result of the Osborne case in 1913, the party's membership ranks contracted, but all other indicators showed expansion.

The high point of the period was reached in 1929 when the party consolidated its electoral gains and emerged as the national government, albeit still in a minority capacity but with sufficient parliamentary seats and authority to make credible its capacity to govern. This success eradicated at long last the image created by the debacle of 1923-1925 when MacDonald had attempted to broaden Labour's base through attractive-sounding generalizations and a coalition with the Liberals, only to have the Liberals withdraw their support and bring the government down.

In the British Labour Party the impact of social and economic unrest associated with the depression did not become seriously divisive until 1931 when the popular vote declined through Mac-Donald's participation in the national coalition and party membership continued to drop. After 1935 British Labour began to rebuild itself. By the end of World War II, the reversal of the Osborne ruling, which served to increase party membership by forcing union members to "contract out," and the triumph in the election of 1945 served to establish once again British Labour as a powerful and continued contender for government control.

VI. DATA ANALYSIS: BRITAIN

CLIENTELE AND ORGANIZATIONAL VARIABLES

The growth of party membership and popular vote support for the British Labour Party generally follow a positive linear function with some significant curvilinear developments between 1930 and 1940, and a general "trailing off" after 1945 (Figure 3). The curve for membership is sharply curvilinear owing to decision rules concerning "contracting in" or "out." Contracting in has had a decided detrimental effect on the number of members in the Labour Party. After the Osborne ruling was rescinded, permitting the adoption of a "contracting out" rule, the membership reached a very high level in 1947 and continued to increase until 1965, when there was a slight decrease.

LEADERSHIP CHANGE

Until 1956, the circulation index for the British Labour Party is quite stable with most fluctuations taking place in the range between .2 and .4. There are, however, notable exceptions in 1916 and 1948, when circulation is very low. It is interesting to note that in one of these instances, namely 1916, the circulation low is followed by constitutional change in 1918.

Perhaps the most substantively significant feature of the circulation data concerns the consistent decline in leadership change after 1956. Indeed, the data graph as a negative linear function, reaching their lowest level since 1916!

Finally, there is very little relationship between the curvilinear patterns noted in the rate and organizational variables between 1930 and 1940 and the circulation index during that period. The latter remains relatively stable throughout that ten-year period with only minor fluctuation. After 1956, however, the circulation index declines while membership, administrative units, and votes remain relatively high and stable, with some expected curvilinearity in the votes owing to competition.

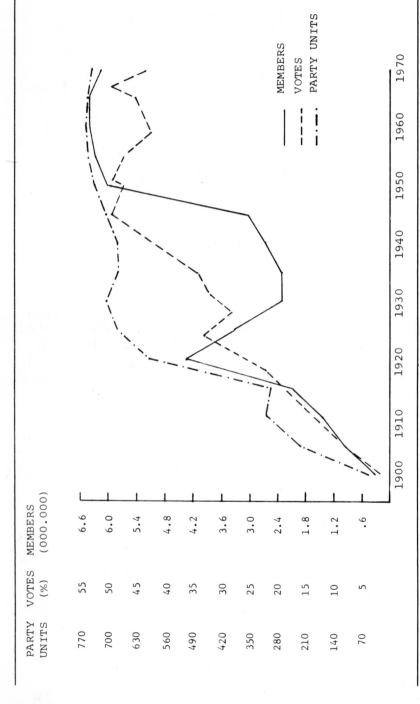

Figure 3: DEVELOPMENT OF THE BRITISH LABOUR PARTY

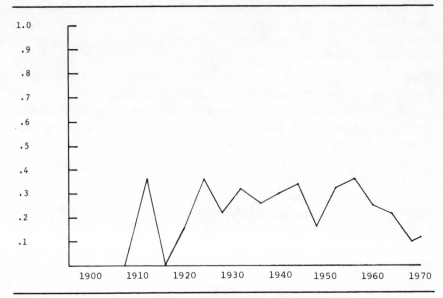

Figure 4: CIRCULATION INDEX FOR THE BRITISH LABOUR PARTY

VII. CONCLUSIONS

The most fruitful way to sum up these research findings and draw meaningful comparisons and conclusions from the data is to divide the development of the two parties roughly into developmental stages. Organizational theorists employ a wide variety of developmental stages to characterize organizational growth and transformation, but based on our previous research (Wellhofer and Hennessey, 1974b), we have found those employed by Selznick (1957: 102-112) to be quite useful. Following Selznick, we suggest the development of both parties prior to World War II could be characterized as embodying two stages of development: selection of a social base, and building an institutional core designed to organize this social base. Selznick proposed, and we have empirically demonstrated elsewhere, the existence of such stages. In the first stage, selection of a social base, the predominant developmental problem is to define a set of groups upon which the organization can be built. Growth during the period is likely to be slow and uneven as the organization experiments with different clientele groups. When the clientele base has been sufficiently defined, the predominant developmental problem shifts to building the institutional core in which emphasis is placed on organization of the clientele base and the development of an administrative apparatus. These two stages capture the nature of the prewar party development in both countries. In both countries the pattern shows an interruption during the 1920s and 1930s when environmental factors or party schisms or both produce a reversal, but the overall trend is clear.

When we consider the circulation index for the two countries during this period, we find that British Labour has a much smaller general range of change than does the Norwegian party. In British Labour the major change in circulation is associated with the constitutional change of 1918 which appears effectively to limit the range of the circulation index after that date. In Norway, on the other hand, there is a much higher level of leadership circulation, and this phenomenon is associated with both organizational change and voter support. That is, leadership circulation in Norwegian Labor appears to be more responsive to organizational dynamics than in British Labour.

The period following World War II is also similar for both parties. Party membership and votes tend to level off if not decline while administrative elaboration declines slightly in British Labour and quite severely in Norwegian Labor. Such a phenomenon in organizational development has been termed "formalization" by Selznick and ourselves.

Turning once again to the circulation index, we observe strikingly different trends in the two parties. In British Labour the formalization period is associated with sharp decline in circulation, followed by an increase, but then succeeded by a prolonged decline to the second lowest level in the party's history. By contrast, in Norwegian Labor the circulation shows a clear stepwise increase although still below the highest points of 1904 and 1920.

These contrasting data demand an explanation. Michels argued that parties are plagued by two organizational diseases: oligarchy and parliamentarianism. It would appear British Labour has contracted both. The presence of oligarchy is clearly suggested by the circulation index, and numerous observers agree the party has tended toward parliamentarianism—an emphasis on vote maximization with consequent atrophy of the party outside parliament (Hanby, 1974: 137-152; Bauman, ch. 4).

The Norwegian Labor Party demonstrates the opposite characteristics: formalization does not lead to oligarchy; rather, leadership circulation is increasing and is associated with competition and conflict over issues resulting in 1961 in a breaking away of the Socialist Peoples' Party.

The differences between the parties is best explained by the differing nature of party membership. British Labour is based upon indirect membership (Duverger, 1963: 13-22) with the vast majority of its members consisting of trade-union affiliates and a significant proportion of these, members by "default"; that is, such members have failed to exercise their "contracting out" option. In contrast, Norwegian Labor is built on direct affiliates who have exercised the affirmative act of party membership. To induce prospective members to make such a commitment, the Norwegian Labor Party has long engaged in a policy of "organizational incapsulation," the provision of a multitude of complex organizations and selective incentives for party members. The effects of this policy ensure a more astute and active membership which can make more effective "claims" on leadership than is true of British Labour. Moreover, the policy militates against the organizational atrophy occurring in British Labour. (We have discussed the full theoretical arguments of this in Wellhofer and Hennessey, 1974a). Indeed, Michels may not have seen the advantage of a powerful, complex, and demanding party organization outside parliament to balance the influence and control of parliamentary representatives.

The implications of this study for the future of political parties are several. First, it seems clear that, contrary to Michels, oligarchy is not the inevitable consequence of organizational growth. Rather, it has been shown that under differing circumstances parties develop along different lines. Thus, the "iron law of oligarchy" is flexible; the future of political parties is not predetermined. Second, it is also clear that the British and Norwegian Labor parties have evolved quite different organizational and membership strategies with important consequences for leadership circulation. In organizations where the constituent units can place effective claims on the leadership, oligarchy does not develop (Edelstein, 1967). In Norwegian Labor the presence of multiple, complex subunits has provided the necessary conditions for sustaining elite circulation. Moreover, such strategies have important implications for the place of parliamentarianism in the party vis à vis its long-standing commitments to its clientele groups; that is, in parties where traditional clientele groups can place effective claims on leadership, parliamentarianism is likely to be contained.

REFERENCES

CAVALA, W. (1974) "Changing the rules changes the game: party reform and the 1972 California delegation to the Democratic National Convention." American Political Science Review (March): 27-42.

BAUMAN, Z. (1972) Between Class and Elite. Manchester: Manchester University Press.

DUVERGER, M. (1963) Political Parties. New York: Wiley.

EDELSTEIN, J. D. (1967) "An organizational theory of union democracy." American Sociological Review (March): 19-31.

GUSFIELD, J. R. (1955) "Social structure and moral reform: temperance union." American Journal of Sociology (November): 221-232.

HANBY, V. (1974) "A changing Labour elite: the national executive committee of the Labour Party 1900-1972," in I. Crewe (ed.) British Political Sociology Yearbook. Vol. 1: Elites in Western Democracies. London: Croom Helm.

HEIDAR, K. and W. LAFFERTY (1973) "Party institutionalization and elite recruitment: a preliminary analysis of the Norwegian Labor movement." Delivered at the Workshop in Pressure Groups in Europe, European Consortium for Political Research, Mannheim, Germany, April 12-18.

McGREGOR, E. B. (1974) "Politics and career mobility of bureaucrats." American Political Science Review (March): 18-26.

MESSINGER, S. L. (1955) "Organizational transformation: a case study of a declining social movement." American Sociological Review (February): 3-10.

MICHELS, R. (1962) Political Parties. New York: Collier Books.

OSTROGORSKI, M. (1964) Democracy and the Organization of Political Parties. New York: Doubleday.

RANNEY, A. (1974) "Comment on 'changing the rules changes the game'." American Political Science Review (March): 43-44.

SELZNICK, P. (1957) Leadership in Administration. New York: Row, Peterson.

SIMPSON, R. L. and W. H. GULLEY (1962) "Goals, environmental pressures and organizational characteristics." American Sociological Review (June): 344-351.

STARBUCK, W. H. (1971) "Organizational metamorphosis," in W. H. Starbuck (ed.) Organizational Growth and Development. Baltimore: Penguin Books.

——— (1965) "Organizational growth and development," in J. March (ed.) Handbook of Organizations. Chicago: Rand McNally.

STINCHOMBE, A. L. (1965) "Social structure and organizations," in J. March (ed.) Handbook of Organizations. Chicago: Rand McNally.

TSOUDEROS, J. E. (1955) "Organizational change in terms of a series of selected variables." American Sociological Review (April): 206-210.

WEBER, M. (1946) "Class, status, party," in H. H. Gerth and C. W. Mills (eds.) From Max Weber: Essays in Sociology. New York: Oxford University Press.

WELLHOFER, E. S. (1974) "Political parties as communities of fate: tests with Argentine party elites." American Journal of Political Science (May): 347-363.

——— (1972) "Dimensions of party development: a study in organizational dynamics." Journal of Politics (February): 153-182.

——— and T. M. HENNESSEY (1974a) "Models of political party organization and strategy: some analytic approaches to oligarchy," in I. Crewe (ed.) British Political Sociology Yearbook. Vol. 1: Elites in Western Democracies. London: Croom Helm.

——— (1974b) "Political party development: institutionalization, leadership recruitment and behavior." American Journal of Political Science (February): 135-165.

WHYTE, W. F. (1948) Human Relations in the Restaurant Industry. New York: McGraw-Hill.

WRIGHT, W. E. (1971) A Comparative Study of Party Organizations. Columbus: Ohio State University Press.

ZALD, M. N. and P. DENTON (1963) "From evangelism to general service: the transformation of the YMCA." Administrative Science Quarterly (September): 214-234.

Chapter 8

AMERICAN POLITICS IN THE 1970s: BEYOND PARTY?

WALTER DEAN BURNHAM

I

The basic shape of American electoral politics has been hugely transformed in the decade since John F. Kennedy was assassinated. The country has witnessed two "abnormal" major-party presidential campaigns (Goldwater's in 1964, McGovern's in 1972), the emergence of George Wallace as a national political force, the miraculous resurrection of Richard Nixon from the politically dead, the destruction of the New Deal presidential coalition, and much else besides. These are changes of overwhelming importance; yet considerable disagreement exists among observers of American politics as to their implications. Controversy has broken out as to whether the country is undergoing critical realignment, as to the appropriate electoral strategies for Democrats interested in winning presidential elections, and as to the "rationality" of the American electorate. It now seems about time to take stock and, by concentrating on the most important dimensions of electoral change, to make a first attempt to order this confusion.

The argument presented here may be summarized very simply. The American electorate is now deep into the most sweeping behavioral transformation since the Civil War. It is in the midst of a critical realignment of a kind radically different from all others in

American electoral history. This critical realignment, instead of being channeled through partisan voting behavior as in the past, is cutting across older partisan linkages between rulers and ruled. The direct consequence of this is an astonishingly rapid dissolution of the political party as an effective "guide," or intervenor between the voter and the objects of his vote at the polls. As a result, critical realignment and party dissolution have uniquely become, in our time, inseparably linked aspects of the same disruptive change in the flow of our political history. It is, in my view, a change of revolutionary scope and implications. First, we shall attempt to describe the empirical boundaries of this change—change as a syndrome of interrelated phenomena. Second, we shall make some effort to identify the leading forces at work which have produced it; and finally, we shall examine some of the more and less probable implications associated with it.

II

We start with the premise that the United States is now living through a critical realignment to end all critical realignments in the traditional meaning of the term. This is a realignment whose essence is the end of two-party politics in the traditional understanding; in short, it is a caesura in American political evolution, a moment in time at which we close a very long volume of history and open a brand-new one. Obviously, putting the proposition this baldly invites the rejoinder that it is not so: tomorrow will continue to look like today, and today's political coalitions and voting behavior have more than a little connection with yesterday's. Agreed. But let us see just how far the argument can be pushed in accordance with the data now available. In doing so, we should look at the meaning of the first operational term, "critical realignment," than at that of the second, "party decomposition" (or dissolution), and finally at the inter-relationship between the two in our time.

CRITICAL REALIGNMENTS

A considerable amount of work has been done since 1967 by historians and political scientists on both the conceptualization of the term "critical realignment" and upon specific historic periods and geographic places in which critical realignments have occurred

(Burnham, 1970; Sundquist, 1973; Holt, 1969; Kleppner, 1970; Rogin and Shover, 1970; Jensen, 1971). This is hardly surprising because these events are highly dramatic and easy to measure empirically. Conceptually, the periodic recurrence of critical-realignment sequences in voting behavior clearly provides an admirable point of entry for ordering, classifying, and interpreting the American political experience in new and fruitful ways. Out of this literature a number of propositions have emerged which set apart critical realignments from other types of elections, for example, those of a "deviating" character, such as occurred in 1904 and 1956. Critical realignments

- are in the nature of relatively short, sharp, and dramatic movements of many voters away from support of one party to another;
- arise as a consequence of severe, cumulative, but uneven stress in the social system (the stress may be of economic, cultural, or other origin);
- are proximately caused by some triggering or "detonating" event or events (e.g., the Kansas-Nebraska Act or economic disruption);
- have historically been periodically recurring phenomena, with peaks spaced approximately 36 to 38 years apart;
- have involved major and intense struggles over the definition and redefinition of the most important national policy agendas of their time;
- have resulted in a new "stable phase" in the electoral cycle, grounded upon durable majorities and minorities in the electorate;
- have been followed by significant alterations in national public policies and by changes in the relative effective political power of our separate national policy institutions.

On its face, this catalogue of "symptoms" appears to fit very closely many salient electoral developments of the past decade. Major crises have erupted in the social system since 1964; we have had, and conspicuously, such normally "anomalous" phenomena as the emergence of the George Wallace (American Independent) movement, as well as striking abnormalities and polarizations within the Republican convention of 1964 and the Democratic conventions of 1968 and 1972, and two extraordinary landslides (1964 and 1972) in the past three presidential elections. Nor can it be seriously doubted that Richard Nixon's election in 1968 was followed by significant domestic policy changes—including, as by no means unimportant or accidental, a reconstitution not only of the personnel but of the policies of the Supreme Court (cf. Adamany, 1973). For those interested in the periodicity phenomenon, 1928 + 36 = 1964 or, alternatively, 1932 + 36 = 1968.[1] And certainly, no one can deny that something very much out of the ordinary electoral routine was going on in both of these latter years.

More to the point, major shifts have taken place very recently in the structure of attitudes in the electorate; and these require some extended discussion. It would necessarily follow from the nature of critical realignments and their relationship to "normal" or "usual" politics that they involve extremely intense issue polarizations by American standards, not only among elites, as in the recent party conventions mentioned above, but also among decisively large parts of the mass electorate. The exceptional nature of the voting shifts that occur in critical realignments—their abrupt departure from hitherto normal standards, their great magnitude in certain parts of the electorate, and the durability of the postrealignment party balance—seems inexplicable unless issue-consciousness and issue-voting among voters were to show massively higher levels than could be expected from reading the collected 1954-1966 works of the Michigan Survey Research Center group (cf. Converse, 1966, 1964). Unfortunately, we can only "prove" the existence of such exceptional issue intensity among parts of the mass public in historical realignments by using the largely qualitative reports of contemporaries and later historians. Modern survey research dates back only to 1935, and survey instruments designed to get to basic attitudinal questions associated with critical realignments were really not available until the early 1950s. This was a time which fell in the midst of a "stable phase," halfway between the class polarizations of the 1936-1940 period and the post-1963 upheaval in the shape of American politics; and the studies produced from these surveys are limited accordingly (cf. Burnham, 1974).

But as attitudinal structures change, so do research findings on the American electorate. Several important studies in the early 1970s have revealed the most drastic changes in the kind and quality of attention the American electorate is paying to politics. Let us recall first what the Michigan group told us about the American electorate in more stable times. First, the most important single determinant of voting behavior, consistently, has been the individual's party identification (Campbell et al., 1960). Second, most voters have extremely weak cognitive maps of the political world: in the overwhelming bulk of cases, they do not respond in a way that reveals what Philip Converse (1964) has called "internally constrained belief systems" about politics. Two corollaries to this proposition are: third, the level of political cognition is very strongly associated with level of formal education among individuals, and that the top 10% or so of the electorate in both categories are in some sense the "keepers of the flame" of democratic values (Converse, 1969: 141); and, fourth, the large bulk of the electorate responds in a heterogeneous way to a number of durable issue clusters in politics, with particularly little relationship or constraint between positions on any domestic issue and issues of foreign policy.[2] Fifth, presidential elections tend to be decided by the least adequately socialized or "competent" parts of the electorate, who come "surging" in under the pressure of short-term stimuli, as in 1952, and then "decline" out in following off-year elections, as in 1954 (Campbell, 1966). It follows from all these and other portraits of the American electorate that it is at once highly subject to manipulative campaign techniques and functionally incapable of providing the necessary mass base for a "more responsible two-party system," as Gerald Pomper (1971) has quite correctly pointed out. It was the popularization of just such findings—more than the findings themselves—which so perturbed the late V. O. Key, Jr., toward the end of his life, and prompted him to dedicate his last book to the proposition that "voters are not fools" (Key, 1966: 7).

Such is, very briefly, the portrait of the American electorate sketched out for us by academic research on voting prior to the early 1970s. It corresponds precisely to what could be expected of the public midway in the larger electoral cycle, when the "old politics" dominates, consensus is high, and issue polarizations are very modest. As we turn to more recent studies, it is at times difficult to believe that they describe the same country or population of voters which was so intensively analyzed just a few years before. Let us briefly summarize the leading findings of this new survey-based work.

In a number of recent articles and commentaries, Gerald Pomper has stressed that a steep upward change has developed in the electorate's perceptions of issue distances between the parties since the age of *The American Voter* (Pomper, 1972).[3] This change did not occur gradually, but was a jump shift associated quite precisely with the 1964 presidential campaign and election. From then on, in a much more sharply defined way than ever before in the history of survey analysis, voters perceived the Democrats to be "liberal" and the Republicans "conservative." Pomper argues two substantive "implications" from this radical change toward "constraint" in the mass electorate: first, the 1964 election was a critical election; second, the existence of a much more clearly issue-polarized competition between the parties, *and public awareness of this issue polarization,* may have created for the first time in this century the essential attitudinal preconditions for the establishment of a "more responsible two-party system" in the United States. Unfortunately, Pomper does not reflect upon one very clear implication of his data: this increasing clarity is associated with increasing conservatism in public attitudes toward the issues and the parties. This shift in opinion has very much to do, it goes without saying, with the shattering of the old post-Roosevelt Democratic presidential coalition, the rise of George Wallace and George McGovern, and the remarkable post-1964 electoral successes of Richard Nixon.

Norman H. Nie (1974) continues the empirical attack upon the Eisenhower-era model of the American electorate in an important article, "Mass Belief Systems Revisited." His findings are very similar to, though richer than, Pomper's. There has been a very steep increase in ideological consistency in public attitudes. This occurs in "breakthrough" fashion in the 1964 election, producing a jump shift in both attitudes and voting behavior in that presidential election and the two that followed. This increase in attitudinal constraint has been an across-the-board phenomenon; in particular, it is found at all levels of formal education in the electorate, which means that the phenomenon cannot be adequately explained in terms of the rapid 1952-1972 growth in aggregate levels of formal education in the adult population. Nor, of course, can it be explained in terms of the strong static relationship between education level and level of attitudinal consistency and political awareness posited by Philip Converse and others.[4] Perhaps crucial to our subsequent argument here is that, in Nie's words, " . . . in the last three presidential elections [1964, 1968, 1972], political attitudes have come to be an increasingly significant force in determining the direction of the presidential vote, while the impact of partisan identification, once predominant, has become much less significant" (1974). He goes on to add, cautiously: "Perhaps voter rationality, like attitude consistency, is also more a function of the political context than a consequence of innate limitations of the mass public"—a point that clearly will have to be kept in the center of scholarly work on voting from now on (1974). Not surprisingly, Nie concludes that this fundamental and sudden change in 1964, coupled with survival of the change thereafter, may very well be associated with an era of major-party realignment. We will return later to some speculations on what party politics might look like in an era marked by high position-issue intensities among the voters and a corresponding decline in "free-floating" party identification as a determinant of voting behavior.

The third major piece of research to have been completed in the early 1970s is a study by a group of Survey Research Center scholars of the 1972 presidential election, based upon the SRC's sample (Miller et al., 1973). Here, as elsewhere, we must remain content with a brief summary of leading findings, coupled with a recommendation to the reader to study the original work. The authors also find that ideological polarizations were vastly more important in 1972 than in earlier decades, with partisan identification playing a much less salient role as shaper of voter decisions. Very suggestively, however, they find that this ideological polarization in 1972 was markedly concentrated among Democrats and Independents, extending much less sharply to Republicans. This reflects a prime reality of contemporary American electoral politics, the disruptive stress the issues of the post-1964 period have placed upon the Democratic presidential coalition:

> Perhaps the most important revelation of the analysis was that the traditional inertial force of party identification proved less potent than the polarizing effects of the specific issues relevant to the election. Indeed, when the relative weights of the three general factors explaining the vote, namely, the candidates, parties and issues, are compared to previous elections, it becomes clear that not only was this an issue election but that it may more appropriately be labeled an ideological election. Above all else, the outcome of the election was the result of the ideological polarization within the Democratic ranks that pitted the left wing Democrats against those on the right. [Miller et al., 1973: 74]

The SRC scholars point directly to a fundamental characteristic of politics in a critical-realignment era: the emergence of profound issue cleavages (involving race, the Vietnam War, and antagonistic cultural symbolisms) which cut orthogonally across traditional partisan commitments in decisively large minorities of the electorate. But they go on to make two points of profoundly disturbing significance. First, these issue cleavages as they have emerged in 1964, 1968, and again in 1972 have contributed to the political discontent of large segments of the electorate. These new issue polarizations severely disturb preexisting partisan commitments by many voters without as yet being able to supersede them. Second, there has been no evidence whatever of any significant conversions within the electorate toward identification with the Republican party, despite the results of the elections of 1968 and 1972. If this is a critical realignment, one is driven to ask, in what sense can it be called a *partisan* realignment?

The authors of "A Majority Party in Disarray" end upon an appropriately cautionary note. For them, a crucial part of the overall context is the steep increase in measurable political disaffection in the electorate over the past decade. As Everett Ladd (1973) also points out, the unresolved crisis within the Democratic Party has contributed to a situation in which, election after election, significant minorities of the electorate—it may be added, different minorities each time—have been left without an adequate perceived choice at a time when they very much want to make one.

> There is a broader question here, namely, the legitimate representation of the American people. In the absence of realignment or a viable third party alternative, it appears that until the polarization within the Democratic ranks is diminished, a major segment of the population will go unrepresented at the presidential level; whether their policy orientation is one of social change or social control, their policy expectations and preferences will go unsatisfied. Such a condition of a perceived nonresponsive government can only lead to further political dissatisfaction, discontent and disaffection. [Miller et al., 1973: 90]

So we may say that many of the most important general preconditions and behavior patterns associated with critical realignments in the past have been manifesting themselves in the current period. Yet something is clearly wrong with this picture as it stands. A quite considerable part of the professional and journalistic literature of the past few years anticipated an old-style partisan critical realignment in our time, or has proclaimed that one is occurring. But—for reasons we shall examine in some detail below—a good deal of this writing is probably an exercise in waiting for Godot. A work like Keven Phillips's *The Emerging Republican Majority* (1969) might have been as well titled *What to Do Until the Critical Realignment Comes.* But suppose it does not come? What if the waiters wait in vain? Suppose that the more probable development, one outlined by me in 1970, is best described in the title of David Broder's recent book, *The Party's Over* (1972)? We may find it very useful under these circumstances to think in other categories, categories that take up the emerging decomposition of party-in-the-electorate and deal with it as of the essence of the current critical realignment sequence. Stripped of all subsidiary or divisible "accidents" of the phenomenon, what is a critical realignment? It is a major change rooted in the behavior of critically large minorities of American voters which durably alters electoral coalitions, the shape of election outcomes, and the flow of public policy. It happens when politically decisive minorities of the electorate stop doing what they have been used to doing, start doing something else, and keep on doing it for a long time afterwards. All preceding critical realignments in American electoral history have been channeled through parties. But if and to the extent that this one is not so channeled—or even more, cuts across and dissolves party—it forms the core of comparative analysis, an analysis through which alone we can comprehend our present political condition.

PARTY DECOMPOSITION

A good deal of work has been done on the phenomenon of decaying partisanship in the American electorate, much of it summarized and elaborated upon in my *Critical Elections and the Mainsprings of American Politics* (1970). This decay in the stability of support for candidates of a given party means several things at once. First, presumably, it entails a decline in the strength and extent of party identification as well as in the degree to which it is autonomously determinative of voting behavior. Second, it is manifested in an increasing longitudinal velocity in aggregate outcomes of presidential elections: the amplitude of partisan swing tends to increase and presidential landslides become common. Third, decay in partisan-related components in voting decisions is reflected in a systematic tendency toward split-ticket voting at all levels of the electoral system (cf. Tarrance and De Vries, 1972). As I have attempted to show elsewhere, the trend toward party decomposition goes back a long way in American electoral history. It was first visible in the 1904-1910 period, reached an intermediate peak in the 1920s, and was reversed to a considerable extent in the two decades following the 1932 realignment. Thus, a clear secular trend away from nineteenth-century levels of partisanship in American electoral politics has existed across most of this century. What is distinctive about the period from 1960 onward is that this decomposition has accelerated at a breakaway pace, reaching all-time highs—so far, at any rate—in the 1972 election.

We have already discussed the recent SRC discovery that autonomous partisan identification in 1972 was much less significant as a determinant of presidential voting decisions than formerly and "ideology" much more. This implies a basic qualitative change in the meaning of such party identification as remains. On the quantitative side, one of the best-known developments of the past decade has been the volatilization of party identification itself; first, the 1964-1965 surge toward the Democrats, and since then a decline among both Democrats and Republicans and a major increase among Independent identifiers. The Gallup data tell this familiar story (Gallup, 1974: 21-22). This upward shift in Independent identification (see Table 1) suggests a corollary to the point made by the 1972 SRC study: if there is any evidence of partisan realignment at all in the contemporary period at this important level of self-identification, the "party" which is benefited by it is clearly the Independents. Moreover, there is every reason to suppose two things about this Independent voter pool: first, it is particularly concentrated among the young and, second, it contains an increasingly large proportion of "new" Independents, that is, those who are more or less actively oriented to the political world, but are alienated from both of the major parties.[5] The first suggests a rather dramatic failure of traditional sources of political socialization of the young, the second suggests what Gallup, the SRC group, and others have identified: a growth in "active" modes of political alienation.

The bulk of the discussion of party decomposition which follows focuses upon leading aggregate changes in American voting behavior which are associated with the contemporary jump shift in split-ticket

Table 1. THE RISE OF THE INDEPENDENT: GROSS PARTY IDENTIFICATION IN THE AMERICAN ELECTORATE, 1940-1974

Age Group	Year	% Democrat	% Independent	% Republican
21 and over	1940	42	20	38
	1950	45	22	33
	1960	47	23	30
	1964	53	22	25
	1970	45	26	29
18 and over	1971	44	30	26
	1972	43	29	28
	1973	43	33	24
	1973/74	42	34	24

voting: it is here that we are confronted with apparently durable behavioral changes of the utmost significance to the future development of American political institutions. The general extent of this post-1960 change can be surmised from examining the data from Milwaukee County, Wisconsin (see Table 2)—perhaps the only jurisdiction in the country which reports the number of straight party ballots cast in general elections.[6] An inspection of the array suggests what a more complete analysis reveals: the decay of straight-ticket voting from 1960 through 1970 is a universal phenomenon, presumably caused by general and powerful processes at work in the political system as a whole.[7]

We now turn our attention to a phenomenon of very great system-level importance. David Mayhew (1973), the first to identify it clearly, refers to it as the strange case of the disappearing marginal seat in congressional elections. The argument is breathtakingly simple. At one time (until the later 1950s), partisan outcomes of contested congressional elections with incumbents running distributed themselves in a rough approximation to a normal curve, with the single mode of the curve falling close to the zone of maximum party competition. Similar unimodal and seminormal distributions could be established for congressional outcomes in seats where no incumbents were running for reelection, and for presidential election results compiled by congressional district. Since that time, the nonincumbent group and presidential elections at the congressional district level have retained this unimodality, the latter of course by no means always with the mode at the area of maximum party competition. The crucial change has come to the

Table 2. SPLIT-TICKET VOTING IN THE MILWAUKEE AREA, 1960-1970*

| Area | Percentage of Straight Ballots Cast | | | | | | % Democratic for Governor, 1968 |
	1960	1962	1964	1966	1968	1970	
Milwaukee City	68.3	52.8	61.6	50.6	36.8	31.7	59.3
Ward 3	68.4	55.3	58.1	50.7	34.5	25.3	42.8
Ward 6 (black)	68.9	59.0	71.1	51.8	51.3	43.7	83.8
Ward 1 (white)	66.6	53.1	66.6	56.5	44.1	35.1	73.7
Greenfield	63.0	x	55.1	34.1	31.9	26.4	51.3
Oak Creek	68.1	50.7	63.0	x	28.7	18.1	45.0
Hales Corners	57.1	40.4	53.2	45.8	39.6	31.9	31.3

*As examples, the most Republican and two most Democratic wards of the city in 1968 (one white-ethnic, the other overwhelmingly black) have been presented here.

incumbent group of congressional seats, always a large majority of all congressional races in the modern period. Here the unimodal "competitive" pattern has been decisively replaced by a bimodality, with each mode quite far removed from the normal competitive range of outcomes. The meaning of this is clear. Presidential "coattails" have all but vanished where incumbent congressmen are concerned. The partisan turnover in House elections has been very much reduced, and the number of incumbents actually suffering defeat has fallen from 50 in 1920 to eight in the equivalent presidential-landslide year of 1972. Congressional incumbents, benefiting by very large-scale ticket-splitting among the voters, have become very largely immune to the tides of politics outside congressional elections and—except in the rare landslide in congressional voting—very largely immune to defeat.

We may begin our discussion of this important phenomenon by extending an earlier discussion of split partisan outcomes as between presidential and congressional elections held at the same time and at the same level of analysis (Burnham, 1970: 100-111). The data from 1940 through 1972 in this regard are reported in Table 3.

While an upward tendency in split outcomes can be detected through 1964, the 1972 election showed a tremendous increase. President Nixon carried 377 congressional districts while George McGovern won 58, in itself an all-time "outcome landslide" for any presidential election at this level. Of these 377 Nixon districts, 188 elected Republican congressmen and 189 elected Democrats. With split outcomes in 192 districts (44.1% of the total), we begin to approach some kind of maximum empirical limit. Assuming a roughly two-party outcome in terms of House seats won, a *complete* rupture of majority coalitions as between presidential and congres-

Table 3. PROPORTION OF SPLIT RESULTS: CONGRESS AND PRESIDENT, 1940-1968

Year	*Number of Districts Analyzed*	*Percentage of Split Results*	*Percentage of Splits Involving Minor Party*
1940	362	14.6	9.4
1944	367	11.2	2.4
1948	422	22.5	33.7
1952	435	19.3	1.2
1956	435	29.9	1.5
1960	437	26.1	2.6
1964	435	33.3	0
1968	435	31.7	34.8
1972	435	44.1	0

sional elections—that is, with the losing party's candidate losing *all* congressional districts, but with his party winning about half of the seats—this limit would be approximately 50% of split outcomes to all district outcomes. As it was, in 1972 Nixon carried over three-quarters (77.4%) of all districts which elected Democrats to the 93rd Congress. One may make the point even more simply: had the electoral conditions of the 1920 Harding landslide prevailed in the 1972 Nixon landslide, the Republicans would have elected about 350 congressmen. Instead, they won only 191, far short of a party majority.

Not only did Republican congressional candidates not "make it" in 1972 despite the Nixon landslide, the President and his advisors adapted their 1972 strategy with this in mind. As Gordon Strachan pointed out in his testimony before the Senate's Watergate Committee, more than a hundred Republican candidates in seats held by Southern and labor-backed Democrats were simply written off by the White House strategists (Ervin Committee, 1973: 2483-2485). This strategy was followed in pursuit of the basic goal of these operatives: the winning of the largest possible majority for the President. Labor, which tacitly supported his reelection, and the Southerners, who openly did so, were not to be antagonized. Thus it is that political elites, in a mutually reinforcing process, adapt to what they see to be the dominant behavioral patterns of electoral politics and, in doing so, reinforce those patterns.

Returning to the "vanishing marginals," a comparison of 1952 and 1972 outcomes reveals this process as it has moved to current levels of coalitional dissociation. As Table 4 makes clear, a major generic change has taken place in the structure of congressional election outcomes involving incumbents. In 1952—excluding the uncontested Southern Democratic "tail" of the distribution—all three categories of elections had a unimodal distribution, though the modes did not coincide for congressional districts with and without incumbents. In particular, there was relatively little difference in distributional shape between the presidential and incumbent categories. Fifty-six incumbent and 28 nonincumbent congressional districts were in the closely competitive 45.0 to 54.9% range, for a total of 84 in all. Because the distribution had remained what it was in 1952, presidential "coattails" still existed and, for the last time in our history thus far, the Republicans won 221 seats to 213 for the Democrats, and organized the House.

By 1972 this picture had radically changed. The presidential and

Table 4. SEPARATION OF VOTING COALITION: OUTCOMES FOR PRESIDENT, NONINCUMBENT, AND INCUMBENT CONGRESSMEN, 1952-1972

Percentage Democratic by District	Percentage of Districts, 1952			Percentage of Districts, 1972		
	President	Non-incumbent	Incumbent	President	Non-incumbent	Incumbent
0.0–4.9	0	0	3.0	0	0	1.6
5.0–9.9	0	0	0	0	0	0
10.0–14.9	0	0	0	0.2	0	0
15.0–19.9	0	0	0	1.6	0	0.5
20.0–24.9	0.2	2.7	0.8	8.3	0	2.1
25.0–29.9	4.6	4.1	3.0	14.9	1.7	10.1
30.0–34.9	9.9	5.5	10.5	23.2	3.4	7.2
35.0–39.9	19.8	9.6	13.8	21.4	12.1	10.3
40.0–44.9	19.3	13.7	12.4	11.7	20.7	5.6
45.0–49.9	14.0	21.9	6.7	6.4	25.9	4.0
50.0–54.9	8.7	16.4	8.8	4.8	10.3	5.3
55.0–59.9	7.6	5.5	5.2	2.5	5.2	7.2
60.0–64.9	7.8	2.7	5.5	1.2	6.9	11.4
65.0–69.9	3.4	1.4	3.9	1.2	1.7	9.0
70.0–74.9	3.0	0	2.5	0.9	6.9	5.3
75.0–79.9	0.9	1.4	2.2	0.5	0	3.7
80.0–84.9	0.7	0	1.1	0.9	3.4	3.2
85.0–89.9	0	0	0.6	0.2	0	1.6
90.0–94.9	0	1.4	0.8	0	0	1.9
95.0–100.0	0	13.7	19.1	0	1.7	10.1
N =	435	73	362	435	58	377

nonincumbent distributions were still unimodal, though with an enormously increased gap between the first mode (30.0-34.9) and the second (45.0-49.9). The incumbent congressional elections, however, had developed a very strong bimodality, centering around 35.0-39.9 and 60.0-64.9. Correspondingly, the number of districts falling into the closely competitive 45.0 to 54.9% range fell to 35 incumbent and 21 nonincumbent, or 56 in all. This represents a decline in the proportion of competitive congressional seats from nearly one-fifth in 1952 to one-eighth in 1972.[8] Clearly, the prime 1972 beneficiaries were incumbent Democratic congressmen, who in most cases have established themselves in their districts quite irrespective of what happens in presidential or any other elections. But the distancing of incumbents from the competitive range essentially favors those of both parties in the long run. What this means, as Mayhew has pointed out, is that even very large national vote swings in these circumstances will have remarkably little effect so far as turnover is concerned. The 1972 results simply reinforce Mayhew's argument as to developments from the late 1950s to 1970.

That this distancing does appear to work to the benefit of incumbents of both parties can be seen by the analyzing paired presidential-congressional outcomes by district in one large state, Pennsylvania, presented in Table 5. This table reveals, clearly enough, the crucial point: the mean percentage for Democratic incumbents increased despite the Nixon landslide of 1972. Moreover, the closing up of the standard deviation reveals a growing homogeneity of such noncompetitive outcomes. Finally, one may note the great increase in the distance between Republican and Democratic incumbents, an increase from 17.9% in 1952 to 29.5% in 1972.

Two objections to all this may be voiced. The first, stressed both by Mayhew (1973) and by Edward Tufte (1973), is that these profound changes are largely the result of structural factors, for instance, collusive reapportionment by state legislatures to protect incumbents. Consequently, they are not—at least not primarily—the result of recent changes in behavior by the voters. The second objection which might be raised is that 1972 is a peculiarly inappropriate bench mark when comparing presidential and congressional outcomes. We may deal in a very preliminary way with this second point by observing that, however unpopular Senator McGovern's unique candidacy may have been among Democrats and Independents, the 4.4% increase in the mean percentage for Democratic incumbents from 1952 to 1972, associated with the fact that the variance among these districts was cut almost exactly in half, makes very clear that processes of coalitional dissociation along

Table 5. INSULATION OF CONGRESSIONAL INCUMBENTS: THE CASE OF PENNSYLVANIA

Year	President Democratic Incumbents	Congress Democratic Incumbents	President Republican Incumbents	Congress Republican Incumbents	Differential (Mean) Democratic Incumbents	Republican Incumbents
1952						
N	12	12	18	18		
Mean % D	57.2	58.5	40.0	40.4	+1.3	+0.4
S.D.	7.37	6.24	5.58	5.28	2.98	2.77
1972						
N	13	13	11	11		
Mean % D	45.7	62.9	32.4	33.4	+17.1	+0.9
S.D.	10.42	4.41	4.00	5.97	9.71	6.84
1952 to 1972						
Mean % D	−11.5	+4.4	−7.6	−7.0	+15.8	+0.5
S.D.	+3.05	−1.83	−1.58	+0.69	+6.73	+4.07

office-specific lines are going on which quite transcend such considerations. We shall, however, return to this point later.

The first or structural argument requires a little discussion here, if only because research on this dissociation is at such an early stage of development and has, in my view, considerably overstated the importance of structural variables in shaping the vast changes we see. No one can doubt that legislatures in recent decades, for example, have typically reapportioned congressional seats in order to protect incumbents of both parties.[9] But we may ask when such practices began, and in response to what changed perceptions of voting behavior in congressional elections on the part of these legislatures.[10] Leaving this aside, it is notable that the same processes of coalitional dissociation and insulation of incumbents can be found in states like New Hampshire and West Virginia, where a single party has controlled the reapportionment process for at least the past forty years.[11]

It is also possible to identify districts without any boundary changes at all for the past several decades. One such district, the 24th Pennsylvania, is presented in Table 6, in part because it permits us to identify the time at which basic changes in aggregate voting behavior began to occur. This is a three-county district centered on Erie, and achieved its present shape in 1941. It was first captured by a Democrat (the current incumbent, Joseph Vigorito) in 1964. As Table 6 reveals, that year marked in more ways than one the beginning of a new era in the district's electoral politics.[12] Obviously, the 1964 election in this district marked the beginning of a breakaway divergence between congressional voting coalitions and those of other offices. This process has now resulted in the emergence of a safe seat for its Democratic incumbent, while the district as a whole remains closely competitive at other levels of election. It is also worth observing that this process of coalitional dissociation was very far advanced by 1970, and was in no way an artifact of Senator McGovern's candidacy in 1972. Virtually be definition, these very recent changes in this district must be attributed wholly to changes in aggregate voting behavior, for there have been no changes in the structural context of voting here.

The explanation for such a profound and rapid transformation in voting patterns may be a relatively simple one. More than a decade ago, Warren E. Miller and Donald E. Stokes of the Michigan SRC group pointed out that voters knew very little about candidates in congressional elections compared with others in more salient

Table 6. THE TRIUMPH OF INCUMBENCY:
THE CASE OF THE 24th PENNSYLVANIA DISTRICT

Year	Incumbent's Party	Percentage for Incumbent	Mean Percentage for Party, Statewide Offices	Differential
1942	R	60.5	60.8	−0.3
1944	R	54.6	54.5	+0.1
1946*	(R)	(63.9)	(64.0)	(−0.1)
1948	R	54.5	55.3	−0.8
1950	R	57.0	54.7	+2.3
1952	R	57.1	57.4	−0.3
1954	R	52.0	49.0	+3.0
1956	R	57.8	57.6	+0.2
1958	R	53.8	52.1	+1.7
1960	R	51.0	52.5	−1.5
1962*	(R)	(51.4)	(52.2)	(−0.8)
1964	R	49.2	42.6	+6.6
1966	D	55.3	49.4	+5.9
1968	D	61.1	50.1	+11.0
1970	D	66.8	53.0	+13.8
1972	D	68.8	51.1	+17.0

*Years with no incumbent running. Party shown is that of the preceding incumbent and the winner in the year indicated. Mean percentage includes president, U.S. senator, and at-large state offices.

contests, conspicuously the presidency (Stokes and Miller, 1966). What little they knew involved the incumbent, and—except in the unusual case—this tended to give incumbents a considerable electoral advantage. Voters seek cues wherever they can, and conspicuously, as a host of writers have pointed out, through the party affiliation of candidates running offices. The American ballot is everywhere vastly more complex than ballots in any parliamentary democracy: both separation of powers and federalism vastly proliferate the number of choices voters have to make in any single election.

It would follow that if, for whatever reasons, decisive minorities of voters do not find party (or their own party identification, if any) a useful frame of reference of voting decisions, they will seek other kinds of cues for those decisions. At the highest level of salience —say, in voting for president, U.S. senator or governor—they will respond to a mixture of candidate appeal, major campaign issues, and, third and last, party in ways similar to those described for the 1972 presidential election by Miller et al. (1973). At lower levels of salience, and especially when this "nonpartisan" minority turns to voting for congressmen, the incumbency effect suggested by Miller and Stokes will have overwhelming importance. Such an effect will, of course, be further reinforced by two other considerations. First, the saturation of the electoral process by electronic media results in severe inequalities of media coverage and increases, very probably, the salience gap as between, say, campaigns for president and those for congressman. Second, there is excellent reason to suppose that incumbents have responded to their electoral context by making themselves as visible as possible to their constituents, chiefly as officials whose basic task is servicing the constituency rather than formulating public policies. And so one would expect to find, and does in fact find, an extremely rapid rise in the volume of mail sent out under the congressional frank from the mid-1950s through 1970.[13]

The institutional and policy implications of this evolution of bimodal congressional-election outcomes could not be more profound. First, as the proportion of incumbents running for reelection increases from five-sixths of the contests in 1952 to seven-eighths in 1972 and the "trough" in the competitive ranges deepens, turnover of personnel in the House begins to approach the minimum possible. This growing stabilization of outcomes—a further move toward "institutionalizing" the House[14]—stands in the sharpest contrast to increasing volatility across time in other election campaigns. Second, until the Watergate affair destroyed the Nixon administration in 1973-1974, all trends pointed toward a decline in the significance of Congress as a whole—and the House in particular—in the national policy process (see Huntington, 1973). Obviously, the march in executive hegemony has been abruptly halted for the time being; but it may well be wondered whether this will prove to be a more than temporary setback. If not, one may anticipate that the House will become ever more clearly a body whose members maintain job security through being *ombudsmen* and constituency advocates before the immense bureaucracy at the other end of Pennsylvania Avenue. But if the collapse of the Nixonian bid for domination of American national politics should presage a permanent shift of influence over policy toward Capitol Hill, another problem is implied by the bimodal distribution. If turnover rates in the House continue to converge as closely to zero as actuarial realities permit, the absence of fresh blood—occurring as it does in a period of the most rapid changes in society and economy—implies a constantly growing gap between a self-insulated House and the needs of the country at large.

In either event, one point stands out with crystalline clarity: at some time between 1960 and 1964, the voting coalitions in presidential and congressional elections became dissociated from one another to a degree unprecedented in the history of American electoral politics since the creation of the party system nearly a century and a half ago. Some years ago James W. Burns (1963) elaborated a theory of a four-party system, composed of presidential and congressional Republicans and Democrats. But the phenomena he described were analyzed at the level of elites. Today we have such a "four-party system" (if such it can be called) at the grass roots. Not only is this situation likely to add a new dimension to the "deadlock of democracy" which Burns described, but it is also very likely to add a most potent behavioral reinforcement of the U.S. Constitution's separation of powers, with consequences which we can barely foresee.

Considerations of space do not permit us as exhaustive an analysis of contemporary party decomposition elsewhere in the electoral universe as we might wish. Further discussion here will be confined to a state, West Virginia, with a very strong former tradition of high turnout, straight-ticket partisan voting, and—except for the realignment era of 1930-1934—a generally stable pattern of both aggregate party affiliation and electoral outcomes across time.[15] In 1938, for example, party registration in this state stood 57.4% Democratic, 41.5% Republican, and 1.1% other or no response—a figure virtually identical with the partisan outcome of the 1940 election for president and other offices. By 1972, the balance had glacially shifted to 64.6% Democratic, 33.8% Republican, and 1.6% other and no response, a pro-Democratic shift averaging 0.2% per year. Clearly George McGovern was exceptionally unpopular in West Virginia: the 1968-1972 partisan swing to Nixon was 18% here, compared with 11.3% nationwide, and McGovern's 36.4% of the vote was the lowest for any Democratic candidate since the abnormal election of 1864. At the same time, Senator Jennings Randolph won reelection with 66.5% of the vote,[16] and the four congressional incumbents won a statewide total of 66.2%, the latter being the highest Democratic congressional percentage in the entire history of West Virginia congressional elections.

A comparative survey of county-level correlations for 1940 and 1972 suggests something of the extent of the deterioration in West Virginia, and indicates that the 1972 presidential outcome alone cannot account very completely for it. The decay in the explanatory power of partisanship in this period is profound, and not merely as between presidential and other electoral coalitions. As Table 7 reveals, there was a single coalition in 1940, one virtually identical with the distribution of aggregate partisanship as revealed in registration data. By 1972, we can see at least three voting coalitions in outline: (1) a presidential-gubernatorial coalition, with one explaining 82.8% of the aggregate county-level variance in the other; (2) a senatorial coalition; and (3) despite the near-identity of gross statewide totals as between senatorial and congressional outcomes, a quite discrete congressional coalition.[17]

We may summarize these developments—and analogous ones elsewhere—by a glance at the basic syndrome of politics described by the late V. O. Key, Jr. (1949), in the "pure non-party" systems of the Deep South a generation ago. His description of Democratic-primary politics in states like Alabama or Arkansas in that era suggests that at the same time were to be found completely ad hoc electoral coalitions from office to office at the same election, and for the same office from one election to the next; very strong evidence of "friends-and-neighbors" effects, that is, abnormal support for a candidate in his home county; as a rule, protection of congressional incumbents; and, of course, low turnout and local-oligarchic control of public policy. For Key (1956), the whole point of competitive party politics was to abolish such dissipation of the potential implicit in electoral democracy, involving—among other things—party as a

Table 7. WEST VIRGINIA: PARTISAN INTERCORRELATIONS AMONG FOUR
MAJOR STATEWIDE OFFICES, 1940 AND 1972*

Office	1940 Office				1972 Office			
	Pres.	U.S. Sen.	Cong.	Gov.	Pres.	U.S. Sen.	Cong.	Gov.
		$r =$				$r =$		
President	1.000	+.988	+.980	+.991	1.000	+.734	+.536	+.910
U.S. Senator		1.000	+.992	+.994		1.000	+.680	+.718
Congress			1.000	+.988			1.000	+.513
Governor				1.000				1.000
		$r^2 \times 100 =$				$r^2 \times 100 =$		
President	100.0	97.7	96.1	98.2	100.0	53.9	28.7	82.8
U.S. Senator		100.0	98.4	98.7		100.0	46.3	51.5
Congress			100.0	97.6			100.0	25.3
Governor				100.0				100.0

*N in both cases = 55. Based on percentage Democratic of total (and two-party) vote.

"solvent of federalism" and separation of powers as well. Something like this was surely his hope for the South. What has happened instead is that these elements of a nonpartisan syndrome have spread outside the South, in many cases (as in West Virginia) for the first time in our political history. In the years since 1960 we find in a state like West Virginia: increasingly discrete (ad hoc?) electoral coalitions from office to office at the same election, and for the same office from one election to the next; emergence of clear "friends-and-neighbors" patterns in voting; protection of congressional incumbents (the last defeated in a general election was retired in 1958); and a rapidly declining turnout. As to the latter, the turnout of 40.3% of the potential electorate in 1970 and 64.9% in 1972 constitute the lowest rate of participation for these respective years since ex-Confederates were readmitted to the West Virginia franchise in 1870. As for "friends-and-neighbors" effects, these have not only been associated with the home counties of congressional incumbents since the early 1960s, but came clearly to the fore in 1972—for the first time on record—in voting for such obscure offices as state auditor.[18] All of this suggests a rapid and increasing deterioration of partisan constraints on voting behavior, a deterioration which may *au fond* be far more a cause than an effect of the 1972 presidential campaign.

Examples of this breakdown could be extended almost indefinitely, but perhaps we have already exhausted the reader's patience: these must suffice as mere fragments of a general pattern. The point must be stressed: if and to the extent that they represent a change in the behavior of politically decisive minorities, a change that is largely irreversible, we have a "critical realignment" of voting behavior. But we also have a critical realignment that works not through but athwart the traditional major parties, and which cumulatively dissolves them as channels of collective electoral action. This dissociation, it would seem, is the most significant electoral development of all which has occurred in the past decade. It follows, quite rigorously, from the basic changes in the electorate's perception of political objects which Pomper (1972), Nie (1974), and Miller et al. (1973) have identified. Bluntly put, to the extent that issues achieve salience and shape voting behavior in the United States of today, the resultant cleavages become both too intense and too numerous to be contained any longer within the traditional two-party electoral matrix. One may speculate that, if electoral law and political tradition in the United States allowed, we would have seen the emergence some time ago of an explicit multi-party system. As it is, we find party decomposition instead. This discussion must now terminate with a brief review of the causes of this decisive change in our electoral politics and a more extended discussion of its implications.

III

The newer electoral literature seems agreed that American voters are polarizing more and enjoying politics less. It also emphasizes a related theme: through a combination of contextual stress (including egregious "imperial" decisions by political elites, such as those that took us into Vietnam) and social change, the electorate is now polarized across at least two orthogonal dimensions. As a result, nothing approximating a majority, however factitious, now exists in the American political system as a whole. One may express this set of orthogonal dimensions schematically (see Figure 1).

As I have suggested earlier, it seems also possible to think about the emergence of these orthogonalities as eruptions of political response to the kind of postindustrial change in social status and functions suggested by David Apter (1964), a response speeded up by the civil-rights revolution and by the Vietnam experience. It is obvious that such a classification nicely elides over many crucial problems of scarcity and political domination in American society. As a "broad brush," however, it is not without some value.

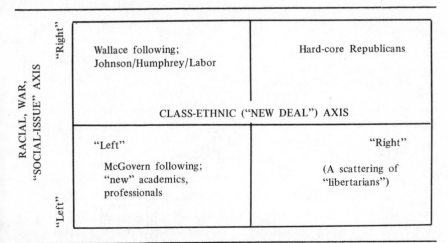

Figure 1: POLARIZATION OF THE AMERICAN ELECTORATE

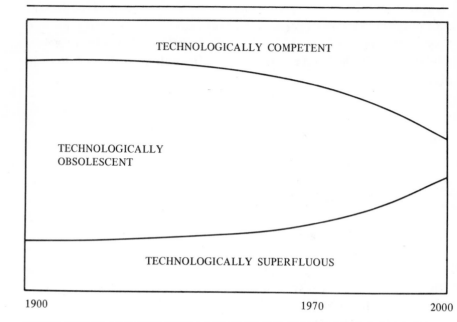

TECHNOLOGICALLY COMPETENT

TECHNOLOGICALLY
OBSOLESCENT

TECHNOLOGICALLY SUPERFLUOUS

1900   1970   2000

Figure 2: POSTINDUSTRIAL STRATIFICATION OF SOCIAL STRATA

Implicit in Apter's argument is that this emergent technostructural stratification of power and influence cuts athwart, without necessarily superseding, the older industrial upper-middle-working-lower class stratification pattern. People in the "technologically competent" strata of postindustrial society, in addition to many members of the more cosmopolitan and older upper classes, would include many of the "newer class" of academics—particularly in the natural and social sciences—as well as many of their students; they would also include journalists and people in the electronic media, particularly those in the "center" as compared with the "periphery" of American society. People in the "technologically superfluous" strata would include those without visible or probable future functional roles in a postindustrial society, because of their lack of necessary competence or acquired skills which are marketable in this emerging form of domination. This population would obviously be quite disproportionately composed of unskilled blacks and members of other racially (and otherwise) handicapped groups in the social structure. The "technologically obsolescent" strata would include a very substantial part of what is called "middle America"—both working-class, white-collar strata and older, largely local or "periphery"—concentrated elite groups.

The logic of justification for the old pre-1929 industrial pattern of domination was the dogma of laissez-faire, Horatio-Alger individualist and capitalist liberalism. Its transitional successor, the "welfare state" born in depression, had for its ethics of rule group pluralism and governmental benevolence. Its technologically oriented successor, pretty clearly, would be grounded in a bureaucratic, "nonpolitical," expertise-oriented ethic, ceteris paribus; and we might count ourselves lucky if it were not to contain a significant element of sophisticated imperialism as well. But perhaps the most significant part of the whole picture is that older logics of justification for social activities and socioeconomic rewards have increasingly—but very unevenly—broken down, while those appropriate to a "technetronic society" have not been in any way solidified. A major consequence of this impaction is, precisely, what Theodore J. Lowi (1969) has described as "the end of liberalism" and the proliferation of social conflicts among a host of groups. In such conflicts, members of the opposed groups typically regard themselves as victims of fraternal relative deprivation: "they" (their antagonists and others) get undeserved social rewards; but "we," the virtuous —for example, "we" who still believe in the older values of self-denial, hard work, patriotism, and the sanctity of the nuclear family—are being deprived of these values by "them," in collusion with the government, and without legitimate right.

Racial antagonisms, arising from the unplanned consequences of such changes as the mechanization of cotton agriculture since World War II, add fuel to the fire. Ex-peasant populations arriving in American cities have always started off at the very bottom of the urban social and economic structure. But as is well known, the experience of blacks in the United States has been fundamentally different even from that of the Irish immigrants of the mid-nineteenth century; and, what is worse, fundamental, technologically conditioned changes in economic production have heavily reduced the social need for the kind of hod-carrying, pick-and-shovel jobs which sustained the Irish for many decades after their arrival. A pool of "technologically superfluous" people at the bottom of the social structure thus collects, grows, and perpetuates itself. To a very large extent, its members of all racial and ethnic backgrounds inevitably become a *Lumpenproletariat* of the sort described by Marx and Engels in 1848. The cultural dissonance which the "lowest classes" present to their white working-class (and white-collar) neighbors is paralleled by the latter's sense of physical and economic threat to their own and their children's hard-won place in the social order.

Moreover, it can hardly be said that as yet those strata who are most likely to benefit positively from a technetronic social universe—academics, students from the older middle classes, technicians, and bureaucrats—have established a logic of justification for domination which is coherent or legitimate, even in their own eyes. To the contrary: for many reasons too complex to discuss here, a very substantial part of this new cosmopolitan elite has rejected the implications of its own dominant position and has come actively to patronize at least those of the technetronic underclass who are members of discrete racial minorities. As it happens, many of these liberal elites—judges, administrators, legislators, academics, and others—occupy a sufficiently exalted position in the social structure to ensure that the direct social costs of combined racial-class integration in the metropolitan area will be borne by those elements of the white population which are both economically and culturally least able to bear them. Except in the very rare case, these costs are not borne by these elites themselves or their families. Those who do bear them—or feel acute anxiety that they will be made to bear them in the near future—know this. The result, visible in case after case, has been the repudiation of these elites by the rank and file who gave them support from the age of Roosevelt to the time of John F. Kennedy.

To all of these pressures must be added the direct costs of the Vietnam War's speedup of cultural conflict in the white population over issues involving definitions of patriotism, life styles, work and leisure, and other primordial values. Out of this transitional farrago of conflict without overarching *policy* legitimacy have come, in direct succession, Barry Goldwater, George Wallace, Richard Nixon, Spiro Agnew, and the McGovern campaign of 1972. Out of it also has come, by the same token, the destruction of the old presidential Democratic coalition. The 1972 Democratic primaries produced national totals divided almost exactly one-third for Wallace, one-third for McGovern, and one-third for the "vital-center" ABM coalition around Hubert Humphrey, Henry Jackson, and the forces of organized labor. This result quite accurately reflects the impaction of one set of issues on another, with no clear way visible now or in the future to resolve the conflicts involved.

The dissociation of American electoral coalitions has thus come to take on a very marked institutional division-of-labor character. The bulk of recent analytical work on presidential elections has made crystal clear that this office—more in the ascendancy than ever before (at least until 1974)—has become the vortex of all the combined passions, intensities, and multiple cleavages over values, relative social status, and relative deprivation which are now at work in the electorate. It is a uniquely concentrated symbolic office: and when symbolisms fall apart, when conflicts escalate as policy legitimacy decays, the symbolisms projected come to dominate outcomes in a highly issue-polarized, near-ideological electoral setting. But the shape of the aggregate data alone also makes it obvious that this pattern cannot readily be extended to other levels of election as a matter of course. On the contrary: the emerging shape of congressional elections, with its growing support for incumbents of both parties, bespeaks quite directly the lack of any ideological polarization at all similar to those operating at the presidential level. As for other levels with some visibility of their own—senatorial elections, gubernatorial elections, and mayoral elections—the pattern is heterogeneous in the extreme: sometimes there are polarizations which parallel those operating at the presidential level, and sometimes there are not. Compare, for example, the two mayoral elections in New York City won by John Lindsay (in 1965 and 1969) with the election won by Abraham Beame in 1973. But there is little doubt that a growing common theme in these contests has been that described by Murray Levin in his analysis of the 1959 Boston election: increasingly, the road to victory lies in a candidate's successfully denying that he ever had anything to do with politics before. And, as Levin correctly observes, this repudiation of politics and politicians is associated with the "alienated voter," the man in the street who finds tremendous cognitive dissonance between what he learns in public-school civics about how the system *should* work, and what he learns in adult everyday life about how it actually *does* work.

Every indicator suggests that there are many more voters with these attitudes in the mid-1970s than there were in 1959. We can present only a few highlights of the most recent survey study which emphasizes this, the study done for the U.S. Senate's Committee on Government Operations (1973) at the end of 1973 by Louis Harris Associates.[19] Among the most significant findings of this study are these. (1) The American people's loss of confidence in their government has now reached majority proportions, though the belief is overwhelmingly widespread that the system can be made to work well. (2) A remarkably sharp divergence has emerged between the public at large and political elites, who were separately surveyed. The public is much more negative about such matters as the evils of secrecy in government, respect for people who run government at all levels, and supposed improvements in the quality of life in the United States than its leaders are. The leaders are relatively contented, if not almost complacent; the public, rather intensely, is not. (3) The discontent is pervasive: of 22 major institutions and the people in charge of them, a majority of the respondents expressed a "great deal of confidence" in only two of them: medicine and local trash collection. By contrast, only 33% expressed this confidence in the Supreme Court, 30% in the Senate, 29% in the House of Representatives, and 18% in the White House (Senate Government Operations Committee, 1973: 37-38). (4) This discontent has grown very rapidly since 1966: the proportion of the sample expressing "a great deal of confidence" in the Supreme Court has declined from 51% to 33% in the 1966-1973 period; in the U.S. Senate, from 42% to 30%; in the U.S. House of Representatives, from 41% to 29%; and, far the most dramatic of all, in the executive branch of the federal government the decline has been from 41% to 19% (Senate Government Operations Committee, 1973: 33). The overall 1966-1973 decline in the proportion of respondents expressing "a great deal of confidence" in the four federal political institutions was from 44% to 28%; while the decline in confidence for eight nongovernmental institutions in this period was from 46% to 37%, suggesting pretty clearly that the decline in confidence is both general and specifically concentrated on political institutions.

Table 8 reveals the same sort of decay in confidence and growth in political and social alienation. A set of projective questions, designed

Table 8. GROWTH OF THE ALIENATED VOTER: THE HARRIS SURVEY, 1966-1973

| | Percentage Agreeing | | | | | Change, |
Statement	1966	1968	1971	1972	1973	1966-1973
The rich get richer, the poor get poorer	45	54	62	68	76	+31
What you think doesn't count much any more	37	42	44	53	61	+24
People running the country don't really care what happens to you	26	36	41	50	55	+29
I feel left out of things going on around me	9	12	20	25	29	+20
Average feeling alienated and powerless	29	36	42	49	55	+26

to tap such feelings, has been asked by Harris since 1966. The results are as follows, and they speak for themselves (Senate Government Operations Committee, 1973: 30). It can hardly be doubted that this across-the-board increase in public discontent is closely linked to the bankruptcy of the existing top-level leadership cadres of both political parties. This bankruptcy, if not total, has been comprehensive: failures of vision, of empathy with the needs and concerns of nonelite Americans of both races, failures in specific policies, indeed, in common honesty and elemental political morality.

It is something of a truism of critical-realignment sequences —though one not as yet sufficiently integrated into scholarly analyses of them—that established "old politics" leadership in any given period responds to growing political crisis by a rigidity and a rejection of the emergent which contributes in no small way to the magnitude of the subsequent explosion, and the completeness of their own repudiation. Thus it was with James Buchanan, Grover Cleveland, and Herbert Hoover. So it has been with the Vietnam warriors of the Johnson administration and virtually the whole personnel of the Nixon administration. Leaving aside the peculiarities of personality, this remarkably recurrent pattern of rigidification, explosion, and repudiation of previously dominant leadership makes sense when one thinks about critical realignments as moments of convulsive transition, moments at which older dominant value sets are being replaced and challenged by newer ones, but where the replacement is still in a very early stage of development. "Bankruptcy" thus tends to take on, as it should, somewhat less of a moralist cast in analysis, and more of a probably systemic consequence of the same political lags, the same gaps between political inertia and social change, which mark these processes.

What is different about the contemporary period in this respect is that leadership has failed the public for so long a time, and that the failed (or repudiated) leadership has included in turn the top elites of both major political parties. By 1976, for example, about 27% of the electorate will be under 30. This very large fragment of the voting population has lived its entire adult life in this cumulative crisis of leadership: the oldest among these young 1976 voters will not have been more than sixteen when John F. Kennedy was assassinated. Moreover, one crucial dimension of this failure has been the emergence of a manifest elitist illusion among top American leadership of both parties. It has been very characteristic of both the Johnson top leadership (especially those involved with the Vietnam disaster) and of President Nixon and his aides to blame the public at large for failure to support their disastrous blunders and, in the case of Nixon personally, to regard adult American citizens as "children." Quite appropriately, and in a very Greek way, this *hubris* has produced its *nemesis* and has led to *ate:* Pride meets its appointed Fate, and Destruction follows. For the realities are quite otherwise. If Key was correct in his generation in arguing that "voters are not fools," and he was, still less are they fools today. In the conclusion to his most recent book, Louis Harris (1973: 286) strikes a most appropriate note:

> The facts in this book have pointed up perhaps more clearly than anything else just how badly the leadership of the country has read the temper, mood and serious intent of the American people. Taken together, the record is a serious indictment of the political, social and economic leadership of this country over the past decade. There is little doubt in this writer's mind that the public, although far from correct in many areas, nonetheless is far more sophisticated, far more concerned, and far more advanced than the leadership believed. It can be said with certainty that the people by and large have been well ahead of their leaders.

Just so; and it may be added that, since this top leadership is ultimately produced by the political parties, we should perhaps not be surprised that repudiation of this leadership and the dissolution of the older parties should move hand in hand together.

When one is in the vortex of a political hurricane, it is particularly difficult to gauge the future with any sense of confidence. Still, the attempt must be made to assess the way ahead. Clearly, the shift toward higher levels of education in the population and radical improvement in the ease of acquiring political information through electronic media and otherwise can be expected to continue. So also will growth in the tertiary sectors of the social structure: across time, professional and technical people will constitute a growing part of the labor force, and organized labor will constitute less. There is no particular reason to assume, on the other hand, that tensions between different racial and cultural groups living in close physical proximity to each other will soon decrease, or that the very high levels of violent crime which now exist will show any tendency toward decline. Just beyond the horizon of current issue problems involving culture, race, and economics lie far larger ones having to do with runaway inflation and a contraction of the available natural-resource base to sustain a social structure grounded upon high mass consumption in its tastes, values, and motivations.

If we assume with Anthony Downs (1957: chs. 11-13) that political parties and their ideologies used to be shortcuts to voting decisions under conditions of imperfect information and widespread economic scarcity, we may view most or all of these prospective developments as unfavorable to the survival of the traditional parties as effective intermediaries between voters and the electoral decisions they make. The massive growth in ticket-splitting and Independent party identification in recent years may well be considered proximate effects of transitional sociocultural stress on one hand and inadequate political leadership on the other. But it also would make sense that, to the extent the costs of political information to voters have been drastically reduced by the new communication technology, many of the older mobilization and concentration functions once performed by the major parties have lost their utility in recent years. Voters can and do make intelligent decisions on the merits, as they see them, of individual candidates and the specific issue clusters which surround their campaigns. Obviously, to the extent that the American electorate in the 1970s and 1980s becomes more affluent, better educated, and with more leisure time on its hands and a number of alternative life styles to choose from, the kind of social structure emerges which alone could undergird the models of the independent, responsible citizen which John Stuart Mill and Moisei Ostrogroski developed. Except as gatekeepers (reducing the number of electable alternatives on the ballot through an enduring monopoly over effective nominations), the parties could then largely disappear and our political democracy would be improved by the disappearance.

A surprisingly large part of political-science literature written by Americans over the past two decades has persistently sought to formulate teleological theories of political development and post-industrial "technetronic" society. At the end of such "development"—very much like the "end of days" posited by Marx a century ago—lies the end of ideology and apolitical bliss. One suspects that such utopias have their function in the practical political sociology of rulership; but as predictions, they will prove as inadequate as most of their predecessors. The old-style American major party-in-the-electorate may very well be on its way out as a channel through which the collective power of the many can at least occasionally control the behavior of the elites who run this political system. If the foregoing analysis of current electoral developments has been correct, this remarkable development would indeed by a "critical realignment to end all critical realignments." But the ultimate results may be very different from those predicted and hoped for by technocrats and democratic elitists from the age of the Progressives to the present. Let us recapitulate—if by perhaps excessive emphasis—what these developments mean in coalitional and institutional terms.

(1) *The presidential coalition.* The most dramatic developments at this level have involved the nationalization of electoral coalitions and the rupture of the older presidential Democratic coalition into three almost equal parts: the supporters of Wallace, the "vital center" groups around organized labor, and the McGovernite "left."[20] These things have happened, as we have attempted to point out, because of the growth of multiple polarizations over race, culture, American foreign and military policy, and economic conflicts. The presidency has increasingly emerged as an imperial office, at home as well as abroad. Dominating the American political system, it has become the vortex for national conflicts over symbolisms and both symbolic and material allocation choices. As a direct result of these conflicts, and the multiple pressures of change playing upon the American electorate, no stable presidential majority coalition can now be said to exist. The results of both the 1968 and 1972 elections would appear to suggest that a predominantly conservative—though hardly Republican—majority may have emerged. Yet such a view reckons without the enduring importance of economic issues. With a combined double-digit inflation rate and recession as of 1974, and with the added short-term impact of Watergate, it would be a hardy spirit indeed who would predict the outcome of the 1976 presidential election.[21]

(2) *The senatorial coalitions.* It is very hard to establish anything like a uniform set of generalizations at this highly visible level of election. In 1972, for instance, the Nixon landslide did nothing to prevent four Republican incumbents from losing their seats to Democratic challengers.[22] It is obvious that Democratic senatorial candidates ran far ahead of their presidential nominee as a rule in 1972. Yet 6 of the 16 Republican incumbents running for reelection actually ran ahead of Nixon in their states.[23] If one were to concentrate on the extreme ends of the Republican incumbent continuum, he could perhaps conclude that in 1972 those who lost their seats were old and tended toward the conservative wing of the party while the incumbents who ran ahead of Nixon tended to be younger and more liberal. But a review of the names in each category

reveals so many exceptions for so few cases that any generalization seems suspect; and that, perhaps, is the point. Some incumbents were popular in their own right, and some were clearly less so; an analysis of the whys and wherefores would thus require a particularized study of the politics of each state involved and an assessment of the relative effectiveness of the candidates as campaigners.

(3) *The House coalition.* Overall, as we have indicated, from about 1956-1958 through 1972 this has increasingly taken a bipartisan incumbent-protection form. In 1972 this development was simply accelerated marginally: the proportion of incumbents running for reelection who were defeated in the general election was 3.4% of all incumbents and 3.0% of the whole House. Overall, the Democratic share of the total congressional vote in 1972 was 52.1% compared with McGovern's 37.5%; Republican congressional candidates won 46.5% of the national congressional vote, compared with Nixon's 60.7%—a *net* split-ticket proportion of 14.4%, as compared with a net split-ticket proportion of 5.1% in 1952.

One is inclined almost to the view that critically large minorities of the American electorate have come to behave in a way which is functionally related to the emerging realities of political power at the center. The imperial presidency, the vortex of all nationwide political conflicts in the United States, is electorally dominated by a network of shifting minority coalitions. The Senate is the more "statesman-like" of the two branches of Congress: the visibility that produces a greater attrition of incumbents than in the House is also the same visibility that produces majorities such as the 82.4% won in 1970 by Henry Jackson (D) of Washington, or the 77.3% won in 1972 by Ted Stevens (R) of Alaska, and that has made the postwar Senate a breeding ground for presidential candidates. The House has increasingly turned to constituency service and ombudsman functions; and its incumbents become both more numerous and insulated from any but the most massive shifts of opinion. What emerges from all this is an immensely significant behavioral reinforcement of the separation of powers.

The reader may well ask at this point, So what? Let us try to answer this from the point of view of, first, the policy analyst and, second, the democratic theorist. The most obvious policy implications of this functional decomposition of voting behavior are, first, a concomitant destabilization of domestic policy initiatives and follow-through; and second, a future for policy making which rests uneasily between the alternatives of reinforced institutional deadlock or executive imposition of policy on the rest of the system. It is clear that a growing fluidity in mass electoral behavior from one presidential election to the next has already meant drastic reversals in a number of crucial domestic policy arenas, particularly but by no means exclusively those dealing with the cities, poverty, and race relations. This is so because, however decomposed the electoral coalitions may be, there is a very substantial and probably growing divergence between Democratic and Republican elites over basic contemporary political issues. To the extent that the presidency changes partisan hands with increasing frequency, to that extent a longitudinal continuity of policy formulation and implementation becomes problematic in the extreme.

Yet it is increasingly obvious that the rest of this decade, and the decades that follow, will be marked by constantly growing pressures for public-sector controls over what used to be regarded as private life. Nowhere more is this the case than with the economy, where multiplying costs of scarce resources are likely simultaneously to intersect with rapid inflation and recession. Eventually, wage and price policies will probably have to be permanently implemented in most advanced industrial societies, including this one. Yet the problem for the policy maker is always how to obtain consent for any such ambitious program as this, and how to insulate it from becoming the plaything of organized sectoral interests. But the United States has always been a country whose policy-making processes have been wide open at all stages to the penetration of such interests. One would suppose that any further *institutional* reinforcement of this American pattern could only make such difficulties worse, yet the current drift toward discrete office-specific electoral coalitions points precisely in that direction. In this context lies a recipe for speeding up the dialectical tension between "drift" (policy deadlock among separated institutions permeated by pressure groups) and "mastery" (executive dictatorship in an atmosphere of acute policy crisis). While "party government" is hardly a panacea, as the current British case amply demonstrates, it is very hard to see how, without it, any prospect for eliminating or softening this excruciating dilemma within the rubrics of democracy can be found.

The energy crisis of 1973-1974 is, or should be, very much like Jefferson's description of the Missouri struggle of 1820 as a "firebell in the night," for the problems it implies, and the demands its successors will place upon political institutions and leaders in the

United States, are at least as profound, and directly involve democratic values at their most basic level. *If* some such massive public controls as those suggested here must be developed and sustained from sheer necessity, they cannot be maintained without consent in a democracy. That consent in turn must be rooted on an ethic of justification. A vital element in any such ethic—assuming that the government must do things that used to be considered possible and legitimate only during a world war, but must now be done in peace—must be equality of sacrifice. If democratic consent is to be won for the very hard public choices that lie just over the horizon, a bona fide, sustained, and more than rhetorical effort to approximate equality of sacrifice will have to be made by policy elites. Unfortunately, nothing of the sort seems possible without a revolutionary change in behavior norms among rank-and-file and elites alike, and in the capacity of our institutions for sustained, integrated, and coherent public policy. How revolutionary this revolution would have to be would depend very largely upon how much time this country has left before really hard allocation choices are imposed on it by brute necessity. But the horns of one further dilemma are already coming into our view. In such an age, policy will either have to be much more social-democratic than it has ever been in the United States, or it will have to be established and imposed by an authoritarian oligarchy, an oligarchy whose first forebears were clearly visible in President Nixon's White House office before Watergate blew it to pieces.

American radicals have long argued that the Democratic Party must be destroyed before any truly democratic structures could be built in the United States. They may now be getting their wish, though not in quite the form they had hoped for. If one assumes that the party decomposition we have been describing is the end of the tale, what follows for the voter? First, he is very likely to become increasingly confused by his enormously complex political system: party is a vitally important vehicle for simplifying and concentrating public choice. Second, he is likely to become increasingly aware that the old party organizations, which control nominations, are in some sense in collusion against his welfare: the lessons Ralph Nader and Common Cause have taught him are not likely to be forgotten, for subsequent experience will most probably reinforce them. Third, he is very likely to find himself being forced to make choices—especially in presidential elections—which do not permit him to do more than vote for the lesser of evils. Fourth, he is very likely indeed to conclude that voting makes no great difference anyway: pressures on him arising from race (from *either* side of that gap), war or peace, and inflation continue to weigh on him despite the promises of candidates and parties. Fifth, as to equality of sacrifice—well really! No one who prides himself on realism about politics in the United States would think *that* a likely outgrowth of this final victory of electoral individualism.

It is hard to escape the conclusion that, if such a process continues to unfold, a true crisis of the regime will emerge, perhaps sooner than later. If "partisan decomposition" continues under these conditions of pervasive public discontent, democracy will be progressively emptied of any operational meaning as executive-bureaucratic imperatives come to dominate the political system. In this case, it may be possible to make a relatively peaceful transition to *Imperium* without much disturbance in *formal* institutional structure. It is worth recalling, perhaps, that the Roman Senate survived not only the accession of Augustus, but until after the fall of the Empire in the West. Alternatively, this decomposition may be reversed by a renewed "critical realignment" which restores the traditional two-party system and produces a durable policy majority for one of its components. Despite the arguments sometimes made to this effect, for example, by James Sundquist (1973: ch. 17), we cannot accept the likelihood of this happening unless we can identify the emergence of forces in society and polity strong enough to overcome those that have produced the evolving patterns of electoral disso-ciation described here. We may doubt that economic stress alone will suffice to restore the party system of the 1930s.

Finally, we may suppose the possibility that a new constellation of parties emerges from the present ruins, broadly arrayed on a "left-right" continuum and not necessarily confined to two major components. Prima facie, the emergence of such a new order of things might seem the least likely of all possible alternatives. More likely, one would have thought, would be a situation in which a man on horseback would emerge at a point when economic and social crisis are in a much more advanced stage than now, and win the presidency on either party ticket or as an independent. Nevertheless: *if* we assume that the electorate as a whole has become more sophisticated from recent painful experience and as educational levels have risen; *if* we assume that there continue to be effective cultural and institutional resistances to authoritarianism; and *if* we assume that outstanding political leadership can be found, can emerge, and can be kept alive, it might happen that political democracy will actually survive. These may appear to be heroic assumptions; but assumptions no less heroic were made *and validated* in past crises, notably the crisis of 1860-1861. Quite possibly, the current dissolution of party-in-the-electorate will turn out after all *not* to be a "critical realignment to end all critical realignments," but the prologue to a revitalization of *democracy through party*.

At the very end, our argument in these pages becomes a truism: each generation must win anew, for itself, its own battle for as much liberty as it can wrest from necessity, or lose what liberty it could have retained both for itself and for its posterity. Now it is our turn to work out this destiny.

NOTES

1. For a remarkable application of content-analytic technique to party platforms, which produces "peaks" of value change precisely synchronous to the midpoint peaks in voting behavior during national critical-realignment sequences, see Namenwirth (1973).

2. This lack of relationship between domestic and foreign-policy attitudes has been a common theme of attitudinal research ever since Gabriel Almond's *The American People and Foreign Policy* (1950). Cf. Campbell et al., 1960: 187-188.

3. The June 1972 issue of the *American Political Science Review* is partly devoted to a symposium on issue voting, of which Professor Pomper's paper (1972) forms a part. See also Boyd (1972), Brody and Page (1972), Kessel (1972).

4. The key to this, of course, is to control for educational levels. When this is done, as the Nie paper points out, the 1956-1972 upward shift in attitude consistency is revealed to be an across-the-board phenomenon, although differentials continue to exist in the predicted direction between better-educated and less-educated groups (Nie, 1974, including Figs. 5 and 6).

5. Cf. Burnham, 1970: 127-131.

6. The data are taken from relevant volumes of the *Biennial Report* of the city of Milwaukee's Board of Election Commissioners. Unfortunately, in 1970 Wisconsin joined the lengthening parade of states shifting their state elective offices to four-year terms, elective in nonpresidential years; hence, there are no such data for the 1972 election.

7. The "test" here is simple, though N is small. First, one computes the time regression line for each ward, 1964-1970 (ward boundaries were changes in 1963). Then one divides b by a in each regression equation to yield standardized rates of decline in straight-ticket voting; and then one correlates the latter with the mean percentage Democratic of straight tickets cast in the 1964-1970 period. Here as elsewhere there are significant differences in aggregate voting patterns between areas populated by blacks and those populated by whites. Excluding the two wards with heavy black concentrations yields an N of 17. The question of the relationship between partisan percentages and the rate of decline in partisan voting in white areas is "answered" by $r = -.330$. This indicates that only 10.9% of the decline can be "explained" in terms of an argument that greater Republicanism is associated with greater propensities across time for aggregate levels of split-ticket voting to increase.

8. This, it should be noted, occurred despite a very sharp decline in the number of uncontested (mostly Southern Democratic) seats between these two elections. If one

computes the proportion of closely competitive seats (45.0 to 54.9% Democratic) to all *contested* seats, they constituted 24.3% of this total in 1952, and only 14.4% in 1972.

9. Though by no means always: in each of the New York congressional reapportionments of 1951, 1961, and 1971, Republicans dominated both branches of the legislature and the governorship. They did what they could to draw lines favoring Republicans and undermining Democrats, conspicuously (and successfully) in the case of the 12th district in Brooklyn (1951), and quite unsuccessfully in the case of the upstate 35th district, represented by Samuel S. Stratton (D) (1961). Remarkable examples of political geography can be found in each of these three New York reapportionments, particularly in New York City.

10. Such is the state of our ignorance about practically all systematic, longitudinal patterns surrounding congressional elections that we are quite without information on this vital point, as on others. It does seem reasonably certain that protection of incumbents of both parties through reapportionments *on the whole* goes back at least to World War II and very probably further.

11. Thus taking 1956 rather than 1952 in these two states as bench mark for comparison, because of a number of turnovers in personal (not party) incumbency in 1952, we find the following pattern:

Year	West Virginia			New Hampshire		
	% D, Pres.	*% D, Cong.*	*Difference*	*% D, Pres.*	*% D, Cong.*	*Difference*
1956	51.1	54.2	+3.1	33.8	38.4	+4.6
1972	36.1	66.0	+29.9	35.0	29.8	−5.2
Shift	−15.0	+11.2		+1.2	−8.6	

The number of incumbents in West Virginia, 1956, was 5 (Democrats), and in 1972 was 4 (Democrats). In New Hampshire, 2 (Republican) incumbents ran for reelection in both 1956 and 1972.

12. The point should be explicitly made here that there have been no significant changes in ballot form or electoral law in Pennsylvania during this period. It is true that, beginning in 1966, the number of statewide office separately elective was reduced by constitutional change.

13. It should go without saying that incumbents in the House—much more than in the higher-visibility Senate—have every incentive to perpetuate the existing state of affairs. This is particularly true so far as proposals to finance their largely invisible challengers from federal funds are concerned. The implications of this for campaign-reform legislation before Congress in 1974 should be obvious.

14. See Polsby (1968) and Polsby et al. (1969). These two articles constitute the first significant effort at the kind of extensive longitudinal and quantitative history of Congress which is so urgently needed.

15. For a general discussion of West Virginia politics, through 1952, see Fenton (1957: 82-125).

16. One major nationwide aspect of the developments we have been describing is the recent emergence—in *some* cases—of extraordinary majorities for senatorial incumbents running for reelection. Senator Randolph's 1972 percentage was exceeded in the history of West Virginia senatorial elections only by Senator Robert Byrd's 67.7% in 1964 (but with Lyndon Johnson also winning 67.9%) and 77.6% in 1970. Other prominent examples of this trend, both very recent, include Senator Proxmire's 70.8% in the Wisconsin 1970 general election and Senator Jackson's 82.4% in the Washington 1970 election.

17. Of course, the standard error of estimate around the regression equations shows an enormous increase between 1940 and 1972. In 1940 the maximum was 2.14 (President-Congress), as compared with a maximum of 7.44 in 1972 (also President-Congress). This represents a *twelvefold increase* in the variance of the partisan vote.

18. It may also be noted in passing that for the first time in the history of West Virginia since the end of the Civil War, a statewide partisan political office (commissioner of agriculture) was won by an incumbent in 1972 *without opposition*.

19. This, incidentally, is the first sample survey ever to be commissioned by the Congress of the United States.

20. Of the 15,993,965 votes cast in the 1972 Democratic presidential preference primaries, the distribution from "left" to "right" was as follows:

Candidate	Percentage
McGovern	25.3
Chisholm	2.7
McCarthy	3.5
Lindsay	1.2
Total "left"	32.7
Muskie	11.5
Humphrey	25.8
Jackson	3.2
Total "center"	40.5
Yorty	0.5
Wallace	23.5
Total "right"	24.0
Others	2.8

21. We note, for example, that Eisenhower had a 15.4% margin over Stevenson in 1956, yet John Kennedy won in 1960; or again, Lyndon Johnson had a 22.6% margin over Barry Goldwater in 1964, yet Richard Nixon won in 1968. Even without Watergate and the economy to concern us, a Nixon margin of 23.2% over George McGovern in 1972 would by no means be enough to give any assurance of a certain Republican presidential victory in 1976.

22. Allott (Colo.), Boggs (Del.), Miller (Iowa), and Smith (Me.), trailing Nixon in their states by a mean 13.2%. One Democrat from the South also lost his seat (Spong, Va.), but ran 16.0% ahead of McGovern. It is worth noting that, while only 3.4% of House incumbents running for reelection lost their seats (including a number who were reapportioned out of them), 5 out of 25 Senate incumbents (20.0%) and 2 out of 9 incumbent governors (22.2%) were also defeated for reelection.

23. Brooke (Mass.), Case (N.J.), Hansen (Wyo.), Pearson (Kans.), Percy (Ill.), and Stevens (Alaska).

REFERENCES

ADAMANY, D. (1973) "Legitimacy, realigning elections and the Supreme Court." Wisconsin Law Review: 790-846.

ALMOND, G. (1950) The American People and Foreign Policy. New York: Harcourt, Brace.

APTER, D. E. (1964) Ideology and Discontent. New York: Free Press.

BOYD, R. W. (1972) "Popular control of public policy: a normal vote analysis of the 1968 election." American Political Science Review 66: 429-446.

BRODER, D. (1972) The Party's Over? New York: Harper and Row.

BRODY, R. A. and B. I. PAGE (1972) "Comment: the assessment of policy voting." American Political Science Review 66: 450-458.

BURNHAM, W. D. (1974) "Theory and voting research: some reflections on Converse's 'Change in the American electorate'." American Political Science Review 68: 1002-1023.

——— (1970) Critical Elections and the Mainsprings of American Politics. New York: Norton.

BURNS, J. M. (1963) The Deadlock of Democracy: Four-Party Politics in America. Englewood Cliffs, N.J.: Prentice-Hall.

CAMPBELL, A. (1966) "Surge and decline: a story of electoral change," in A. Campbell et al., Elections and the Political Order. New York: Wiley.

——— et al. (1960) The American Voter. New York: Wiley.

CONVERSE, P. E. (1969) "Of time and partisan stability." Comparative Political Studies.

——— (1966) "Information flow and the stability of partisan attitudes," in A. Campbell et al., Elections and the Political Order. New York: Wiley.

——— (1964) "The nature of belief systems in mass publics," in D. E. Apter (ed.) Ideology and Discontent. New York: Free Press.

CUMMINGS, M. (1967) Congressmen and the Electorate. New York: Free Press.

DOWNS, A. (1957) An Economic Theory of Democracy. New York: Harper.

Ervin Committee (1973) U.S. Senate, 93rd Cong., 1st Sess., Select Committee on Presidential Campaign Activities, Hearings. Washington, D.C.: U.S. Government Printing Office.

FENTON, J. H. (1957) Politics in the Border States. New Orleans: Hauser.

Gallup (1974) Gallup Opinion Index. No. 105 (March).

HARRIS, L. (1973) The Anguish of Change. New York: Harper.

HOLT, M. F. (1969) Forging a Majority. New Haven: Yale University Press.

HUNTINGTON, S. P. (1973) "Congressional responses to the twentieth century," in D. Truman (ed.) The Congress and America's Future. Englewood Cliffs, N.J.: Prentice-Hall.

JENSEN, R. (1971) The Winning of the Midwest. Chicago: University of Chicago Press.

KESSEL, J. H. (1972) "Comment: the issues in issue voting." American Political Science Review 66: 459-465.

KEY, V. O., Jr. (1966) The Responsible Electorate. Cambridge: Harvard University Press.

——— (1956) American State Politics: An Introduction. New York: Knopf.

——— (1949) Southern Politics in State and Nation. New York: Knopf.

KLEPPNER, P. (1970) The Cross of Culture. New York: Free Press.

LADD, E. C., Jr. (1973) "The dynamic of contemporary American electoral politics." Typescript.

LOWI, T. J. (1969) The End of Liberalism. New York: Norton.

MAYHEW, D. (1973) "Congressional elections: the case of the disappearing marginals." Delivered at the 1973 New England Political Science Association convention in Boston.

MILLER, A. H. et al. (1973) "A majority party in disarray: policy polarization in the 1972 election." Delivered at the 1973 American Political Science Association convention in New Orleans.

NAMENWIRTH, J. Z. (1973) "Wheels of time and the interdependence of value change in America." Journal of Interdisciplinary History (Spring): 649-683.

NIE, N. H. with K. ANDERSEN (1974) "Mass belief systems revisited: political change and attitude structure." Journal of Politics 36.

PHILLIPS, K. (1969) The Emerging Republican Majority. New Rochelle: Arlington House.

POLSBY, N. W. (1968) "The institutionalization of the House of Representatives." American Political Science Review 62: 144-168.

——— et al. (1969) "The growth of the seniority system in the House of Representatives." American Political Science Review 63: 787-807.

POMPER, G. M. (1972) "From confusion to clarity: issues and American voters, 1956-1968." American Political Science Review 66: 415-428.

——— (1971) "Toward a more responsible two-party system? What again?" Journal of Politics 33: 916-940.

ROGIN, M. P. and J. L. SHOVER (1970) Political Change in California. Westport, Conn.: Greenwood.

STOKES, D. E. and W. E. MILLER (1966) "Party government and the silency of Congress," in A. Campbell et al., Elections and the Political Order. New York: Wiley.

SUNDQUIST, J. L. (1973) Dynamics of the Party System. Washington, D.C.: Brookings.

TARRANCE, V. L. and W. De VRIES (1972) The Split-Ticket Voter. Grand Rapids, Mich.: Eerdmans.

TUFTE, E. R. (1973) "The relationship between seats and votes in two-party systems." American Political Science Review 67: 540-554.

U.S. Senate Committee on Government Operations (1973) "Confidence and Concern: Citizens View American Government" 93rd Cong., 1st Sess. Washington, D.C.: U.S. Government Printing Office.

CONTRIBUTORS

WALTER DEAN BURNHAM is Professor of Political Science at the Massachusetts Institute of Technology. He is author of *Presidential Ballots, 1886-1892,* and *Critical Elections and the Mainsprings of American Politics,* and co-author and co-editor of *The American Party System.*

GERALD FINCH is Assistant Professor of Political Science at Columbia University.

JOHN J. GARGAN is Associate Professor of Political Science and Associate Director of the Center for Urban Regionalism at Kent State University. He is the author of several articles on New York State politics during the Rockefeller years.

VINCENT J. HANBY is Lecturer in Sociology at the University of Stirling. He is the editor of *Political Sociology* and has written a number of articles on European political parties.

TIMOTHY M. HENNESSEY is Associate Professor of Political Science at Michigan State University. His articles and reviews have appeared in many scholarly journals in the United States and Europe.

JOHN E. JACKSON is Assistant Professor of Government at Harvard University and the Urban Institute. He is the author of *Constituencies and Leaders in Congress* and a co-editor of *Public Policy.*

DAVID KEMP is on leave as Lecturer in Politics at the University of Melbourne, Australia, while serving as Senior Advisor to Malcolm Fraser, Federal Leader of the Liberal Party.

LOUIS MAISEL is Assistant Professor of Government at Colby College and co-editor of the series which this volume inaugurates. He has served the Maine Democratic Party as a county chairman, member of the state committee, and delegate to the national and state conventions.

RICHARD J. TRILLING is Assistant Professor of Political Science at Duke University.

E. SPENCER WELLHOFER is Assistant Professor of Political Science at the University of Denver. He has published extensively in the fields of comparative politics and political sociology.